An Eye for Innovation
The life of Austin 'Clarence' Farrar

An Eye for Innovation

The life of Austin 'Clarence' Farrar

David Chivers

Austin Packard Farrar
C.Eng. FRINA
1913 – 2004

First published in 2007
Second edition published in 2016
Copyright 2007, 2016 © David Chivers
All rights reserved.

Published by Boatswain Books • www.boatswainbooks.uk

ISBN: 978-1-912724-08-6

Designed and produced by Robert Deaves

All rights reserved. No part of this publication may be reproduced by any means, electronic or mechanical, including photocopy or any information retrieval system without the prior written permission of the copyright owner.

CONTENTS

CHAPTER 1	THE FAMILY HERITAGE AND CHILDHOOD	7
CHAPTER 2	APPRENTICESHIP, PHILIP & SON, DARTMOUTH	17
CHAPTER 3	THE FIRST JOBS	59
	JOHN SAMUEL WHITE LTD. AT COWES	
	'CLARK AND SYNNOTT', LONDON	
CHAPTER 4	THE WAR YEARS	85
CHAPTER 5	WOOLVERSTONE SHIPYARD	98
CHAPTER 6	SAILMAKING. SEAHORSE SAILS, SEAHORSE OFFSHORE AND AUSTIN FARRAR SAILMAKERS	130
CHAPTER 7	POST WAR DINGHY SAILING, THE OLYMPICS, THE IYRU AND THE LITTLE AMERICA'S CUP	157
CHAPTER 8	RETIREMENT? & OTHER PROJECTS	183
APPENDIX 1	INTERNATIONAL 14 DINGHIES TO AUSTIN FARRAR DESIGN	203
APPENDIX 2	OTHER ASSOCIATED ARTICLES	207
INDEX		223

CHAPTER 1

THE FAMILY HERITAGE AND CHILDHOOD

That Austin Farrar should turn out as an innovator and leading designer of his generation should not be a surprise when one considers the legacy of his family. Over several generations, both sides of the family have shown themselves to be people who were not afraid to experiment and move forward by their own efforts. His paternal family came from a long line in the colonial service and his maternal family were Suffolk farmers who became agricultural fertilizer merchants, the Packards.

The Packard family name can be traced back many generations in Suffolk with Thomas Packard being initiated as Prior of the Priory of Woodbridge in 1467 and the family is listed as originally from Rougham and Witnesham not many miles away. Austin's great great grandfather John Packard was a farmer at Hasketon, just outside Woodbridge in Suffolk and his second son Edward – Austin's great grandfather – was born at Thorpe Hall on January 5th, 1819, a house which had been in the possession of his family for a considerable time. Edward Packard had an elder brother John so it is unlikely that he would have ever inherited the farm. He was educated at Woodbridge Grammar School and on leaving was articled to Mr. Francis Cupiss of Diss under whom he studied pharmaceutical chemistry, obtaining the diploma of the Pharmaceutical Society.

He set up business in 1841 at Saxmundham and was quickly successful, serving the town and supplying medicines for animal husbandry. He was determined to improve the farm service area of the business and, putting a manager into the shop, he went to Kings College, London to study under Dr Nesbit to enhance his knowledge of agricultural and analytical chemistry, returning to Saxmundham on completion. Here he gave talks at local Farmers Clubs and sold bone based fertilizer to several farmers, dissolving the bones in sulphuric acid as recommended in a book by Dr Justus Leiburg in 1839.

About this time an article appeared in the 'Journal of the Royal Agricultural Society of England' written by Professor Henslow, who had discovered the presence of coprolitic nodules in the Red Crag. In analysing these he found them to be rich in phosphate of lime, suggesting that they would form an excellent substitute for bones as an agricultural fertilizer. Edward Packard realised the possibilities at once and obtained a bushel of coprolites to experiment with. There was no machinery suitable for grinding them and so initially all the work was done by hand in a mortar and the result dissolved with sulphuric acid in the same way as bones. Whilst similar experiments were being carried out by Sir J.B. Lawes the two men were completely independent of each other and probably both deserve equal credit for the introduction of artificial fertilisers.

Edward Packard was producing fertilizer from crushed bones and in 1843 he started producing a commercial product from coprolite nodules, after his successful experiments. He tried to establish machinery to crush the coprolite at Snape, but failed to secure suitable land to build and so he turned his attentions to Ipswich. Here, in 1851, at Ipswich Docks, he established a works in a former flour mill along with a plant to produce sulphuric acid, in what is now still known as Coprolite Street down by the wet dock. The coprolite was obtained locally from the Red Crags and imported from other phosphate deposits in Germany and France on a considerable scale. By its nature, being fossilised dung, there is a limited supply of natural coprolite and he eventually discovered how to manufacture the final compound chemically. One of the constituents needed from the beginning was sulphuric acid and although it was produced in Ipswich it was not a suitable site amongst the local houses. The rapid expansion of the business saw a specific sulphuric acid factory established on land at Bramford in 1854 and the first deliveries of artificial fertilizer to Scotland soon became exports to Ireland and Russia. He was the first person to establish this trade. In later life he suffered from rheumatoid arthritis, retiring from the company in 1886 and handing the reins to his sons Edward Junior, born 1843 (Austin's Grandfather), and Henry, in partnership as Edward Packard and Co. Until his death in 1899 however, he continued to serve and enjoy the things he had done most of his life. He was the Conservative representative of St Margaret's Ward, Mayor of Ipswich and then Alderman until 1889 when his health required him to spend winters abroad. He served on the Ipswich Dock Commission and, with his love of science, supported the Ipswich Museum assisting with buildings, exhibits and equipment for the Schools of Science and Art in Ipswich and Framlingham College, for the latter offering the annual 'Packard' Science Prizes.

From 1886, Edward Packard (Jnr) and his brother Henry (d. 1912) guided the company from strength to strength despite competition from foreign imports. The latter caused Edward to be a leading member of the newly formed 'Fertilizer Manufacturers' Association' in 1895 which reduced competition in the home market and he was elected President in 1926. The company was reformed in 1895 as E. Packard and Co. Ltd until in 1929 when it became 'Fison, Packard and Prentice Ltd.' with Edward Packard as Chairman. The Fison name is the name we know today as a final amalgamation of the various companies. Like his father he had a good education from Bury St Edmunds Grammar School and Kings College, London where he studied Chemistry and Engineering. He followed this with time at the Royal College of Agriculture at Cirencester where he gained a love of farming and farming stock that stayed with him for the rest of his life. For over twenty years he ran an experimental farm at Saxmundham where various trials were carried out and the results are still on record. Edward and Henry were also successfully associated with shipping as 'The Ipswich Steam Shipping Company' which owned and ran small coasting steamers between Ipswich and the North of England until the company was wound up in the First World War when shipping came under direct Government control.

Edward continued the good works started by his father and was Vicar's Warden of Bramford Church for fifty years, Town Councillor, Mayor and Alderman of Ipswich for fifty-five years, a member of Harwich Harbour Board for fifty-two years and a member of the Council of Fertilizer Manufacturers from its formation for nearly sixty years. He was also chairman of the Ipswich Dock Commission, responsible for seeing the Dock Gates re-sited to allow larger ships in. He was eventually honoured as High Steward of Ipswich and in 1922 he was knighted for services to the town.

Edward Packard married Ellen Turner in 1867 and they went to live at Grove House in Bramford, close to the works in Paper Mill Lane, which was given to him by his father on his marriage. They lived there all their lives and had twelve children, six sons and six daughters – Austin's mother was about half way – expanding the house as the family grew. It was a happy house and in the surrounding fields he bred Suffolk horses, his favourite breed. The greatest loves in his life were art, painting and the water. He had rowed at Cirencester and continued successfully at the 'Nautilus' Rowing Club at Ipswich which he helped to found, and in his early twenties he had a 14 foot sailing dinghy which he raced against similar boats on the river Orwell. He had some art lessons from W.R. Symonds and he became a prime mover in starting the Ipswich Art Club as its first secretary and treasurer, the latter post he was to hold for the rest of his life. He was a proficient artist and many of his paintings survive in the family and at the Ipswich Museum. He never stopped painting water-colours of his beloved Bluebell Wood at Grove House and the peaceful meadows around his home. He frequently travelled and would paint at every opportunity.

Sailing was a passion and for many years, he was Rear Commodore of the Royal Harwich Yacht Club and Commodore of the Orwell Corinthian Yacht Club after its formation in 1888. Edward Packard owned a succession of yachts and Austin searched various records such as *Hunts Yachting Magazine*, which includes Harwich Regatta reports, to try and identify these vessels.

Edward Packard's first boat was probably from his childhood and referred to in speeches by him as '.......with the aristocratic name of the Bug.......' He presumably started his sailing with other people and his first memorable race was in 1863, aged twenty, from Erith to the Nore, although the boat is not mentioned. In 1864 he built his own 14 foot dinghy, probably called 'Rosebud', and his name is linked with several other boats although it is not certain whether or not he owned them. These were the 'Bessie', 10 tons of 1860, the 'Madge', designed by G.L. Watson and later found in America where she outclassed all the American boats of her size, and the 'Anita', a 43 ton schooner in which he raced in July 1870 from Harwich to Hull.

In 1875 Edward designed the 10 tonner 'Aveyron' which was built by E. Robertson of Woodbridge. He was head of the 10 Ton Class which then raced on

Water colour of una rigged Vigia by Austin's mother

the East Coast and was successful in winning the Prince of Wales Yacht Club's 50 Guinea Challenge Cup three years in succession, an achievement of which he was very proud. In 1881 he owned the large 80 ton yawl 'Atlanta' and by 1888 he owned a Una Class called 'Puritan'. These were descended from the American Cat Boats and sometimes known as Cowes Una Boats as the first group was built there in the mid 1850s, based on the design of the Cat Boat 'Una' which was imported from America in 1853 by Earl Mountcharles and from which the class took its name. By 1880 the class had broken up and several boats migrated to the East Coast and continued racing there with at least two new boats built by local builders, until the late 1890s. It is uncertain who built 'Puritan' but it is likely that she was built in Cowes, probably by C. Corke in his yard in Birmingham Road. The boats offered good racing and day-sailing, but could provide a wet and wild ride in less than perfect weather. Today, few Una boats remain, although a sister ship to 'Puritan', the 'Vigia', built in 1872 has been restored by Peter Sainty and for many years she lay in the creek at Brightlingsea, although gaff sloop rigged. 'Vigia' is now in the Maritime Museum in Newport on the Isle of Wight, where she is to be returned to her original rig.

Racing was still a key effort in 1891 when Edward purchased the 5 Rater 'Valentine'. These were out and out racing craft built for speed and not for a long life. This boat had been designed by G.L. Watson and built by Camper & Nicholson in 1890 for Mrs G.A. Schenley, a renowned lady sailor from the Solent. The boat was successful and in her first season she took 5 firsts and four other prizes out of twenty-seven starts.

In 1894 he purchased his last yacht, a 40 ton schooner called 'Britannia'. This was one of several vessels of that name, there being no rule in Lloyds to prevent this. In 1895 Edward Packard and Austin's Mother, Celia (1871–1960), cruised right around Britain. They travelled up the East Coast, which they did not greatly enjoy and passed through the Caledonian Canal to spend a month around the Clyde with various members of the family joining and departing, and staying in a rented house on the shore. They returned down the west coast, along the south coast and to the Solent in time for Cowes Week. From this voyage came a beautiful set of water colours by Austin's mother, who was the only one of the family to sail the whole trip round Britain. Austin does not remember his grandfather sailing, he was by then in his seventies, though he can, however remember him in his eighties re-rigging a bone prisoner of war ship model for the Ipswich museum.

All the family sailed at one time or another but most not seriously, except for Edward Packard himself, Celia (Austin's mother) and one of her younger sisters Nina.

Together Celia and Nina shared an Orwell Corinthian One Design, at a time when it was most unusual for young ladies to go sailing at all. That sailing was in her blood is indisputable when one considers she was still sailing her Royal Harwich One Design when she was eighty years old. During her days at kindergarten she made life long friends with William Burton, later Sir William, who became an influential person in her son's life on several occasions and was a leading light in yachting, locally, nationally and internationally.

The Orwell Corinthian One Design class was designed by H.C. Smith of Burnham-on-Crouch and was one of the earliest one design classes, racing actively from around 1899 until the mid 1930s. The class also raced at Burnham-on-Crouch as the Crouch One Design and the Ipswich boats were later sold there when replaced with the Royal Harwich One Design in 1937. The Orwell Corinthians were half decked keel boats of 18 feet LOA, 15 feet LWL, 5 feet 2 inches beam and only 2 feet 9 inches draught. The boats were originally Gunter rigged, although the boats at Burnham eventually raced with Bermudan rigs. The boats proved to be good sea boats, sailing up and down the coast competing at regattas at Aldeburgh and Burnham. Celia Packard owned with her sister Nina (b.1876), Orwell Corinthian O.D. number 2 called 'June', a name that would continue onto the Royal Harwich O.D. Her friend, Sir William Burton, owned number 3, 'May', named after his wife. 'May' and 'June' were two of the first batch of six Orwell Corinthians probably built in Burnham, but looked after by W. Orvis & Co who built some later boats at the end of the dock in Ipswich, and it was here that the boats were wintered and laid up for the First World War. The Packard boat was attended to by Bill Read, the paid hand, who worked in the Packard factory as a crane driver. He also served as steward aboard Edward Packard's yachts, in particular 'Britannia'.

Celia Packard was a determined and successful racing helmswoman and is regularly mentioned in the regatta reports. Austin had two beautiful silver cups won by his mother outright at Burnham-on-Crouch in 1899 and the Aldeburgh regatta in 1901. She was not afraid of adventure or travel and the taste for the latter must have set in at an early age when she attended a finishing school in Brussels enabling her to be fluent in French.

The paternal family was a mixture of 'Austin' and 'Farrar' and came from the Caribbean area. The first Farrar to settle in the area was a missionary who went out in the early 1800s, but the Austins had been out there since the early 1700s. The first Austin was shipped to the West Indies as a convict by Judge Jefferies for some peccadillo. Presumably the offence was slight as no doubt he would otherwise have been hanged. He was shipped out to work as a slave on the plantations, but with the chance to earn himself a piece of land by the end of his sentence. Having completed his time he settled on the piece of land and expanded from there, with one of his descendants becoming a Bishop in the West Indies. Another descendent moved to British Guiana and at sometime there began the criss-crossing of the family tree as an Austin married a Farrar cousin, and visa-versa down the generations. They all had large families with many child deaths and it has left a complicated legacy of ancestors.

Austin in kindergarten

Austin's father came from the British Guiana branch and was indeed born there and (Austin believed) educated there before joining the Colonial Service.

Austin had no recollections of his father, who was killed in 1916 after his ship was torpedoed whilst returning home on leave from Sierra Leone in West Africa. He had been in England when Austin was born in 1913 but returned to Sierra Leone some time in 1914, where he worked as a Colonial Administrator. Austin knew less of his father's side of the family as they were more spread out and he very much grew up in Suffolk, the home of his mother's family. Austin's mother and father met in Sierra Leone. Celia Packard was a most adventurous woman and was in Sierra Leone housekeeping for her eldest brother who was a Judge. He was a bachelor and needed someone to keep house for him and to act as a companion. This was at a time when West Africa was regarded as the white man's grave. Austin's father and Celia Packard eventually married in 1905 in Bramford, the family home, and their first son, Norman, was born in 1907.

After the war, as a war widow, Austin's mother kept house for the family and immersed herself in good works. Once Austin and his brother were ensconced in school, she did a great deal of travelling. She was prominent in the Women's Institute and travelled extensively, visiting her in-laws in British Guiana and the West Indies at least twice, as well as America and Canada, often on Women's Institute business.

AUSTIN PACKARD FARRAR was born on 21st February 1913 at Felixstowe and lived with his mother in Ipswich during the First World War, usually in rented accommodation, starting off near Henley Road, then Fonereau Road where news of his father's death reached them. A bungalow was rented in Manor Road and then they moved to 107 Constable Road which was unfurnished and much of the furniture bought then survived in Austin's home until his death. Austin's schooling began at kindergarten during the war in 1917 at the age of four. This was part of the Ipswich High School for Girls in which its kindergarten section also took boys. The High School has recently moved from Ipswich to take over the Old Woolverstone Hall where many years later after the Second World War Austin was to run the Boatyard. These two points were, Austin regarded, as reason to claim Old Boys status. One of his teachers at that time was Enid Blyton working as a trainee teacher before going on to write her many books. Much later, after a letter requesting assistance in the local East Anglian Daily Times, Austin was able to help one of her biographers by producing a group photograph showing himself and her circa 1918. His friend Harry Rackham is also in the photograph. He lived next door to Austin in Ipswich and rose to become City Engineer of Salisbury. They stayed loosely in touch through the years and Austin found himself invited to Salisbury in the early 1980s to give a talk to the local yachtsmen.

In 1920 the family moved to Felixstowe, starting in lodgings and subsequently having a house built at Lark's Rise, Links Avenue. This house backed onto the old Eastward Golf Links and part of the requirements for the new houses was that they must have chain link fences so that golfers could retrieve their lost golf balls. Austin's mother and father had lived in lodgings in Felixstowe before the war. Here Austin attended Pre-Prep School before moving on to Imperial Service College, Windsor, to their Junior School (Prep) in 1922. This was part of the main college about one mile away and Austin remembered walking across the fields to the main school Chapel. In January 1924 Austin entered the main College to complete his schooling until July 1930. *'Life at school seemed to take such a long time. To work out that I really could only have been at the junior school for two years, but it seemed like five or six at the time'.* Austin remembers at pre-prep school when the term stretched away into infinity, you couldn't imagine how far away the end of the term was. Looking back, his main thoughts on school were that he hated it and it probably hated him. Like many of his generation he suffered from Rheumatic Fever and missed a year of schooling. He spent much of the time in a wheelchair and had to learn to walk again using a stick in the early period. To finish schooling required a great deal of cramming on subjects such as calculus and no doubt he was glad to move on.

Austin's mother at the helm of June, the Royal Harwich OD

Apprenticeship was to be the next step and a marine connection is hardly surprising. Austin had been building model steam boats since Prep School and a career as a Marine Engineer would seem a logical step. He recalled that the first model did not have a very clever hull nor was the machinery very good. The machinery had been selected from a catalogue full of exciting things from a company in London called Stevens' Model Dockyard – the boiler and oscillating engine came from this catalogue. The boiler was soft soldered together and unfortunately it did not take very much of getting up steam for the solder to flow. If you boiled it dry it, of course, fell apart. It did however teach Austin to solder.

June on the Orwell

Austin's first memories of sailing were around 1920 when he was seven and it was Bill Read, his mother's boat hand, who taught Austin much of his early knowledge of boats and the sea, including how to swim. The 'June' was much used for picnics and sails down the river. Although his older brother Norman joined his Mother for racing, Austin has no recollection of racing until his days of apprenticeship. Whilst still sailing in the summer holidays, at the Imperial Service College, he took up rowing like his grandfather before him and this was his main sport until the 1930s.

AUSTIN TOLD OF his early sailing in one of his many written anecdotes, this from 1993:

"Some of my earliest memories are of being taken sailing by my mother in 'June', an Orwell Corinthian One Design which she shared with her sister Nina Packard. Grandfather Packard had been a considerable yachtsman in his day, owning a string of yachts from the 1860s onwards, some of which he had designed himself, and raced with some success as evidenced by the array of silverware on his sideboard. However, of a family of 12, only the two girls had taken seriously to yachting, and they raced 'June' together since the class started in 1899, at a time when it was most unusual for young ladies to take an active part in yachting. I started at about the age of six, when the boats were fitted out in 1919, after being laid up for the duration of the War.

At that time the One-Designs were kept on moorings at Pin Mill. We used to go from Ipswich in one of the paddle steamers, 'Norfolk' or 'Suffolk', which plied from new Cut East down the river to Felixstowe Dock pier and Harwich; with a request stop at Pin Mill. Those who know Pin Mill today will know the hard, with its dog-leg, as being one of the longest in the country, but never quite reaching low water springs. This is because dredging of the main channel has encouraged silting, and the more the Dock Commission dredge off the end of Potter Point to get big ships up to Ipswich dock the more it silts up off Pin Mill. In those days before Cliff Quay was built, when the Australian grain ships would moor to large buoys in Buttermans Bay below Pin Mill and unload into sailing barges which ferried the grain up to Paul's and Cranfield's mills in Ipswich dock, there was enough water at high tide for the paddle steamer to put her bow in opposite the dog-leg in the hard. Here passengers would scramble from one of the paddle box sponsons into a boat pulled by one of the Ward family and be ferried ashore.

During the trip down the river I would be glued to the plate glass windows which gave a view into the engine room, fascinated by the gleaming steel rods and copper pipes of the paddle engines, and this is probably what started me wanting to be a marine engineer. I never had a desire to be an engine driver.

'June' had a paid hand, Bill Read, whose official job was driver of the steam crane in Grandfather's factory, but who doubled as steward in his 40 ton cutter 'Britannia' and looked after the One-Design. When we were going sailing Bill would make his own way to Pin Mill by bus or steamer and have the covers off and everything ready when we arrived. We would have a leisurely sail down river, kedge in shallow water for a picnic lunch, and Bill would give me my first lessons in swimming.

June and the paddle steamer Suffolk

I was too young to be taken racing, but I remember an expedition in 1919 or 1920 to Harwich Harbour to see the Royal Naval review. The Harwich Destroyer Force were there anchored off Shotley Spit, and the King had come in the 'Victoria & Albert' to inspect them. Incidentally, he knighted Sir William Burton on board the 'V & A', for his wartime work in food rationing. We sailed round looking at the destroyers, which looked enormous to me, got too close to one of them and caught our topping lift on her boat boom. We could not sail it clear because of the tide, and a sailor had to go out along the boat boom and cut our topping lift. A bearded and very senior-looking naval officer leant over the rail and laughed at our predicament. Mother worked out afterwards that it must have been King George V himself!"

It was also in 1920 that Austin and his brother Norman were taken on his first trip abroad to British Guiana to visit his father's family. They spent most of the summer visiting the various family plots. His father had also been one of twelve or thirteen children and so there were various aunts, uncles and cousins scattered across the West Indies.

Cycling was seen as an excellent form of holiday transport and the first cycling holiday with his mother and brother had been when Austin – still at pre-school – could only just ride a bike and the three of them cycled to Kent. This involved cycling down through Essex to take the ferry from Southend-on-Sea to Sheerness and then on to Canterbury, visiting various cousins in the area. Later, during his prep school years, the family holidayed in France at St Cast, in Brittany, taking bicycles with them and touring the area. On returning to England on the St Malo to Southampton ferry, they then proceeded to cycle to Dorset staying at Bed & Breakfast along the way to visit yet more cousins.

Austin's future career was greatly helped by the long time family friend and mentor Sir William Burton. William Burton was born in Suffolk and was educated at the Ipswich Grammar School, living in Ipswich or nearby for all his life. A local businessman, his firm 'Burton, Son and Sanders' was sited in Key Street, Ipswich and he was knighted in 1921 for services during the First World War. He enjoyed the countryside and was master of both the Staghounds and the Essex and Suffolk Foxhounds, but like his friends the Packards, sailing was very important. He began his racing with a half-rater called 'Lollipop' and also raced the Orwell Corinthian One Designs and later supported the new Royal Harwich One Design. He entered first class racing in 1897 with a 52 Rater called 'Penitent' and was Commodore of the Royal Harwich Y.C., the Royal Thames Y.C., and the Royal Victoria Y.C. at various times. It was to yachting management that he made the greatest contribution and by 1905 he had been elected to represent the United Kingdom at the conference to form a universal measurement method and the formation of the International Yacht Racing Union, reformed as the International Sailing Federation. In 1907 he sailed a 12 Metre 'Britomart', winning twenty firsts and twelve other prizes out of forty-five starts. 1909 saw 'Ostara', a 15 Metre, and 1911 'Octavia', a 19 Metre, both equally successful.

William was by now heavily involved with the Yacht Racing Association – now the Royal Yachting Association – and in 1919 visited Scandinavia to discuss common rating rules. This was a subject that took up many committee meetings over the years. He was an excellent racing helmsman, his wife Lady Burton was usually with him as his timekeeper, and in 1920 he helmed 'Shamrock IV' in the unsuccessful Americas Cup Challenge of Sir Thomas Lipton.

In the early 1930s he sailed the 6 Metre class, representing Britain at the Olympics, and in 1927 he started a long and successful association with the Twelve Metre Class and four yachts to that rating, ending with 'Jenetta' which was hastily laid up at Brightlingsea in 1939 on the outbreak of war. Sir William never sailed again as he died in 1942. He had been involved with the formation of the International and National classes and worked with committees on the racing rules. As a Vice President of the Y.R.A. and Chairman of the Permanent Committee of the I.Y.R.U. he gave thousands of hours to the workings of these two organisations and laid the foundations of the sport as we know it today. He was elected President of the Y.R.A. in 1937 and is remembered today in the trophy presented by him to the National Twelve Class in 1936. 'The Burton Cup' is still raced for to the present day. With this background, he was able to make the first introductions for Austin's apprenticeship.

CHAPTER 2
APPRENTICESHIP, PHILIP & SON, DARTMOUTH

Schooling completed, Austin began his apprenticeship in the autumn of 1930 at the Yards of Philip and Son in Dartmouth. His intention was to train for the position of a Marine Engineer and to this end his apprenticeship indenture stated he was to learn the 'Art of Fitting and Turning, with a year in the Drawing Office'. The choice of firm was helped by the family friend Sir William Burton, who at this time was having his new motor yacht, 'CALETA', built by Philip and Son, and gave good references for Austin. Burton was by this time racing Twelve Metres and had been using his old Nineteen Metre 'Octavia', as a tender. However, with a Centenary Regatta being held in Sweden, he wanted a boat that could tow his Twelve Metre to the Baltic. This was to be Caleta's first job. Above the water she looked like the steam yachts of old with her clipper bow and counter stern, but below the water she was a Philip tug. She was built in steel and styled by Burton's designer Alfred Mylne.

The firm of Philip and Son had two yards in Dartmouth. They owned the old Simpson Strickland Steam Launch Yard known as the Sandquay Yard on the Dartmouth Bank, with its foundry and engine shops and the facilities for building wooden yachts up to 50 tons. On the Kingswear bank and upstream from the town, they owned the Noss Yard with the main shipbuilding and fitting shops for tugs up to 100 feet. This yard had very poor access with no road, only a path and the main access was by water. There were no mains services and the yard had its own power station running on producer gas from anthracite delivered by water. Two big Crossly gas engines provided the power for the whole yard and the main burners had smaller ovens around the sides to enable lunches to be heated up during the morning. Most men took baskets with food ready prepared for lunch. Austin's landlady provided his, and a yard hand would collect the meals during the morning and have them ready to be distributed at lunchtime. Austin remembers fondly the real 'Devon' pasties made by his landlady, some ten or twelve inches long with meat at one end and apple at the other, being made ready and piping hot for lunch. Care needed to be taken to make sure you started at the right end. This facility ensured the men had regular hot meals at the right time of the day.

To start an apprenticeship as a Marine Engineer in the 1930s proved to be a less than sound choice, as this was the start of the Depression and the slump in shipping which became progressively worse and worse. However, for Austin it provided more variety in the yard as he was able to move around the various departments gaining more experience than might originally have been expected. Like many others in shipbuilding, Philip and Son suffered during the Depression, temporarily mothballing the Noss Yard around 1933 and sometimes laying off men or transferring them to other jobs.

Austin arrived at Philip and Son 'talking posh' and unable to cope with the Devon dialect. By half way through the first morning nobody on the fitting shop floor had bothered to ask his name, but he was addressed as 'Clarence'. It seemed a reasonable handle and he accepted it as a sort of 'nom de voile' and it was used ever since throughout the marine industry. Austin started work at the Noss Yard and this was his base for the first couple of years. He started working on the steam engines for the third Torpoint Chain Ferry then being built. The yard had built two ferries the previous year and this was to be the reserve boat to allow one vessel in for service with two always running. The previous generation of ferries had been built by Philip and Son and these were their replacement. They have subsequently been replaced again with more modern diesel engines ferries. However these three were powered by compound steam engines driving a toothed wheel for the chain. Austin worked in the fitting shop and his very first job was cutting the ends off large two-inch diameter bottom end bolts. Bolts this size could not be bought and were turned and the threads cut on the lathe. The end where the lathe centre had been, needed cutting off and filing up by hand. Austin was handed a saw with the dreaded words 'don't break the hacksaw blade, boy' which, as we all know, guarantees that this is exactly what will happen. However, this was not held against him and he worked his way through various small jobs in the fitting shop.

The Torpoint Ferry safely afloat

February of 1931 saw the ferry ready to launch and the events of the day left a lasting picture. The ferry, hull complete, sat right at the top of the long slipway, a tug having been built below her. The engine and boiler were ready and would be fitted once launched, using the sheer legs on the end of the quay. These were massive sheer legs some one hundred feet high and lifting 60 tons. Here on the quay berth the vessels would be finished before sea trials.

The appointed day dawned and all was ready with the drag chains in place and the ways prepared. First thing in the morning, the officials from Cornwall County Council had arrived and the Chairman's wife was ready to knock the champagne over one corner of the ferry, the ship not having a normal single bow. The ceremony took place but, instead of a grand launch, absolutely nothing happened. They heaved and they pulled but the ferry remained firmly in place. Being early in the year, she had frozen onto the ways. The drag chains were removed and hydraulic jacks tried, along with blow lamps, all to no effect. At this point it was decided to take a wire from a bollard on the ferry, through a snatch block on the quay and up to the sheer legs. All these things had taken some time to try and the morning had warmed slightly. They were just about to try winching from the sheerlegs when the ferry began to move. Austin was watching from the end of the quay and a slightly blurred photo taken on his box camera looking back on the ferry shows one of the hands frantically casting off the wire from the bollard to prevent the sheerlegs being pulled over. By now the tide had dropped and instead of a smooth path into the water a six foot drop waited at the end of the ways. With no drag chains, the Ferry accelerated down the ways, over two hundred feet of clear slip, cleared the six foot drop and they later reckoned that she must have hit the water at close on 30 knots. Being flat bottomed; she planed across the river and hit a moored steamer on the other side. Fortunately the only damage was a badly buckled brow on the ferry and some dented plates on the steamer. As Austin said, 'never a dull moment.'

The Torpoint Ferry frozen at the top of the ways

As the shipping slump worsened, the last vessel at the Noss yard was a ninety-six foot tug built on spec, known to all as the 'Stock Tug'. The hull had been finished and there being no more orders, the platers were paid off. The fitting shop continued to build and install the engine although with no further jobs the yard worked at a more relaxed pace than normal.

The cylinder block had been finished on the boring machine and all the cylinder head bolts, some 2 ½ inches in diameter, specially made. All the nuts and bolts had to be individually made, being lathe cut. The nuts and bolts were numbered to ensure that they could not be mixed up as there was no guarantee that they would interchange. Whilst it did not seem so at first, Austin was told that this was a relatively small engine, with a fifteen inch diameter high pressure cylinder and a thirty-two inch diameter low pressure cylinder, with a twenty-four inch stroke. Larger engines were encountered, however, in the steamers laid up on the river. Because of the shipping slump there were a string of twenty or thirty steamers moored up the River Dart and occasionally one would be sold to a Greek owner.

Although a caretaker would be on board, the yard would be called in to check the engines and raise steam before the ship departed. The freighters were around three to four thousand tons, but there were a couple of small liners. One of these turned out to be the sistership of the ship that Austin had travelled in, to British Guiana in 1920. Then she had seemed enormous, the 'Arzila' of the Royal Mail Steam Packet Company. However, after a little research to establish that the vessel laid up was indeed a sistership, it came as a bit of a shock to find that she was only three thousand tons. This is considerably smaller than the cross channel ferries in use today. One job ordered was to check the main cooling water inlet which seemed to be partially blocked. This was known as the Kingston valve, although why is not known, and was some eighteen inches in diameter and two feet long. The lid was taken off, and inside was an eel that had obviously got in through the outside grating when it was small and had lived in there for some time, then being too big to leave. By this time it was about six feet long and it escaped onto the engine room floor. The ensuing chase across the steel plates would have done credit to the silent movies.

The shipping slump, however, provided Austin with a golden opportunity. Whilst admitting he was scared stiff of the Managing Director, Mr Sauter, he summoned the courage to ask, 'would it be possible, since there wasn't going to be much more work in the fitting shop, could I move around the yard into the other departments and widen my experience?' Mr Sauter pondered, but said, 'yes' and Austin was able to spend roughly six months in each of the coppersmith's shop, the foundry and the blacksmith's. This was wonderful experience and Austin became quite good in each department, particularly enjoying the coppersmith's shop.

A propeller on the lathe

Austin then moved across the river to the Sandquay Yard to begin his time in the foundry and the blacksmith's shop. The foundry had a team similar to the coppersmith's shop with a foreman, two men and four boys, completing complicated tasks. One of the first jobs in the foundry was to make a spare propeller for the 'Stock Tug' before she departed. Casting a propeller is a complicated project, because the pattern only has one blade. This allows a three or four bladed propeller to be formed by careful alignment with the various pegs for the centre boss.

Whilst still in the fitting shop, Austin had been mate to one of the turners, Joe Maginnis, who worked the big lathe when turning the original propeller. This was a lathe with a ten foot diameter faceplate capable of turning a propeller to bore it and do the taper. Austin had worked with this turner on nearly the whole engine for the 'Stock Tug'. The crankshaft forging weighed over a ton and was laid on the marking out table for Maginnis to mark the two cranks at right angles and centre the unit with its forged-on flanges. The crank throws were solid blocks growing out of the central shaft and the middle was cut out by drilling hundreds of holes. The main parts of the shaft were turned whilst the cranks were still solid and the crank pins had dummy centres set up to allow them to be turned. These centres were marked from special castings that were bolted on to the flanges that had already been turned. Because turning the crank pins required the whole assembly to be off centre, the unit was wildly out of balance, rotating around its crank pins. To try and help, various iron balance weights were hung and bolted on, although the turning still had to be dead slow. The lathe for this was enormous with a twelve foot face plate which dipped down into a recess in the floor. Joe Maginnis was a small man and needed a pair of steps to get up to the cross slide which was about six feet off the ground. The propeller shaft was made on a special long bed lathe which had been made for gun boring at the Royal Arsenal.

The coppersmith's shop was probably the most impressive for Austin because, during this time, they made and installed all the piping for the 'Stock Tug'. The Tug had now been launched and was lying alongside for fitting out. Most men had been laid off and the boys actually did the work, in teams of two, under the guidance of the foreman. Austin worked with one of the other boys, Johnny Caulder. This was the finest way to learn rather than the traditional method of one man and the boy to fetch, carry and mostly watch. At this time there were four boys, one man and the foreman, Jim Meakin, in the coppersmith's shop.

The pipe work involved bending the main steam pipe, which was of six inch diameter heavy gauge copper, from the boiler to the engine, and the exhaust pipe which was of eighteen inch diameter and needed two bends of ninety degrees quite close to each other. This exhaust pipe was about eight feet long and the bends were in two planes giving a full twisted 'S' bend. The pipe had its ends stopped and was filled with natural resin to support the walls, and was bent with the aid of a 50 ton jack and various pegs and wedges to control the bend. With this pressure, and despite the best efforts, the walls could not fail to collapse a little. After the bending was complete, the pipe was heated and the resin melted. Water was used to cool and anneal and these areas were hand worked back to circular. The pipe was large enough for the smallest apprentice to actually lie inside and armed with ear plugs, work the crinkles out.

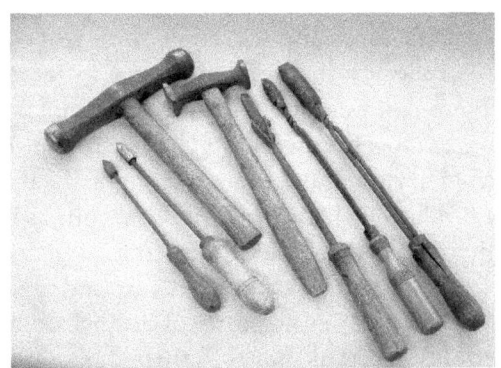

Planishing hammers and soldering irons

As normal with most apprenticeships, tools were made during the training and in the coppersmith's shop Austin was able to make various planishing hammers, which he used all his life and which I continue to use today. Having completed the copper pipe work, the shop then began all of the iron water piping. There was a tremendous amount of this piping to be completed for numerous tasks such as bilge pumps and fire pump outlets. Most of this piping was of three inch diameter and filled with sand and then bent hot. Patterns for the pipe runs were made from quarter inch iron wires which were bent to follow exactly the path from flange to flange, ensuring adequate clearances along the route. This pattern was taken back to the shop and the pipe was bent to exactly match the template. This was then offered up to check and, assuming all was well, it was returned to the shop to have its flanges fitted. The flanges were gunmetal castings brazed to copper pipe, or iron flanges screwed to iron pipes and obviously they had to be exactly square. The pipe would then be returned to check its final fit. If all was well the expression in the yard was 'it fitted so well it left my hands and floated up into place.' When this happened without correction on pipes such as the steam and exhaust pipes, it showed the real skills of these workers, and gave enormous satisfaction to the job.

Many skills were learnt in the coppersmith's shop including brazing, although to his regret Austin never had the chance to learn welding. There was one welder only with the firm and the welding equipment was portable and kept in a work boat to be available in either yard. The engine to power the generator came from a First World War tank. A job learnt and relished during this time was the making of a cowl ventilator with a dovetail join down either side, totally in copper. This join was cut on one side in a dovetail pattern and then lapped over and under the uncut edge. The whole assembly was then hammered down smooth and brazed. Once cleaned off it gave the impression that was all from one sheet.

AT THIS TIME Austin teamed up with another apprentice, Arnold 'Sam' Price, to build a model. Under the watchful eye of the coppersmith's shop foreman, Jim Meakin, they decided to build a scale model of the 'Stock Tug'. There was obviously no problem in obtaining the lines plan from the drawing office and the hull was constructed in wood at Sam's house and was some three feet overall. They then set about constructing the machinery at the yard, which was now fairly quiet and where there were spare lathes. The boiler was a twin drum water tube boiler built from bits of scrap copper tube all brazed together with ⅜' tube linking the two in a loop and a header tank above. The single cylinder engine was a slight cheat in that they were able to obtain a complete cylinder block casting ready machined from Stuart Turner. This was the only way they could get a cylinder casting.

The engine was then built around this as a vertical engine. The Stuart No. 10 could be finished as either vertical or horizontal and the cylinder and valve chest came all ready. The crankshaft was turned from a ⅝ 'bolt down to about a ¼' diameter for the shaft and the head of the bolt became the crank disk. Another smaller bolt screwed into that for the crank pin. The guides for the cross head con rod were machined from solid metal and the finished engine was set up on the bench and run on compressed air. The boiler was tested and the whole assembled in the hull. The model was finished with the details to the decks and superstructure and painted in the correct colours. It was then tested on the river. It worked supremely well and would tow a large rowing boat quite happily. However the boat never had a feed pump installed so her only disadvantage was that she had a limited steaming time before the boiler needed to be refilled with water. This at least controlled her range. 'Sam' Price had lived locally, but his parents moved away and 'Sam' went with them, never finishing his apprenticeship at Phillip & Sons. Austin gave his share of the model to Sam when he left, but it is to be hoped that the model is still safe and in steaming condition somewhere.

The 'Stock Tug' was in time finished and surveyed for tonnage. This procedure starts with the total volume of the boat, part of which can be classed as tonnage area or cargo carrying potential, and the remainder as allowed areas. These allowed areas include the engine room, ventilation shafts and accommodation. The survey complete, Austin remembered being given a hammer and chisel and the job of cutting the registration number into the steel engine room bulkhead. The number was as given and the tonnage was nil. The surveyor, having started with the whole and methodically subtracted the allowed areas, had eventually arrived at a zero tonnage. This is not quite so odd if one considers that a tug would not ever carry cargo and could not therefore be taxed for this purpose.

They then heard that the RAF was interested in the Tug to go out to the seaplane base in Singapore. This was being organised from the RAF Flying boat base at Plymouth, where they were developing seaplane tenders and similar craft. A sea trial was requested and its organisation was put in hand. Austin was part of the engine room party, having worked on the installation. This had to be meticulous in its accuracy. There were no flexible couplings available then and the shaft and engine had to be in perfect alignment. The engine was blocked, wedged and bolted solid and the flanges adjusted with feeler gauges all round. This had to be completed when the ship was afloat as there would be a slight movement when she lay on the mud alongside the fitting berth. After installation, if the ship took the ground then the whole set up would move as one. The engine had been turned over with a worm drive to check the valve timings etc. but had never raised steam. The yard had two tugs of its own, one of which was nearly always in steam for general shifting jobs on the river and her engineer came to raise steam on the 'Stock Tug' for the first time. Also on board was the leading hand fitter who had actually installed the engine.

There came the day when the 'Brass Hats' arrived from Plymouth in a seaplane tender to go out on trials and joining them was a rather scruffy individual who arrived on a motorbike. All was ready and Alec Philip, younger son of the old man George Philip, was skipper for the trials. He went to the bridge and stood by the wheel and telegraph. 'Cast off for'ard.' She was laying along side the floating dock, and he let the bows swing away with the tide.

'Cast off aft, slow ahead.' At that moment the engine turned for the first time. Austin remembers being much impressed by this, and it is an example of the confidence the management had in their product and the skills of their work force.

The ship left for trials in Start Bay, including a time trial over the measured mile, but to ensure a modicum of safety they had borrowed two lifebuoys from a local yacht; these were marked 'Grey Goose' and were now hung on the front of the bridge. Austin overheard the scruffy individual remark to one of the 'Brass Hats' that he wondered if the name 'Grey Goose' was an intentional joke seeing as the boat was painted grey and it was being sold to the RAF Austin could not recall whether the 'Brass Hats' had lunch onboard, only that in the engine room they had brought their own lunches which were duly warmed up on the boiler.

The trials completed, the ship returned to her berth and the scruffy individual departed on his motorbike. One of the 'Brass Hats' then took Austin on one side asking him if he knew who the scruffy individual was. 'No, sir.' He was Lawrence of Arabia. At this time he had taken the name 'Shaw' and had joined the RAF as an aircraftsman. He was working from the RAF base at Plymouth and with the British Power Boat Company at Hythe, on the development of high speed seaplane tenders.

There was a grapevine in the trade, as always, and Austin recalls that, although he cannot remember exactly how he found out, he learnt that Shaw was working on the spray breakers on the chines of high speed launches. Shaw had worked out that these breakers had to be horizontal to be effective. This was to be very useful to Austin when he designed his first boats some years later.

There were many trials held on boats from the yard, and one particular problem occurred with the propellers of the 'NAGMATI', built in 1932 for his Highness the Maharoo of Kutch. The full story is told in Appendix 2.

In the blacksmith's shop, Austin worked on fittings for the yachts being built at the Sandquay yard including wrought iron floors, knees and hanging knees for wooden yachts. These were worked with a steam hammer and the floors required careful planning to ensure that when the arms of the floor were bent up the changing angles of the hog and hull matched exactly. This was a work of art for the smith to get the offset angles right so that they matched when bent. This was beyond Austin's initial skill, although he did say he made a lot of bolts. He worked at his own anvil and forge, and learnt to keep a forge going.

The NAGMATI

At other times he would work with another person, both striking to work metal down. One of the useful things that Austin learnt was the technique to ring the bell at the fair. This test is not, as supposed, a test of strength, but a knack. The wooden mallet that you are given is not heavy and it is the speed not the actual strength of the blow that will ring the bell. You must start with the mallet right up above your head and then accelerate to hit the button as fast as possible. This technique, mastered in the blacksmith's shop, proved profitable at the local fairs and again much later in the 1960s when on the IJsselmeer at Hoorn at their local fair. Here, Austin's success proved a little unpopular with the stall holder.

About this time they had a very old wooden lightship in for repair. This vessel was over one hundred years old and needed work on her planking. The Trinity House surveyor had gone over the boat very thoroughly, and he had several bolts drawn for inspection. These proved to be in perfect condition but new ones had to be made to replace them, as the old bolts could not be re-used due to the damage caused to them driving them out. Austin worked on making the new bolts, but the old ones were used to make soldering irons for his tool box. I am now using them and they are as fine as ever. The bit was forged and a hole punched through. A piece of quarter inch iron wire, as used for templates, was posted through the hole, turned back on itself and twisted red hot. The two ends were then brought up and welded together, beaten square and formed into a tang for the wooden handle. Throughout an apprenticeship, the student was expected to make many of his tools and the time and materials were provided. These tools would often last a lifetime and beyond.

THE REPAIRS TO the Lightship remained vivid in Austin's memory and he wrote an article in 1990 recalling the event:

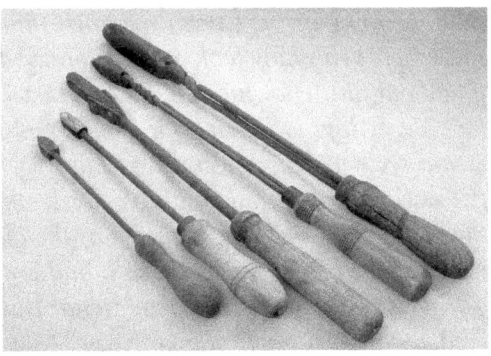

Soldering irons

"While I was an apprentice at Philip & Son at Dartmouth we used to do quite a lot of repair work for Trinity House on lightships and their tenders. One tender, I think it was the 'MERMAID', was docked for a routine survey and regular maintenance work on hull and engines. The floating dock, showing its age somewhat, was quite difficult to handle, and required all the skills of Jo Thorsen, the dockmaster, to bring it up level, controlling the air vents from the separate tanks by wooden bungs driven into their outlets. On this occasion it came up under a shoal of grey mullet – normally very difficult to catch with rod and line – and every one in the yard had fresh mullet for tea while a wagon load was dispatched on the night train to Billingsgate.

The specification for the overhaul called for all the paint on the superstructure to be burnt off down to bare steel, because many layers of paint over the years add up to a considerable weight which could affect the ship's stability. But the mate, who stayed on board as Ship's keeper, would have none of it: 'Don't you dare touch my paintwork: it's taken ten years to get it as good as this and I'm not going to start all over again'. How he squared it with the management I never knew but the superstructure got one coat of enamel; the mate signed for it having been burnt off, primed and undercoated, and the yard made quite a saving on the job.

The Seven Stones Lightship was a hundred years old when she came in for overhaul. Built in about 1830 of oak, and copper fastened, her scantlings were near enough the same as those for 'HMS VICTORY', built 60 years earlier and more than twice the size. Her outer planking was 8in thick, then there were grown frames 8in square and placed so close that they almost touched, and inside a 'ceiling' 6in thick, laid like another skin and caulked. The copper was stripped off the bottom and the surveyor had several of the copper fastenings driven out for examination; they were all in perfect condition and new ones were made to replace them. I was working in the blacksmith's shop at the time and managed to scrounge a piece of one of the old bolts 1in in diameter out of the sternpost, and forged it into a huge soldering iron, which I still possess.

The only timber which needed replacing was the forward end of the garboard strake on the starboard side. It had been badly scored, presumably by floating wreckage, and about 15ft back to the first scarf was to be renewed. Imagine the garboard strake of a wooden dinghy and how it twists from the angle of the bottom up to vertical on the stem, bending at the same time, then think of making it 8in thick and 15in wide. The shipwrights carefully took out the damaged length of plank and made a template of it as if laid out flat. They then sawed and adzed a new plank to the template and steamed it for several days to soften it for bending into place. But the new plank would not respond at all; securing the aft end and pushing the fore with hydraulic jacks only damaged the steel plating of the floating dock, so they contemplated carving another one out of the solid. However, examination of the old plank confirmed that the grain of the oak followed the curve and twist, so it had been made straight. There must be some way of getting it to go round. The traditional Dutch ships were all built of oak, and had even greater curves in their planking.

At about this stage a Dutch motor coaster came into Dartmouth and the shipwrights, finding the elderly skipper in the pub, asked him how the builders of the traditional boats used to get their planking round the bow. He told them that this was a trade secret, jealously guarded by the Dutch builders. So they plied him with drink all the evening and when it was near closing time one of the shipwrights said 'go on – you don't know how it's done, do you?' 'Oh, yes I (hic) do – they light a fire on one side and pour water on the other and it goes round on its own.' And so it did. But only because oak has such a large swelling and shrinking effect when wet or dry – any other timber would not do it."

LATE 1934 SAW Austin enter the drawing office for the last year of his apprenticeship. Here he began to see the design side of the business and have his first serious contact with yachts that would find his future employment. Although he was not formally trained as a Naval Architect, he spent many hours teaching himself the basics that he did not learn at work. His first dealings with successful design, however, were slightly earlier when Austin designed the steering gear for a new yacht.

This major project was a new yacht for Admiral Goldsmith, on which Austin would do a lot of work. This venerable character had gained a 'reputation' during the First World War when he commanded the Destroyer Flotilla at Harwich. He was also known to have taken a Destroyer through the small craft passage between Drake's Island and the mainland at high tide, but at full speed. Drake's Island can be found in Plymouth harbour and the narrow passage between it and the mainland, whilst safe for small craft, is not suitable for large modern warships. The new yacht was designed by the Chief Draftsman with Admiral Goldsmith looking over his shoulder, for the Admiral knew exactly what he wanted. The new vessel was to be a modern 'old-timer' with a straight stem and transom stern of some 41 tons and around 34 feet. During the designing and building project, the Admiral lived alongside at the yard on his current yacht, a 35 ton ketch called 'ENIADÆ' (built by Philip's in 1925), so he was always around. Austin visited him regularly during the evenings for a chat as his stories were always entertaining, supper was often forthcoming, and they became good friends.

The Admiral had been Captain of the Dockyard at Plymouth before his retirement and still had a house at Cawsand Bay near Plymouth. However, he was now living alone on his yacht, having moved out when his mother-in-law moved in, he not being able to stand her. His wife, mind you, must have been a woman of inexhaustible patience. He was adamant that he would not return home whilst his mother-in-law was there and lived a happy bachelor existence in Dartmouth being seen around with his trousers always rolled up to mid calf and his booming voice heard all over the yard. At one time he was asked to read the lessons in Kingswear church. However, it was reckoned that you did not need to be in the church to hear them; he could be heard in Dartmouth. One morning, Austin went down to the Admiral's yacht to find it dressed overall. Slightly puzzled, he was greeted by the Admiral on his way out with the words, 'mother-in-law's died, I'm off to the funeral'. He left with his lunch in a little bag and caught the bus to Plymouth. Later that evening he returned looking pleased with himself, declaring it a splendid funeral. He had waited till everybody had left, then sat on the grave to eat his lunch.

Admiral Goldsmith's new yacht progressed steadily and he eventually sold his current yacht. The new boat was quite special and great attention had been paid to detail. All the deck fittings and many of the internal fittings were of solid Monel metal (an alloy of copper and nickel which can be polished but settles to a light grey colour). He did not want polished brass and chrome was not yet acceptable. These were as usual done in house, cast, filed up and polished. When the steering gear was needed, there was really only one worm gear available on the market, but this only worked down one side and required the wheel to be skewed in the cockpit and was not very satisfactory.

Austin had observed the big Thames Sailing Barges that worked down Channel and become friends with the skipper of the 'LADY DAPHNE' who would come into Dartmouth with cement. Having seen the very neat gear used on the barges with a double thread on one shaft, Austin suggested to the Admiral and the drawing office that this system might adapt very well to the Admiral's yacht. This was agreed and Austin was given the task of designing the steering gear. He went aboard the 'LADY DAPHNE' to take the measurements and returned to the drawing office to produce a final scaled drawing for the yard to work from. Patterns were duly made and the castings produced and the shaft machined up with its double thread. The unit was installed and worked beautifully.

As can be imagined there was a grand party when the launching time came and Admiral Goldsmith's three daughters were there together with a niece who was always in the party and treated like a fourth daughter. The yacht at 51 feet and 44 tons was duly christened 'MADALÉNA', and the four girls were launched with the ship on August 22nd 1934.

The worm drive steering gear

One of the Admiral's daughters at the helm

The yacht was moored alongside to be rigged and fitted out. She was a mixture of the old fashioned and the very new, being gaff rigged with a standing squaresail yard but with the latest hollow laminated boom, gaff and yard from McGruer in Scotland. The mast was however a solid pole mast. She was fitted with a Kelvin single cylinder, twenty horsepower diesel – which started on petrol. It was a complete diesel engine with an auxiliary combustion chamber and a screw shut off valve. The auxiliary chamber had a spark plug and a carburettor that was rather like Aladdin's lamp in that you poured petrol into it. The engine was turned over by hand a couple of times to draw up the petrol and then the impulse magneto would turn over and provide a spark. As the engine picked up, the decompression lever was closed and the full diesel would fire and run. This used about a tablespoon of petrol in all.

The skylights, doghouse windows and portholes were all fitted with toughened glass when this material was very new. The yacht received a dispensation from Lloyds that brass rods were not therefore required over the skylight glass as would be normal. The glass was proudly shown off to guests who were handed a ball pein hammer and invited to try and break the glass. Needless to say no one succeeded. Austin believes he probably came closest when working aloft at the crosstrees. He dropped his iron marlin spike and remembers time standing still as he watched it spiralling down. It

Madeléna under sail

turned in the air falling big end down and striking the main saloon skylight. It bounced off the glass turned again in the air and embedded itself point down in the deck.

Come November the yacht was finished and Austin was invited to join for the shake down cruise along the West Country coast. The yard was very quiet and the Foreman was quite happy for Austin to be away for a fortnight, partly because it would be one less person to find a job for. Having loaded the yacht with stores, they motored upstream to anchor in Old Mill Creek past where the old training ship 'HMS Britannia' had lain. Next morning, when it was time to leave, it was found that the anchor was well and truly foul. The yacht was fitted with a hydraulic capstan, driven off the engine and under full load the yacht was at least a foot down by the head. They backed the capstan up with handles and eventually managed to raise the anchor to where it could be seen in the clear water. The anchor fluke had gone through one of the links in the old Britannia mooring chains that had been left there when the ship was removed. These links were some two inches square iron and two feet long. The Admiral eventually slid down the anchor cable and standing knee deep in water managed to get a rope under the links. They were able to free the anchor and then cut the rope, freeing the yacht with a tremendous surge, but a lesson in seamanship.

They left Dartmouth with the Admiral, his wife and the three daughters with the intention of calling into some of the local ports. Austin shared the Foc'sale with a Scotsman known as Scotty

Freeing the anchor

Dunlop and they were very comfortable with good pipecots and nine foot headroom. Austin cannot remember visiting Salcombe – probably because of their deep draft, but they spent some time around Plymouth which was the Admiral's old stamping ground. They motored up the Tamar finding that you could not always trust your eyes. They were slightly concerned going under the Saltash bridge which looked far too close to the mast head. There was at least fifteen feet of clearance according to the pilot guide but it still looked too close. The Tamar opens out above the bridge and as they proceeded on up they were horrified to find high tension power lines stretched across the river in catenaries with big loops hanging down with the lowest apparently above the main channel. They edged up to them, gingerly feeling their way, and with everyone standing well away from any metal work until they passed underneath – apparently only just clearing them. That afternoon they picked up a mooring at the village of Cargreen and later, ashore in the local pub in conversation, expressed their concern about the power lines further down the river. 'You don't need to worry about them,' they were told, 'they are forty feet higher than the Saltash bridge.'

The yacht was very comfortable, with the Admiral's wife and the girls aft in the ladies cabin. The Admiral had the owner's or navigator's cabin and one man on the saloon settee, called Harry Mainsty. Forward of the saloon was the galley one side and the heads the other, and forward of this the Foc'sale with Austin and Scotty Dunlop as mentioned earlier. At Fowey, however, Harry Mainsty had to leave to return to work and Austin was invited to

Going under the Saltash Bridge

move into the saloon. Austin duly moved but for one night only. There was six feet between the bulkheads, but by the time the cushions were fitted there was a good deal less than six feet. Austin then realised how short Harry Mainsty was as Austin needed six feet two inches to sleep out and he had one of the most uncomfortable nights he has ever spent, unable to stretch out, and the next night he moved back to the foc'sale. That morning they had all been to church in Fowey, it being Sunday. The problem for the crew however was to keep straight faces when it came to both the lesson and the sermon. This is believed to have been taken from 'The Second Book of Kings' and is etched on Austin's memory. 'The bed is not long enough that a man may stretch himself thereon nor the covering wide enough that he may wrap himself therein,' the gist of the sermon being that this was the acme of discomfort and the cause of great mirth in their pew.

From Fowey they cruised onto Falmouth, visiting Restronguet Creek to go ashore and anchored off King Harry Ferry. They did not stop at Falmouth itself, being unable to pick up a mooring, but cruised on to the Helford River to 'worship at the shrine of St Claude.' This was of course Claude Worth who lived by the Helford river and was regarded as one of the fathers of modern yacht cruising. He was by this time a very old man in his eighties, but still reasonably active and not overly liked by the people who had to deal with him. He was certainly not popular with the men at Philip and Son, where he had had his last boat built, – 'Tern IV'– and Austin had heard many stories about him from the men. The chippies working on 'Madaléna' had said what a pleasure it was to work for a nice gentleman like the Admiral, not like Claude Worth. Worth created bedlam and seemed to go out of his way to cause trouble and was generally an unpleasant character. Worth had designed 'Tern IV' himself and had a contract to build with Philip and Son. This contract called for all timber to be free of knots. However he had specified a Canadian Rock Elm capping to the bulwark in one length which in itself was difficult enough to find.

Despite regular visits, he waited until the capping was finished and varnished before pointing out that there was a very small knot half way along. Rock Elm has by its nature small pin head knots and it was one of these. However he insisted that the whole lot was ripped off and replaced. One story was that, on one of his visits, he came upon a chippy fitting a galvanised Runner Chainplate through the covering board to bolt onto the topsides. Where it went through the covering board there was as necessary a slightly loosing fit, and the chippy was making good with a little teak coloured putty. Worth came along with the words, 'Is that how you cover up your mistakes my man?'

The reply was swift and short, 'Yes, Doctor, the earth covers yours.'

As the 'Madaléna' entered the Helford River, they passed a little cutter sailed by the old man Warrington-Smythe. They picked up Claude Worth's mooring in the Helford River; he no longer owned a yacht but still had a mooring off his house. Warrington-Smythe was an old friend of the Admiral and once secure came alongside in his dinghy loaded with apples from his orchard and the hearty greeting

'Big chief Warrington-Smythe bring present for white man'. The apples lasted for some time. Later the Admiral and Mrs Goldsmith went ashore in the dinghy to call on Claude Worth, and invited him onboard to look around and come for a sail. Next morning he was fetched in the dinghy and brought aboard.

Despite his age and his irascible nature Worth had a sound knowledge. He walked to the foredeck and tapped the self tacking foresail sheet horse. This was a piece of inch stainless steel shafting with a Monel metal fitting at either end bolted through the deck. 'Your foresheet horse is a foot too long.' He was absolutely correct, as only that very morning they had decided it was too long and that they would have to blank off six inches at each end to sheet the sail to the correct angle.

Sailing with Claude Worth

Worth settled in the Dog House to keep out of the chilly day and was going on about this and that. Scotty Dunlop quietly remarked to Austin that it sounded exactly like his book. They listened for a little longer and Scotty became even more sure. He leapt down the foc'sale hatch and into the saloon to find the book. On return they found that Worth was repeating his book word for word as necessary and completely verbatim. They eventually departed for a sail and Worth sat in the helmsman's cockpit sheltered from the wind. Here Austin was able to take a photograph of the famous man. This was Austin's only experience of the man but it was quite enough and he was not sorry when Worth departed later that afternoon. The fortnight's meanderings were too soon over and from the Helford river the 'Madaléna' returned to Dartmouth., and early the following year the Admiral left for the West Indies, taking with him as crew a local friend of Austin's, Marco Martin. He also had a Dart Dinghy and had been a protégé of MacAndrew, a local racing enthusiast, who was also to help and influence Austin, and of whom we shall hear more later.

A steady supply of work for the yard over the years had been the repair of lightships and the lightship tenders used to service these vessels. At this time the yard received a contract to build a new batch of lightships which would allow the Noss Yard to be restarted. These lightships were used all round the British Coast and many are still in service today from the 29 ships built over a 30 year period after this time. This contract was one of the first projects that Austin worked on in the drawing office. Another class of vessel that had provided regular work was the steamer tenders, some 100-120 feet long and very beamy, for the shipping lines that had regular services in and out of Plymouth. These tenders would collect the passengers from the station or quay and take them out to the liners lying in the Sound. As with the lightships, these were in regularly for survey and repair. Often these were in a sorry state and were put in to the floating dry dock for work on the bottom. Austin remembers that whilst the dock was being pumped out, the surveyor would go round the vessel and throw every lifebuoy into the water. These were the old fashioned cork ones and most of them would sink. This was a regular occurrence.

The contract for lightships was a fruitful one and went on long after Austin had left the firm. As with most building contracts at Philip and Son the entire job would be completed in house, from the drawings to the finished vessel, with very little bought in. The only major component not built by them was the boilers for tugs. The first design work had been done on the hull shape of the lightships and a half model made of around four feet long. Austin was helping one of the senior draftsmen to do the shell plate development. It was not possible to take the plates directly from the plate development drawing because this gives a distorted picture. Therefore, using the half model and pieces of paper, the model was plated up and it was then possible to see the plate runs and those difficult areas that would require smaller plates and hot workings. An element of trial and error was used and the plates drawn onto the model. The little paper patterns of the plates were then measured and the actual plates ordered from them to be the right size on arrival. Whilst a large ship would have many plates the same size, a lightship that tends to be shaped all over has many different shaped and sized plates. This complicated job was excellent experience.

Austin completed many standard jobs in the drawing office. One job that always had to be done was the redrawing of the accommodation plan on the stock designs from Captain O.M. Watts. Austin had first encountered Captain O.M. Watts in 1932, when he and his partner Captain Sullivan put into Dartmouth on passage, delivering a motor lifeboat to Ireland.

They were already established as yacht chandlers in a back street of Mayfair, not far from their later shop in Albermarle Street; yacht design was one of the services offered. Most of the yachts built by the Sandquay yard were not designed in house and many were built to stock designs from other designers. Captain O.M. Watts did not design his own boats, but employed a draftsman to draw up the work. The designs produced good sailing yachts that, whilst a little chunky, sailed well but the interiors needed to be redrawn. Captain O.M. Watts' draftsman never seemed to be able to grasp the fact that the accommodation plan does not go straight down from the deck plan. The heads would be shown half way up the hull side with little chequered floor tiles that would be impossible to use. If the heads had been placed where shown it would have meant a hole in the hull side and the heads half in and half out of the boat. This meant a little in-house reworking to allow for the hull curves.

Several Captain O.M. Watts' designs were built whilst Austin was at Dartmouth, and he was able to go on the delivery trip for one of them from Dartmouth to Bembridge on the Isle of Wight. This yacht was the 23 ton 'Evelyn' built for Mr Ferris St George of Bembridge, around thirty-five feet with an early diesel auxiliary, and Austin was there nominally as engineer (things were again slack in the fitting shop), although he had not been involved with its installation. They had fair wind up Channel until near the Solent when, with a dying wind, they decided to start the engine. Although the engine must have been run at the yard, Austin found that it was totally impossible to get the thing started. There was not enough room to turn the starting handle fast enough to enable the engine to start. There was nothing for it but to have patience and to sail to Bembridge with no doubt a less than pleased owner. Unfortunately Austin cannot remember the final outcome to this incident. However, there was one diesel that Austin had learnt to start, whist he was still in the fitting shop.

Austin wrote of this vessel in one of his articles in 1989:

"A regular trader on the River Dart used to be the 'Annie', a Plymouth barge which must have been a fairly rare breed even in the 1930s. With her Cornish skipper and his mate she would sail, if there was a fair wind, or motor up the Dart to Dittisham where there is a large bay opposite the village with a sandbank in the middle built up by silt from the faster flowing upper reaches. 'Annie' would be grounded on the sandbank on a falling tide, and at low tide skipper and mate would load her with sand using a hand winch and a basket 'skip' slung from a derrick. At high tide she would float off and proceed down river to unload alongside Dartmouth quay into builders' carts.

One tide she didn't float off. The frequent grounding had loosened the caulking in her seams, and she filled up till the deck was underwater and the stowed sails soaked.

The yard tug was dispatched on a salvage mission, and when the tide had left the deck awash and the hatch coamings clear, the 6in suction pipe of the salvage pump was lowered into the hold and the water, and most of the sand, was pumped out. Then, with the pump still running, she was towed alongside back to Philip's yard. The engine was lifted out and brought into the fitting shop, and 'Annie' was grounded on a slipway for re-caulking between tides as there was a lightship in the floating dock.

The engine was a hot-bulb, two-stroke, semi-diesel Bolinder, with a cylinder about 10in giving 40hp, and a huge flywheel, a type of engine which was still in use up to 25 years ago in most of the Baltic fishing boats. It had once had compressed air starting, with a hand pump and air bottle which would give it one kick over for 20 minutes' pumping, at which it might, or might not, start. We had it in the fitting shop and stripped it to dry it out. Harry Inder, the foreman, asked the skipper if we should give it an overhaul while we were about it. 'Oer naw,' he said, 'Er don't want nothing done to she; us just wants you make she goo.'

So the engine was re-installed, water drained out of the fuel tank and pipe line, and I took lessons from the skipper in hand starting it, which with a little practice was much easier than pumping up the air bottle. The starting handle pulled forward out of the rim of the flywheel, against a spring. After using a five-pint blowlamp to heat the 'bulb' on the cylinder head to a dull red heat, one grasped the handle and swung the flywheel to and fro, bouncing it against compression each way (top dead centre was with the handle at the bottom): gaining momentum with each swing until an extra big one was enough to work the fuel pump, when it would fire and start on the rebound. There was no gearbox or clutch, and the engine was described as 'direct reversing'.

The fuel pump was worked by a cam on the crankshaft and included a wedge with a handle which slid in and out as a throttle and governor to adjust the length of the stroke

Stepping the mast in Carmela

which the cam gave to the pump plunger. By holding the wedge up with its handle the pump gave no fuel until the engine (which only did about 150 rpm anyway) slowed right down and almost stopped: then, at the critical moment when it was coming to dead centre for the last time, one gave the pump a full stroke with the wedge, and it would fire and go off in reverse. If the 'engineer' got it wrong he had to start again with the handle – which could be embarrassing – but with practice I learned to come in to the pontoon, give her a 'touch astern' and stop alongside."

It is doubtful if the health and safety people would welcome that engine today.

In 1934, the firm built another larger O.M. Watts design, 'Carmela', a 59 foot, 35 tonner for Major Gerald Potter of Brixham. As with 'Evelyn' she was a heavy cruising type with teak planking on grown oak frames, and cutter rigged. After launching her it took most of the chippies and apprentices to manoeuvre the solid wood mast through the yard to the crane to step it, where Jack Flahraty, the rigger, took over to splice the shrouds to length. She was to be based at Brixham and therefore there was no delivery trip. However, Austin managed to get out on the sailing trials. 'Carmela' had a paraffin-driven refrigerator, and since it looked like being a hot day, the owner told the acting steward in charge of the lunch hamper to turn the fridge well up to get the beer nice and cool. This he did. The wind died away, the sun beat down and it was good weather for stretching the sails if not actually sailing. Austin was sent off in the dinghy with the yard photographer (and his own camera) to get some pictures.

Aboard again for lunch, the bottles of beer were brought out of the fridge - frozen solid. There was not time to wait for them to thaw, so the only thing left was to crack the glass off the bottle-shaped ice-lollies, break them into manageable sized lumps and suck them.

The drawing office provided Austin with valuable experience and the chance to hone his skills as a draftsman. However, the precise skills of design were learnt through long hours of self-study and experiment. His set of ships curves were a twenty-first birthday present, made of pearwood. He used them all his life and after his death they were passed to Euan

Carmela photographed from the dinghy

Seel. At the time, he had a subscription to the magazine Model Engineer, taken out when building the model Tug, and in it he found an advertisement for a Planimeter. This was purchased and passed to me after a lifetime's use. When he went to work for Robert Clark, he found that Clark did not have one and would borrow Austin's. When Austin left he presumed that Robert Clark had to go out and buy one, or return to his previous technique of counting squares.

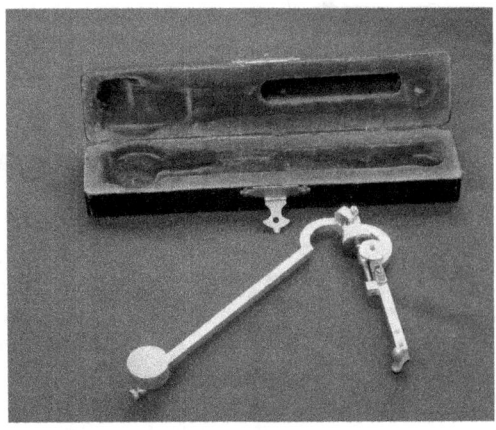

Planimeter

There were no regularly available text books on yacht design, and much of his early knowledge came from observation and studying the articles in '*Yachting World*'. An early foray into journalism (See Appendix 2) with a short article published in '*Yachting World*' on October 11th 1935 earned him the funds to purchase Uffa Fox's first book, '*Sailing, Seamanship and Yacht Construction*'. (Austin has written many articles over the years and some feature in this book.) Other books followed over the years, including Uffa's other books, bought with further '*Yachting World*' articles. The classic '*Skene's Elements of Yacht Design*' followed as soon as possible and '*Naval Architects, Shipbuilders and Marine Engineers Pocket Book*' by Clement Mackrow and Lloyd Woollard was purchased during the war in 1943. Design competitions were run by '*Yachting World*' and whilst he did not have great success it provided a regular opportunity to present finished designs. Meanwhile, in the drawing office, Austin worked on the drawings for fittings and modifying interior drawings. If a yacht came in to have a different cabin arrangement, Austin would be required to measure and draw the existing arrangements from the boat and then work out the modifications to fit in the same space and provide the new drawings. This work gave a close understanding of yacht interiors, and was good practice for later work at Robert Clark.

OUTSIDE WORK TIME, there was leisure, and although Austin had continued to row for the first year at Dartmouth he could not give over six evenings a week when he was asked to join the Junior four in 1932 and was promptly asked to leave the club totally. Work was Monday to Friday and Saturday morning on top of which there was studying to be done. Austin was also trying to brush up his mathematics on a correspondence course which he completed – although he admitted to never fully mastering calculus again as he had at school. There, he had completed enough to pass the school certificate and then forgotten the lot. He never fully regained that understanding and admitted to using graphic methods instead, although there were only two occasions when he remembered using simultaneous quadratic equations. The details of one are lost but the other was to work out the runner positions on

Hugh Falcus with Mudlark

one of Robert Clark designs. The runner block tail and tackle needed to be the right length to stow right forward when cast off to allow the main boom to free right away. This calculation was methodically worked through to give the desired result but the method was not used again.

Although work did not allow the time commitment demanded for the rowing club, there was time for sailing both in dinghies and big boats. Austin had teamed up with another apprentice friend, Hugh Falcus. Hugh Falcus lived with his family (his father was retired) on a houseboat on the Dart and rowed across to the yard each morning in the dinghy. One weekend in late 1932 or very early 1933 the two were exploring a laying up boatyard in Old Mill Creek above Dartmouth. The yard did not build boats and was a collection of slips and sheds for storage and laying up. There they found a 'Thing' which for the princely sum of £7 10s 0d was to become their first 'yacht'. With wages of 7s 6d per week this was a considerable sum. The 'Thing' was a half decked keelboat of around fourteen feet long and looked like a miniature metre boat, or a small Swallow. There was just a hull, almost derelict and very neglected. She had an unballasted wooden fin keel and internal ballast in the form of rusty rivet punchings. They were told that the previous owner had found her rather tender, which was hardly surprising. However, not daunted by this fact or that the rig had disappeared, the purchase was completed and Hugh Falcus towed the boat back to Philip's yard with his parents pulling dinghy, where some drastic alterations were planned. The exploits of getting her back afloat led to her being named 'Mudlark'. On arrival at the yard a corner was found, the boat cleaned up and work started to fit a rig and ballast.

Austin takes up the story from part of an anecdote from August 1989:

Mudlark awaiting a rig

"We scrapped the remains of the lugsail rig, which seemed inappropriate for the hull, and changed to Bermudan with a home-made mast and some sails cut down from old ones off my mother's boat. We felt we could not cope with a proper hollow mast, but at that time there was a lot of publicity for the 'Jecketo' mast which was claimed to cause less of a wind shadow on the sail. It was a narrow tripod with metal brackets between the legs, the sail set on a jackstay down the aft side, and we built one with spruce battens for the legs. Looking at the photo now, I think that the wind shadow may well have been less, but the legs must have acted as spoilers to cause turbulent flow over the sail.

The biggest problem was to make her stable enough to carry sail. To do this we cut through the iron keel bolts, removed the bottom section of the four pieces of elm which made up the fin keel and used it as a pattern for the yard foundry to cast in lead, which we then put back with new keel bolts.

During this operation I lost my partner. Hugh went off on a nature expedition/treasure hunt to the Cocos Islands in an old topsail schooner called 'Mynonie R. Kirby', which had been refitted at the yard after being seized for debt in Brixham. She did not get very far as the masts fell down when she met the Atlantic swell. I finished the refit myself."

Mudlark with the Jecketo mast

(Although Hugh Falcus did not get very far on the 'Mynonie R Kirby', his new interest in nature was to prove his life work and he abandoned his apprenticeship to become a full time naturalist. Austin did not hear of him for many years until he happened to see the credits on a BBC programme from the nature unit at Bristol and there was Hugh's name.)

"It never occurred to me that sailing a ballasted keel boat with no buoyancy and very low freeboard was dangerous, but fortunately the home-made mast collapsed before she capsized. It was my first dismasting, and how peaceful it was when everything had subsided. Some empty paint tins lashed under the deck did for buoyancy but I needed a proper mast.

So on a Saturday afternoon I took the train to Teignmouth to see if Morgan Giles could help.

The treasure hunter Myomnie R Kirby

The great man, builder of the early 14ft Internationals, was there in his yard and was kindness itself. He listened to my tale of woe and said he thought there was a 14-footer mast up in the loft which had warped after glueing, but there might be enough straight length for what I wanted. We went up into the loft and he brought the mast down and dusted it off. The top 18 inches was hooked off to port. He fetched a saw and cut the top off for me to take as well because it contained the halyard fairlead. He explained that he never fitted a sheave as they always seized up, and half a sheave fitted through the mast as a fairlead saved weight aloft.

I forget what I paid for it, but certainly less than £1.0s.0d. and I managed to spring it through the train door and into the corridor to take back to Dartmouth. The mast was near enough the right length, but the mainsail luff needed converting to a boltrope and the yard sailmaker (who had been in square rig) showed me how to do it. The new rig was fine. I never dared go outside the harbour, but I had some exciting sailing 'til the end of the season, when I sold the boat for enough to buy one of the local class Dart One-Design dinghies, designed and built by Morgan Giles."

REALISING THAT 'MUDLARK' was not the sort of boat he wanted to stay with for very long, it was duly advertised for sale in *Yachting World* and received an instant reply. Someone in the Channel Islands would have it, and it was sold for £20.0s.0d, realising a reasonable profit and enough to buy a tatty 'Dart Dinghy'. This dinghy had belonged to the Captain of the Royal Naval College and needed some attention before sailing again, particularly to restore the colour of the Honduras Cedar. Once completed, Austin's spare time was spent racing either the Dart dinghy or the big boats. Often for the evening races in the Dart Dinghies they were joined by the cadets from the 'Naval College', sailing some of the twelve boats that MacAndrew had presented to them, although they did not turn out for the Saturday afternoon races. The Dart dinghies often visited the regattas at places such as Torbay, towed by MacAndrews. It was here that Austin was first able to watch with envy the International Fourteen footers, a class on which he was to later have a profound influence. Austin recalls his first Dart dinghy and some of the sailing in an article from 31st March 1989.

Austin's Dart dinghy with her wishbone rig

"My first dinghy was one of the Dart One-Designs, designed and built by Morgan Giles. She was No. 7 of the first batch of a dozen to be built and was called 'Dart'. Clinker built of cedar, 12ft 6in long with a gunter lug sail of about 100sq ft, and a heavy cast iron centreboard, she had had a hard life, and 'worked' a bit when sailed hard. Before I bought her from the Captain of the Royal

Naval College, she had been maintained in the College boatshed, which meant that she was varnished with pusser's copal varnish, a relic of the Victorian Navy and still standard issue during the second world war. In Naval use it needed renewing every few months and had the effect of bleaching the wood under it, so that when I got her 'Dart' was almost white, and I set about scraping her inside and out to restore the colour of the cedar.

It's probably just as well that I scraped the inside first, or I would never have faced such a task. After using varnish stripper I became very skilled at sharpening a 'dummy' or joiner's scraper (the Skarsten was unheard of at that time), and scraping the clinker lands behind the timbers with broken hacksaw blades. It took every minute of my spare time for six weeks, after which scraping the outside was a blessed relief, but I swore I would never scrape another clinker boat, and I never have. The bottom was white enamelled, as most of the class lived afloat on moorings.

The Dart dinghies were a little short of buoyancy, and very difficult to bale out after a capsize as they floated with the gunwale awash. They also had a tendency to drive under on a run and continue sailing like a submarine with only the rig and the crew's head and shoulders above the water. After some experimenting with blocks of Onozote foam lashed under the forward thwart we changed the class rules to make the boats a lot safer. We had some marvellous racing mid-week evenings in the river off Dartmouth, and at weekends at Dittisham, where the Dart opens out into a wide shallow reach with room for a good triangular course.

The father of the class was Vernon MacAndrew. He had presented 12 boats to the Royal Naval College for the cadets to sail, and used to tow a string of boats up river to Dittisham behind 'Raven', his speedboat, which then acted as committee boat, and we all gathered round after racing for a picnic and to discuss the race.

For Torbay Week we used to tow round behind Mac's motor cruiser, 'Harpado', which acted as mother ship while he raced in the West Solent Restricted class. After two seasons of this, Mac called a meeting of the DOD Class and told us that we should have to look after ourselves in future, as he wanted to spend more time with the West Solent.

I found myself promoted to Class Captain, and one of my first jobs was to organise the expedition to Torbay for the 1935 regatta week. I managed to borrow a launch from some friends. 'Lady Blanche' was 36ft long and 6ft beam. She had been a steam tender to a large yacht but now had a petrol engine geared down to the original large propeller, and would make 9 knots without a ripple. She towed six of the DODs while Commander Martin's 'MARTLET'

The Dart dinghy awash

Towing a string of Dart dinghies past Berry Head

towed another four. I made up and issued to each dinghy 15ft length of tow rope with a large toggle in one end and a becket in the other and a tail looped round the mast. So after a race we could very quickly make up a tow in any order with the boats equally spaced by coupling up toggles and beckets. The boats spent the night in Torquay, Paignton or Brixham, wherever we had been racing and the crews went home by bus. I became very adept at manoeuvring 'LADY BLANCHE' in close quarters by kicking the stern sideways with the big propeller. On one occasion I turned her round in Torquay inner harbour with less than a yard to spare between two stone walls. For the long tow to and from Dartmouth we took the heavy centreboards out of their slots and laid them on the bottom in the stern, which kept the bow up and made the boats tow better."

THESE DINGHIES HAD been well supported by Vernon MacAndrew, who was part of the MacAndrew shipping line and very much a local benefactor, and would become one of Austin's regular crewing positions. Vernon lived in a very nice house near the entrance to the harbour and when Austin first met him he was racing 'NATICA', a 'West Solent Restricted' class although he later raced Twelve Metres. He also owned a speedboat in the ChrisCraft style and a motor yacht called 'HARPADO', which was used to tow the 'West Solent Restricted' round to Torbay for the regattas, and was sometimes shipped aboard one of the MacAndrews steamers to cruise the Mediterranean or Red Sea where he indulged his passion for collecting shells. He was very supportive of the Royal Dart Yacht Club and largely responsible for getting the Morgan-Giles designed Dart Dinghies started. Initially Morgan-Giles built six and then MacAndrew had a further dozen built by local Dartmouth boatbuilders to present to the Royal Naval College.

Another had been on permanent loan to Marco Martin when still a schoolboy and before he set off with Admiral Goldsmith to the West Indies. His father was an Engineer Commander and a master at the college teaching engineering. Marco was about two years younger than Austin and during term time was at boarding school. However during the holidays he seemed to live in his dinghy or on other people's yachts. Both Marco and Austin were regular crews for MacAndrew and Austin stayed in touch with Marco – who would always look in the sail loft when in the area – until his death. Marco had followed his father into the Navy as an Engineer, with an excellent career specialising in gunnery both before and after his retirement. After leaving the Navy, he became the English agent for the Italian gunmaker, 'Oto Melara', having made contacts during his time as Naval Attaché in Rome and Stockholm.

At the end of the slump the MacAndrew Shipping Line was obviously doing well and MacAndrew moved up to racing Twelve Metres. When this happened, Austin, who was by now experienced on Sir William Burton's Twelves, had the option of which boat to sail on. MacAndrew's first Twelve was the Nicholson designed 'Trivia' tendered to by his new Norman Hart designed motor yacht 'Campeador'. 'Trivia' was the most successful Twelve until the arrival of the American 'Vim' in 1939. She was then sold to Norway and re-named 'Norsaga' during the 1950s, but bought back again as a trial horse to 'Sovereign' in 1964 – she has subsequently been fully restored and is again sailing the classic circuit. 'Campeador' had been built on the East Coast but proved to be not large enough, and he had a larger Norman Hart design built by Philip and Son called 'Campeador II'. Austin divided his Twelve Metre crewing between MacAndrew and 'Uncle' Willy Burton and Marco lived aboard MacAndrew's yacht and crewed for him. At the outbreak of war a few years later, MacAndrew signed 'Campeador II' over to the Navy and then went along as Captain with some friends as crew, including a couple of retired Admirals as sub-Lieutenants RNVR. This was fine until Churchill got to hear of this and said it would not do at all. The answer was to promote them to full Lieutenants. They undertook patrol work but sadly were mined and the yacht was destroyed with the loss of all hands bar Stanley Vercoe, the deck boy, who was on deck at the time and blown clear.

Sir William Burton's yacht the SY Caleta

The racing was, however, a passion and MacAndrew was a very competent helm. When the 'Trivia' arrived from Nicholson's, it would not go despite best efforts. It took six weeks of hard work and an almost total re-rigging of the boat to improve her performance. It appeared that Nicholson had not thought things through. Initially it was impossible to straighten the mast because of the poor runner arrangement which had to be rebuilt. Originally the runners were on slides along the gunwale but these proved impossible to tension and were re-worked with purchases and Highfield levers as on the Burton boats. Austin's experience on at least three of the Burton Twelves was very useful as these were all competitive and had been designed by Alfred Mylne. The steering on 'Trivia' was so stiff that it took brute strength to turn and you could not feel the boat. MacAndrew's engineer from the motor yacht discovered that there was a wooden drum on the wheel shaft with wires that lead around pulleys to a sliding lever arrangement on the tiller. This arrangement had so much friction and poor alignment that it would never work and between them MacAndrew and his Engineer

The 12 Metre Veronica

rebuilt the system with a quadrant and chain drive from motorcycle chain around the correct size pulleys. This time the steering was finger light.

The big boat season consisted of regattas around the country, starting with Harwich on the East Coast moving down to the West Country, up to Scotland and back again in time for Cowes week at the beginning of August and then again to the West Country for the end of season events. Although Austin had only started at Philip's in the autumn of 1930, the West Country regattas of 1931 saw him aboard the Twelve Metre of Sir William Burton, 'Uncle Willy'. She was called 'Veronica' and Sir William's reputation as a helmsman was forged over many years. In 1906, on 18th January, the paper 'The Yachtsman' said of him; '*Great Britain, Mr WP Burton, a businessman and member of the YRA council reckoned to be the only Corinthian to handle a yacht with the skill of a 'professional'.*' The summers for the next several years were to be taken up with yachting and the Twelve Metre class in its heyday.

Austin crewed for the early and late season regattas and Torbay week 1931 proved a windy affair as recounted by him here:

"Torbay Week in August 1931 started as usual with Brixham Regatta, a two day affair with the Brixham trawlers racing in two classes while the Big Boats and the 12-Metres had different courses in the bay.

I joined Sir William Burton's 12-Metre 'Veronica' at Brixham having walked the five miles from Dartmouth with a kitbag on my shoulder because the buses did not seem to be running. Fortunately the launch was waiting at the steps and put me on board in time for the race.

After Brixham the fleet moved across to Torquay where 'Britannia' and the other big boats anchored outside, while the Twelves and their tenders berthed inside the outer harbour. My mother had joined us and can be seen in a photograph seated between Sir William and Lady Burton in the group aboard 'Caleta'. We were against the outer harbour wall and got the full brunt of the easterly gale which blew up overnight. 'Britannia' and her attendant destroyer and the others moved back to Brixham for shelter but those in Torquay had to ride it out.

I worked all day with the crew of 'Caleta' fending off from the wall and there was a scend of about 15 feet so that one moment we were looking over the harbour wall at the huge seas that filled the bay, and the next looking up at it as a wave broke right over it and down our funnel. Ordinary yacht-type fenders did not last very long but Mrs Hugh Paul of 'Astra', who had stayed on shore, led a contingent from a garage bowling old motor tyres along the wall between waves, and onto our deck. We finished with black circles all along our topsides which took some scrubbing off but it was better than dented plates.

Our neighbour in the harbour was our near sister-ship Sir Alfred Goodson's 'LADY MAY' and she fared worse than us. When 'Caleta' was built her skipper asked if she could have a fisherman's anchor instead of one of the stockless ones as specified. He explained that he would rather spend a little longer anchoring in doubtful weather and be able to lie safe in his bunk. We lay safely thanks to the fisherman, laid out well ahead as we came into Torquay and veered back into our berth but 'LADY MAY' only had her two stockless ones which dragged so that she went back and battered in her stern plating on the bow of a converted Brixham trawler, which lost her bowsprit in the mêlée. Eventually they managed to get a rope out ahead to one of the 12-Metres (which were all lying to their regulation fisherman anchors as specified in their rules) and that held her. In the photographs the 12-Metre's crew have just secured a rope from 'LADY MAY's' bow ready to be hauled on.

Whenever there was a lull in the storm extra ropes were run out to a yacht ahead or, if long enough, to a ring in the harbour wall, so there was a spider web of ropes just below the surface all over the harbour. Shortly after the scene in the photo the 12-Metre crew set off in their dinghy rowing side by side on the middle thwart to take a rope to the steam yacht lying ahead. Halfway there all the yachts rolled to a wave so as to tighten the spider web, and lifted the dinghy clean out of the water. We watched, expecting it to spill the crew who were looking over the side wondering what next. Then everything slackened, the dinghy was lowered into the water again, and the crew carried on rowing as if nothing had happened."

BRITANNIA off Babbacombe

Gale in Torquay Harbour

Astra with Hugh Paul at the helm and George Paul behind him

Securing a rope from Lady May's bow

It took some time the day after to sort out all the extra ropes and lines that had been run out, but as soon as possible racing resumed. This was the heyday of British yachting and Austin was fortunate to be involved with it at first hand. Those formative years enabled him to see and race with the cream of British yachtsmen. The very rich would own a J-Class or 23 Metre, whilst the successful businessman would own and race a 12 Metre. The Big Class was headed by the King's 'Britannia', her normal crew topped up when racing by ratings from her attendant destroyer. King George V used to take the helm when he was on board, though at other times she was raced by her sailing master Sir Philip Hunloke. The other members of the Big Class were 'Astra', 'Candida', Cambria', 'White Heather', 'Shamrock V' and 'Endeavour'. They did not all race regularly, but the owners and their guests lived on board with the 20 or so crew. Sir Thomas Sopwith had bought 'Shamrock V' after her unsuccessful America's Cup Challenge of 1930, and used her for rig development before challenging himself with 'Endeavour' and later 'Endeavour II'. Bill Stevenson, who managed the English branch of Woolworth's, built 'Velsheda' to the J- Class, her name made up from his three daughters Velma, Sheila and Daphne. T.B. Davis was a colourful character who had made a fortune as a stevedore in South Africa, and retired to Jersey where he kept the schooner 'Westward'. She had been built by the famous designer Herreshoff and raced with the Big Class. Like all schooners, she was at her best on a reach, but could not hold the cutters to windward. She had a basic crew of about fifteen and he recruited as many again from 'Britannia's' escort destroyer. He still used a stevedore's vocabulary when racing, and there was once a complaint from the naval ratings about his bad language.

At least four of the Twelve Metre owners out of about seven regulars used to live comfortably aboard. Johnny Payne of 'Vanity' was known as Fiddler Payne from his habit of playing the violin in the cockpit on quiet evenings. However, not every one lived aboard and certain standards were to be maintained at all times. Most of the larger boats and several of the smaller vessels including the Twelve Metres had their attendant tenders. These were often magnificent vessels in their own right. Sir Thomas Sopwith had the 500 ton 'Vita' later replaced with the 1600 ton 'Philante'. This beautiful Nicholson designed vessel is still in use today as the Norwegian Royal Yacht, 'Norge'. 'Velsheda' had her tender, the 457 ton 'Malahne', using the rest of the girls' names and MacAndrew had 'Campeador II' as tender to his Twelve Metre. Sir William Burton had the 140 ton 'Caleta' as a tender to a succession of Twelve metres. On board the highest standards were maintained and dinner jackets were worn every evening after racing. The only exception was Sundays when blue suits were acceptable.

This was an age of yachting that no longer exists today and Austin was privileged to take part. Although he had limited time off, he raced regularly with Sir William Burton and MacAndrew. The yard being quiet, an occasional early Friday afternoon could be gained to join the yacht and in 1933 Austin managed to take part in the Falmouth regatta, Lymington Regatta and the Torbay Fortnight as well as sailing his Dart Dinghy. Lady Burton raced with Sir William and acted as timekeeper for the starts, sitting in the hatchway and holding the stopwatch which was also large enough for Sir William to see.

L to R: K5 Vanity V, K6 Marina, K18 Little Astra

This was a very special time in British yachting and Austin recalls some events from that period:

12-Metres in Strong Winds

"People writing about the America's cup racing in Australia have thought it remarkable that the 12-Metres should go out in 30 knots of wind. However, this used to be quite normal. They have just become soft in the balmy winds off Newport.

Back in the 1930s, (before the sailmakers had mastered the art of cutting genoas which would go to windward, when we still used to change from a working jib on the windward leg to a genoa for the reach) the mainsail would be reefed if a strong wind was expected for the race. This was done before it was hoisted, and the pennants were laced around the boom, but it was also possible to have a slab reef (as we used to call it) in the luff by a spiral lacing through eyelets a few inches back and round the luff rope. There was no question of reefing during a race but, if the wind lightened, the reefs could be shaken out. The lacing would be cut along the foot, and a hooked knife, with a down haul line laid into the slab reef, was pulled down to cut the luff lacing.

Sometimes we got caught out. During Torbay Fortnight in 1933 we went round the corner one day to race in Babbacombe Regatta. About half an hour before the start 'Britannia's' attendant destroyer received a gale warning by wireless and sent a launch round the fleet to tell us. Aboard 'Veronica', with Sir William Burton, there was no time to reef as the mainsail was already set, but we did take off the light weather mainsheet and reeve off a stronger lightly tarred Italian hemp one. 'Astra', the old 23-Metre, found time to reef, but 'Shamrock V' did not and 'Britannia' revelled in it with full sail.

Seven 12-Metres started. We had working jib for the start, and bore away almost at once for a spinnaker run to a mark off Teignmouth. We were close hauled to a mark out to sea and then during the beat back the wind struck. It was hard going and wet. 'Shamrock V' was dismasted and most of the other big boats gave up, but 'Britannia' carried on and won her race.

In the 12-Metre race 'Morwenna' had some trouble and gave up; 'Iyruna' was also over-canvassed and retired. We were certainly over-canvassed, but what at any other time would have been a disaster saved the day. A call for another inch on the jib sheet was too much for the bolt holding the halyard block aloft and the jib came down followed by the halyard and block; the second halyard block was on the other end of the bolt so there was no question of resetting it. We eased the mainsheet a bit to reduce weather helm, but Sir William was having to use all his weight on the wheel and we actually went faster. So we won the race under mainsail only in gale conditions.

The next day we raced at Brixham and, against a backdrop of trawlers, saw 'SHAMROCK V' anchored outside the harbour with just the stump of her wooden mast. There was a slight swell in the aftermath of the gale, and without the steadying effect of her mast the 90-ton pendulum of her keel had her rolling uneasily. We heard later that her skipper had to ask for volunteers from the crew for the tow back to Gosport because the motion was so violent.

The West Country in 1934

Racing at Falmouth early in the season had an added interest, as we sometimes saw one or more windjammers at the end of their Grain Race from Australia lying in the roads awaiting orders. One we saw was the 'ARCHIBALD RUSSELL' in 1934.

We also saw 'ENDEAVOUR' sporting her Park Avenue boom for the first time. Its purpose was to act as an endplate at the foot of the mainsail, and in plan it traced an aerofoil section with transverse sliders so that the sail would run to the lee side and take up its proper section with the lee side of the triangular boom continuing the curve. First time out though, the sliders were jamming and the sail would not run across, so we saw half the crew up on the boom busy kicking the sail across.

For the passage to Plymouth 'VERONICA' would normally have been towed by 'CALETA', her tender, but it was a beautiful day so it was decided to make an early start and sail. This was a wonderful opportunity to sail a 12-Metre myself and find out what it felt like. Yes – I was at the helm. Unfortunately by mid-day the breeze had dried up completely, so 'CALETA' caught us up and passed a tow line. She had already picked up 'Morwenna', which did not have her own tender, so we towed abreast for the rest of the way. 'VERONICA's' tow rope was a brand new hemp mainsheet that had been stretched and made a bit supple before being put into use.

During Plymouth week Sir William and Lady Burton and the rest of the afterguard were invited to dinner with the Sopwiths aboard 'VITA', Sir Thomas Sopwith's 500-ton tender for 'ENDEAVOUR' ('Caleta' was only 140-tons). After dinner Sopwith said 'Well, Willie, I expect you'd like to see my new boat.' So we all piled into a huge speedboat lying alongside.

ENDEAVOUR **with her Park Avenue boom**

Sopwith pressed the starter switch and the engine spluttered into life. 'She's missing on two cylinders,' he complained. 'Er-yes, sir,' said the wretched mechanic. It was probably firing on about ten cylinders, but Sopwith was a perfectionist. 'Well, get me another boat – I'm not going in this.' So we transferred to a slightly smaller speed boat and went about a hundred yards to where 'ENDEAVOUR' was anchored.

After getting used to a 12-Metre the J-Boat seemed enormous. The forecastle reached back about to the mast and there was a huge galley and cabins for the skipper and mate. The rest of the ship was proper accommodation (unoccupied) with a vast saloon and numerous cabins. Sopwith pulled up a grating at the bottom of the companion stairs and switched on a light. We peered down and in the depths we could see a Stuart Turner lighting set, mounted on the keel. 'There you are, Willie,' said Sopwith, 'there's room for your 12-Metre down there,' and apart from a few pillars under the saloon floor, there was too!

I heard afterwards from Frank Murdoch, who was Sopwith's stress man and looked after 'ENDEAVOUR'S' rigging, that when her mast (which was a welded steel oval tube about 24 inches by 18) was stepped, Lady Sopwith had dropped a silver five shilling piece into the recess for luck. At the end of the season, with the mast moving ever so slightly and under a compression load of about 300 tons, the silver Crown had spread out to fill the entire mast step.

Plymouth Sound

Anyone who has sailed in Plymouth Sound will be familiar with the huge wall that backs a shooting range on the cliffs on the eastern side. The wall is big enough to deflect the wind under certain conditions, and when the wind is a little west of south it sends a local squall across the main wind and downwards into the sound. It can be enough to capsize a dinghy, and on one occasion it was enough to put our 12-Metre 'MARINA'S' spinnaker aback, up over the masthead and down in two pieces on either side of the mainsail. It also broke the spinnaker pole.

This was on the first run into the sound from the breakwater. On the next beat out we repaired the pole by 'fishing' it with four spare crosstrees. We set another spinnaker on the second run and the same squall struck again, wrecking our repair to the pole but not, mercifully, the sail.

On the following beat we repaired the pole again, this time with our emergency iron tiller, and this time the tiller bent almost double and the sail tore, so we had nothing to set for the final run. We were just ahead of 'FLICA', our favourite rival, at the beginning of the run, and she would have gone straight past us with her spinnaker had we not started a luffing match. We luffed her right across under the cliffs and got her spinnaker in a twist, and then gybed and luffed her right across the other way, and repeated this about four times. Stan Bishop was trying to control the mainsheet during the gybes and got his hands badly burned, but we managed to stay ahead and just took the gun.

There is an old saying 'the ships will drift together in a calm'. Shades of the Ancient Mariner, the doldrums and the Sargasso Sea. But one day we saw a perfect example of

Repairs to the spinnaker pole

this phenomenon in a 12-Metre race off Plymouth, so it's not a legend but scientific fact, though I'm not sure what causes it.

The wind was light at the start, and by the second spinnaker run from the Knap to the Tinker buoy outside the eastern entrance there was barely a ripple on the surface, although there was an uneasy ground swell probably left over from an Atlantic gale hundreds of miles away. The spinnaker needed some coaxing, but we could just keep steerage way. Inside the Sound there was a light but very variable breeze – a thermal caused by the land heating up – and on the next beat out we took a long leg into Cawsand Bay, out again and in towards Penlee Point looking for an inshore breeze. There was none; the sails hung limp and we just stopped.

Then we had a grandstand view of the two yachts ahead of us, which had been a hundred yards apart, rolling slightly in the ground swell with sails flopping uselessly from side to side. They slowly moved together until they had to use fenders to prevent damage. This lasted several minutes, and then a very light breeze filled in and off we all went.

How did the boats move sideways, towards each other? It is possible to fan along a light boat in a calm by rolling her from side to side, but then the boat tends to go forwards. A heavy boat like a 12-Metre will roll in a swell with the keel acting as a *pendulum. A photograph shows our jib going across on its own, and one of the two boats ahead has her main boom further off than the other. This difference may have caused one to move sideways towards the other, but it all adds to the legend.*

Racing Moments

At Plymouth Regatta in the Thirties, the Big Boats and the 12-Metres were expected to provide a

The 12s drift together in the calm

spectacle for the public on the Hoe, and were set a course accordingly.

The starting line was right off the Hoe, with the first mark only a few hundred yards away, and the yachts then sailed out through the western entrance at the breakwater.

The 12-Metres sailed a figure-of-eight course, round the Knap and Tinker buoys (about a mile outside the western and eastern entrances respectively), in through the eastern entrance, round a buoy between Drake's Island and the eastern end of the Hoe (the Melampus, I believe) and across the line, four times round.

The Big Boats were sent on a longer course round marks out by the Eddystone, still a figure-of-eight but fewer times round, so while we were milling round what was little more than a dinghy course in the Twelves, we only saw the Big Boats occasionally.

*Once, I remember, we saw them with a vengeance, our respective courses coincided in the Sound. We had done our short leg off the Hoe and were making our way close hauled on starboard tack. Our fore hatch was open, ready to change from working jib to genoa for the reach from the Knap to the Tinker buoy (cotton genoas in those days weren't any good to windward, so we had a headsail change for each leg of the course). Suddenly 'V*ELSHEDA*' came up from astern going half as fast again than we were and displacing 150-odd tons to our 25. She very decently went through our lee so as not to take our wind, but only about 10 or 15 yards away from us. Her quarter wave picked up our stern and we surfed forward on it at nearly her speed with our whole foredeck under water up to the mast and a cataract going down our forehatch. We continued our plunge until her wave passed under us; our bow surfaced and pointed to the sky and several tons of water surged aft through our accommodation. It took most of the race to bucket and pump out the water we had taken in.*

Sometimes we went the other way round to suit the wind direction, but usually it was a beat out through the western entrance, a reach across outside the breakwater, and a run back through the eastern entrance.

*On another occasion we were following 'F*LICA*' out of the Sound, about a boat's length astern, when one of her hands fell overboard from the bow. We all saw it happen, but Stan Bishop our skipper worked out that the man, who must have gone right under the bilge, would surface just astern of her and to leeward. Without a word he went to*

Close racing in 12 Metres

our lee shrouds and hung over the side. The man surfaced right alongside and Stan grabbed him by the back of his overalls and swung him inboard with his momentum. The man had the water emptied out of him and was taken below to recover.

When 'Flica' was within hailing distance (it must have been on the reaching leg) Hugh Goodson shouted 'Can we have our man back please?' 'No! Sorry, we should lose our place if we tried to put him aboard. He's quite safe with us'. So 'Flica', having lost a man overboard and not recovered him, could not sign her declaration.

'Yankee' in England

In 1935 the Big Class was enlivened by the visit of 'Yankee' from the USA. She had been an unsuccessful contender for the defence of the America's Cup the previous year, when 'Rainbow' had been selected to race against 'Endeavour'. There were some who thought that 'Yankee' should have been selected, and it was only because her owners and Frank Paine her designer hailed from Boston and did not belong to the New York YC that Vanderbuilt and 'Rainbow' were chosen.

'Yankee' was purchased by Gerald Lambert who had owned 'Vanitie' since 1929 and, while she was not fully competitive, had sailed her as a trial horse against the new 'Rainbow' in 1934. 'Yankee' was fitted out in 1935 to sail across and race with the British Big Class which comprised 'Endeavour', 'Velsheda' and 'Shamrock V' as true J-Class yachts, with 'Britannia', built in 1893 but still very competitive in a breeze with the Bermuda rig, 'Astra', 'Cambria', 'Candida' and 'White Heather', all former 23 or 24 Metres and receiving a time allowance, and the schooner 'Westward'. They seldom appeared all at once.

J Class racing

Lambert already owned the 185ft schooner 'Atlantic' which held the transatlantic record under sail from 1903 to 1983. She had been neglected and her rig taken out, but on buying her he had re-rigged with three old wooden J-Class masts but correctly with gaff sails. 'Atlantic' was tender and accommodation ship for 'Yankee' and the two had a friendly race across the Atlantic which 'Yankee' under a reduced rig for the passage just won.

After fitting out with her racing rig at Gosport, 'Yankee' joined the Big Boat racing circus at Southend, Lambert having watched the first race at Harwich from the shore and been rather startled to see the close quarters at which these large yachts manoeuvred, as he was more used to match racing in the open sea off Newport, Rhode Island.

I did not see 'Yankee' until I joined the Burtons to race in 'Marina' at Plymouth, where we attended a splendid party aboard 'Atlantic'. There I met Sherman Hoyt, the American helmsman and tactician, who was pulling Bill Stevenson's leg about his 'five and ten cents store' in Plymouth. Stevenson owned 'Velsheda' and was head of the British Woolworth's. At 532 tons this three-master was the largest sailing yacht I was ever aboard, and as an engineer apprentice I was fascinated to find that she had a steam auxiliary engine with a flash boiler and a telescopic brass funnel.

'Yankee' was an interesting contrast to the English J-Class yachts I had seen. She was all bronze built – which may seem terribly extravagant for a short life racing yacht but in fact it made sense, as the bottom was polished metal – no paint or antifouling – so as smooth as could be. Several American aspiring defenders for the America's Cup had been built of bronze, and then re-cycled when their racing days were over and the metal used to build a new one, so it is probable that 'Yankee' was the reincarnation of some earlier yacht. She in turn was re-cycled in a way: Gerry Lambert was a great Anglophile, and soon after the beginning of the Second World War he had 'Yankee' melted down for scrap and the proceeds sent to pay for a squadron of Spitfires.

I did not see much of the Big Boats during Torbay regattas as I was racing (in Torbay) in the 12ft Dart One-Designs, of which I had been promoted to class captain.

Cutting away the broken mast from Yankee with the help of Evadne's boat davits

Yankee being towed in with her masthead dragging on the bottom

Trouble with the twin forestays. Note the vertical slab reef

At Dartmouth the DODs had a small triangular course just outside the entrance, and we had a grandstand view of the Big Boats starting, but we missed seeing 'Yankee' lose her mast on the other side of Start Bay when she was leading from 'Endeavour' in the last race of the season. We did, however, sail out to see and photograph her after she had been towed in and was lying alongside 'Evadne', Dick Fairey's tender to 'Shamrock V', while the sails and rigging were cut away, as the masthead was dragging on the bottom and she could not reach her normal berth.

The twisted and torn remains of the mast finished up on the shipyard scrapheap and I took a hacksaw and cut off a small piece as a souvenir. I kept this little piece of rusty steel in my collection, and nearly fifty years later had the pleasure of presenting it – in a fancy casket – to Gerry Lambert's daughter, Lily Lambert McCarthy, who is as much of an Anglophile as her father, and had just been made an honorary vice-president of the Society for Nautical Research which looks after HMS 'Victory' and to which she has been very generous.

Headsail changing and Weymouth Regatta

Most of the pre-war 12-Metres had twin forestays. Frequent headsail changes from working jib to genoa for the reaching leg and then the spinnaker meant running up the next sail on the spare forestay and then peeling the used sail, to avoid sailing bald-headed during the change. This was easier if the spare stay was to leeward as otherwise the windward stay would drag across the leeward one as the sail filled, with a fair chance of one of the piston hanks hooking itself over both stays. When this happened it meant either lowering the sail, or both if the new one had been hoisted, or a climb up the forestay for the bowman to clear the mess.

In a photograph showing the bowman at work in

Taken in Cowes Week, Sir William Burton at the helm, with SHAMROCK astern

his bos'n's chair, the bunch at the luff of the mainsail is a vertical slab reef – in the old sense of the term – laced in when the sail was hoisted to flatten it. It could be shaken if the wind lightened during the race as a line was led up the luff inside the lacing with a special hooked knife on the upper end, pulling on the line brought the knife down, cutting the lacing as it came.

On the way west between Cowes Week and Torbay in 1935, the Royal Dorset YC put on a regatta in Weymouth Bay with races for the Big Class and the Twelves. 'MARINA' had full accommodation and Sir William Burton used to sleep aboard her sometimes on principle though he normally preferred the greater comforts of 'CALETA', his motor yacht. As 'CALETA' was rather large for an already full Weymouth Harbour, and the holding ground out in the bay not to be trusted with an onshore wind, he decided to send her on ahead to Torquay and spend the night quietly aboard 'MARINA' – only to find that he was invited to the Royal Dorset's annual dinner and as chairman of the (then) YRA and president of the IYRU he was to be guest of honour – and his dinner suit was aboard 'CALETA' on the high seas.

Sir William was quite a wit, and got his own back on the Royal Dorset for the late invitation in his speech replying for the guests. He apologised for appearing improperly dressed in a blue suit but said, 'I did try to hire a dinner suit,' (this was totally untrue) 'I went round the likely shops in Weymouth but was told, 'Sorry, they're all out – didn't you know, sir? It's the night of the Royal Dorset Yacht Club Dinner Party.'

SIR WILLIAM'S FIRST Twelve Metre in 1927 was called 'IYRUNA'. As chairman of the International Yacht Racing Union he had a hand in the development of the Metre boat classes and this was the start of the name. The last two letters stood for National Authority, as Sir William was also President of the Yacht Racing Association. The choice of names was not always so convenient and often caused much searching. With many boats to name over the years, he would offer a prize of five pounds for the suggestion of a suitable name. The only stipulations were that there should not be that name already in Lloyds list, that it should end in 'a' and be suitable for 'hailing'. 'Veronica' was named this way at a garden party where the Vicar's daughter suggested that the yacht should be named after her. After checking the Lloyds list and finding no Veronica, the lucky young lady earned herself five pounds and used to send a sprig of Veronica shrub to tie on the stem.

The Twelve Metre class was one of the finest Metre classes providing a good seaworthy racing yacht with comfortable accommodation. They were designed and built by the best designers and usually to the highest standards. This was helped by the requirement to conform to the scantlings laid down by Lloyds. An example of the high standards is recalled by Austin on the Belgian owned Twelve 'Cerigo'. She had been designed and built by Fife's for a Belgian millionaire in 1926 and well maintained but never raced in the class. Around 1934/35 she was sold to Dr Ward from Totnes who was locally known to buy and sell yachts fairly regularly. He collected the yacht from Ostend with his regular skipper and sailed back to Dartmouth. The skipper, knowing Austin's interest, called him aboard to look round. Considering that the yacht had just sailed the North Sea and the English Channel, the Skipper pulled up the floor to show Austin the bilge. There in the heel of the bilge was a spider's web and a few shavings. She had never made water in her life. Taking him into the saloon, he explained that they had a surprise on taking the yacht over. Opening the green silk lined, glass fronted cabinets there stood six half pint and six pint tankards all in solid silver. The drawers below revealed silver cutlery and all pieces were engraved with the yacht's name.

Once the sailing season had finished and the winter set in then free time was spent designing boats and walking in the countryside around Dartmouth. Austin had taken his bicycle down to Devon with him at first, but found the pedals of no use when the cycle required pushing up the hills and freewheeling down. It was disposed of when Austin realized that the 3d per week storage was adding up. Occasionally he would take the train over to Torquay on a Saturday afternoon to do some shop gazing. It was here he remembers buying his early drawing instruments. These were second hand but lasted him for some time.

There was really no way of earning a spare penny to supplement the 7s 6d per week, so any overtime jobs were always gratefully received, although they were often not the easiest of jobs. Austin remembers one such job, fairly early on, when a merchant ship came in for repairs to her steering gear. There was a separate steering engine driving worm gears onto the rudder quadrant. The ship had taken a large wave on the rudder and the force had driven the worm gears and engine off to one side. The new engine had been ordered by radio and delivered by rail. It was craned into the launch and craned aboard the ship. Here it was found that it was impossible to fit through the entrance to the steering engine house. Austin and two others were put aboard to work almost constantly for three days. They lived and ate aboard, and Austin remembers a pillow of cotton waste and trying to grab a bit of sleep on top of the low pressure cylinder of the main engine. The old steering engine was dismantled and removed through the doorway, the new one dismantled to bring in and then reassembled in place.

Austin's mother paid for his lodgings and keep whilst he

Austin's mother seated between Sir William and Lady Burton

was in Dartmouth and after the first year or so his mate from the fitting shop, Joey Maginnis, informed him that his missus took in lodgers and Austin moved there for the rest of his time in Devon. The house was on the road out to the point on the Dartmouth side and Austin had a sitting room and sleeping cabin on the top floor with views straight out over the harbour mouth. Mrs Maginnis was an excellent cook and Austin enjoyed his time there, not least because just over the road was Lidstone's Boat Yard. They would talk boats into the evenings and it was also where he kept his dinghy. Phil Lidstone asked Austin if he would like to have a go at designing a speed boat for one of the local pilots who wanted to run trips round the harbour, whilst ships for pilotage were scarce in the slump. It had to look like a speedboat and more modern than the regular tripper boats, to attract the customers, but wasn't to be a real speedboat as there was a strict speed limit in the harbour and Alf Langmaid the pilot could not be seen exceeding it.. The psychology worked, and 'SCARLETT RUNNER' was duly designed and built to look fast. She was designed as a displacement boat with the transom just dipping into the water so as not to drag a wave. She made 8 or 9 knots with a converted car engine and could keep pace with other local boats without getting into trouble, and had the layout of a speedboat with room for eight people facing forward and a car type steering wheel. The pilot ran the trips in his off times and was very successful.

However, another pilot – Bill Chapman – saw this and decided to enter the same business but this time with a real speedboat and trips outside the harbour where the speed limit did not apply. Austin had studied the speedboats working off the beach at Felixstowe and knew their claims of 'Thrills with safety at 40 miles per hour' were highly exaggerated. In fact he once challenged an operator who admitted that his Chris

SCARLET RUNNER

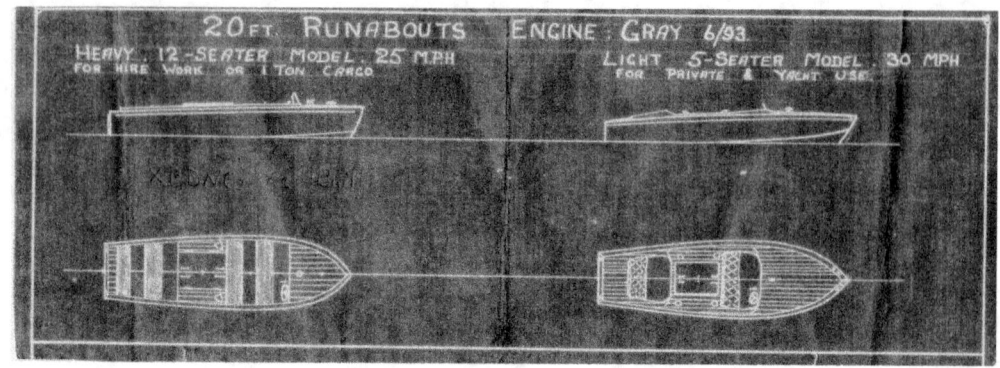

Blueprint of EXPDNC on the left

Craft with its 100HP engine would do about 25 knots flat out or about 18 when loaded. 'But,' he said, 'it looked and felt fast, and that was all they wanted.' 'EXPDNC' was designed, appropriately, looking similar above the water but very different below, built with sawn mahogany frames, carvel spruce planking and with a varnished mahogany deck and trim. She was fitted with a six cylinder, 93hp American Grey Marine engine imported from the USA – there being no British marine engines at that time, only conversions from car engines – and made 23 knots on the measured mile. Austin had spent time making sure his details were correct and the boat was fitted with spray breakers at the horizontal angle that Shaw had worked out and these proved very successful. At 23 knots the boat would be perfectly dry. A fortnight later the client returned to the yard to ask for the spray breakers to be removed because they were not what the customers wanted.

Putting the finishing touches to EXPDNC

As Austin says, in his innocence he had not realised that people go in a speed boat to get wet, and they were complaining that they were not getting wet enough. The spray breakers were planed back until they faired into the chine, the spray blew aboard and everyone was delighted. These fast boats provided the next step in life.

ONE FINAL STORY from this period, also with Lidstone's, taught Austin a valuable lesson in the designer's 'eye':

"I had explored by bike as far as Slapton Sands where the open Seine boats were in regular use. They were especially busy

when the annual shoals of salmon were making their way along the coast to their home rivers to spawn, and a watcher on the cliff above would spot a shoal and call out the fisherman. These large pulling boats were double enders of a classic shape – really beautiful – which I have never seen anywhere else, and must be directly descended from the Vikings. So I was very interested when I heard that Lidstone's were going to build a new one. One of the Slapton Sands fishermen had come to the yard to say, 'That boot yer faather built,' (about 25 years before), 'er's getting a bit limber (nailsick) and us wants yew tu build we a new un but that want tu be just a little finer in the starn.'

Mr Lidstone had helped his father build this boat when a young man, as he must have all the half a dozen or so then working, and he wanted to refresh his memory because there were of course no drawings, nor ever had been. So the two set off by bus to Slapton and Phil told me about the visit later. The old boy had walked round that boat's sides to fix the shape in his mind. Then the same at the stern except that he 'squeezed' the shape with his hands a fraction finer in way of the waterline. They caught the next bus back to Dartmouth, where a single mould for midships was brought down from its nail on the wall and set up on the building stocks. They shaped the clinker planks and built the boat entirely by eye. The planks did not touch the midship mould anywhere – it was merely a guide to measure from.

This made me realise how vital it must be for a builder or designer to be able to hold a shape in his mind and then express it either in wood or on paper and I set about practising what must be a form of art rather than just a craft.

Sadly, old Mr Lidstone took a chill the following winter and passed on. Phil, who was married but had no son to succeed him, took charge of the small yard and we had many discussions of an evening about shapes of boats.

At the far end of Slapton Sands the Beesands fisherman had motor boats which they launched down the steep beach to work crab pots round the rocks of Start Point. In complete contrast to the beautiful Seine net boats these were very functional, and had straight stems and transom sterns. When Phil Lidstone was given an order for a new crab boat to replace one which had been lost, I dared to suggest that the basic shape could be improved to make it a better sea boat by raking the stern forward and flaring the bow a little, so as to be more like the Seine boats at the other end of the Sands.

The boat which was being replaced had been landing with her catch and pots in a rising onshore gale. She had run up on the beach between waves and the crew jumped out, but before they could couple up the winch wire to haul her out, the next wave had broken over her stern and filled her, and then the undertow had dragged her down into deep water and oblivion. No amount of grappling at low water when the weather had moderated had succeeded in locating her. She was a total loss, so my suggestion for improving the seaworthiness of her replacement was well received by both Phil and the owner, and an oak crook was found to make the raking stem.

When she was approaching completion and the engine, a two-cylinder Brit from Bridport was being installed, the owner came to the yard and was delighted with her smart appearance – though with such a functional boat the idea of improving her looks had not formed part of the suggested change of shape. When Phil remarked, 'I suppose you'll have her black as usual,' he came out with, 'Oer naw – uss'll 'ave she greeeen, zo as 'er'll look like a yaaaacht.' The yard had no slipway, so the finished boat was eased out of the doorway which had a sheer drop to the water, and lowered by a crane with a huge handwheel.

A year or more later another gale spewed up the remains of the lost crab boat on the beach not far from where she had sunk. There was not much left of the planking and the transom had gone, but the 8HP Stuart Turner engine was still bolted to the bearers on either side of the keel and it still retained some green paint. We had it in the fitting shop at Philip's to see what could be done with it. All the nuts unscrewed for stripping, the piston needed some coaxing out of the cylinder, but the bearings were still oily, and with some new piston rings and a new coat of paint (green for reliability) it was good enough to go into another boat."

CHAPTER 3

THE FIRST JOBS
JOHN SAMUEL WHITE LTD. AT COWES
'CLARK AND SYNNOTT', LONDON

ALTHOUGH AUSTIN HAD stayed on at Philip and Son after his apprenticeship had finished, there came the time to seek a new job and further opportunities. There appeared in January 1936, in *Yachting World*, an advertisement for a designer of High Speed Wood and Metal Boats. The advertisement gave no details and only a Box Number. With the confidence of youth, a reply was duly written and sent. To this day, Austin is convinced that he must have been the only applicant as the position was confirmed by post with no interview. As he says, it must have been a very good letter. The job was as a designer for John Samuel White & Company Ltd, Ship, Boat and Aircraft Builder in Cowes. The idea behind the advertisement had apparently been to attract the famous power boat designer Fred Cooper, but he had not fallen for this attempt. Things moved very quickly and by March Austin started on a short but interesting time in Cowes.

The company had not built high speed boats before, being primarily builders of larger vessels including submarines and destroyers. The firm covered a large amount of ground in both East and West Cowes, with the drawing office and engineering on the West side of the river and the main ship building on the East Cowes side. They launched a destroyer whilst Austin was there and he remembers climbing up into the big hammer head crane to get a better view. This crane still stands as a land mark in Cowes today. They moored a wooden lighter against the wall almost under the crane to act as a buffer for the destroyer should things not go quite perfectly, as there was only just enough room to

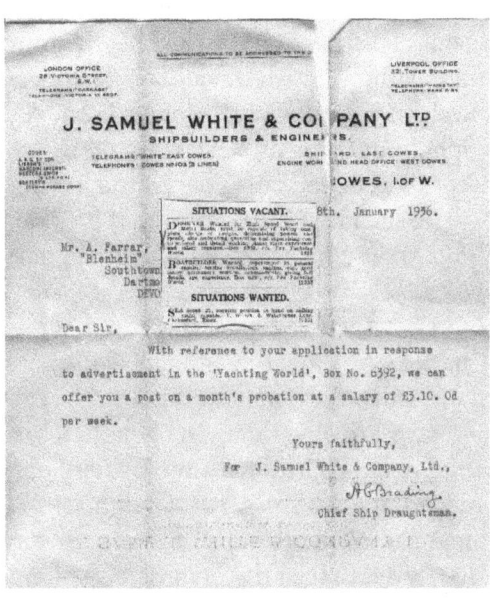

The letter confirming Austin's position

The crane in Cowes

launch across the river. There was a press photographer already in the crane and Austin said, 'I suppose you are hoping it's going to hit the other side.' 'Oh no,' he said, 'our ethics don't allow us to hope things like that. We're just here in case they happen.'

Having located new digs in Cowes and completed the task of moving, Austin joined the team in the brand new 'Fast Boat Design Office' – upstairs in the attic. This was completely separate from the main drawing office where the ship designs were completed which was off limits due to the military nature of the contracts. The team of four people, including Austin, plus the section leader, worked on various proposed designs, some of which were built, but not many.

Although the working environment was not ideal and they tended to be a firm where you started and finished on time, it did however provide an opportunity to expand his knowledge in detail. He mastered rudder and rudder stock design and how to stress them and developed complicated steering gears. He learnt how to design a twisted bottom vee chine boat which has become one of the standard power boat forms. This design was used on the MTB's and Royal Air Force boats right through the war and had been refined by Hubert Scott-Paine and his team at the British Power Boat Co. at Hythe on Southampton Water. Austin worked on a great number of projects, many remaining only as quotes, but again the estimating of materials and quantities such as the number of nails of a certain gauge for a double skinned bottom was a valuable lesson. Austin's section leader taught him about the rudders, pointing out the error in the text book about where the centre of effort of a rudder ought to be. The text book tells you that it must be a third of the way back but if this is done the boat goes round in circles because once the helm is turned the force will be such that the boat cannot be straightened out of the turn. In fact the centre of effort should be not more than one quarter of the way back.

AUSTIN EXPERIENCED THIS at first hand some years later during the war. His friend Charles Currey, with whom he would sail International Fourteens from 1939 on, was stationed in the Solent evaluating an American copy of the Scott-Paine MTB, using it as a target towing boat. The boat had boxes of ballast to represent the torpedoes and armament. Charles Currey was very experienced in handling the Scott-Paine boats and had invited Austin down to have a look at the new boat. Austin was working for the Admiralty at the time and managed a pretext to visit the South Coast and Cowes. He arrived to find the boat tied up alongside the Island Sailing Club pontoon. After lunch they took the boat out and headed off towards Ryde at full speed. Charles warned Austin and the engine room to hold tight and gave the wheel no more than two spokes of turn. The boat immediately turned hard to port, the wheel spinning out of Charles' hands, and the boat continued in ever decreasing circles until Charles cut the engines. The boat would always do this and no one could hold the wheel or turn the boat out of her turn. Shortly afterwards they slipped the boat and with a hacksaw cut the leading edges of the rudders off to move the centre of effort forward to the 25% position. From that time on there were no problems.

Austin always regrets that he never met either Scott-Paine – the man behind Supermarine and the British Power Boat Company – or Peter Du Cane, the Director of Vosper's. However, the man who eventually became managing director of Vosper-Thornycroft was at school with him. John Rix was about one year younger than Austin but knew that he had gone into a shipyard apprenticeship. John Rix's father wrote to Austin saying that John was also interested in working with boats and could he visit him in Dartmouth to see what went on? This was arranged and shortly after John Rix gained an apprenticeship at Thornycroft's in Woolston in Southampton. He served through his apprenticeship and then moved to Vosper's. At the outbreak of war, he was running an MTB repair shop for Vosper's at Wivenhoe in Essex, to service the boats from HMS Beehive in Felixstowe. Austin stayed in touch with him and recalls visiting Wivenhoe during the war and being given a run in one of the repaired MTBs under trials on the Colne Estuary. At the end of the war John moved back to the South Coast working his way up to the M.D.'s position and a knighthood, and taking over his old firm of Thornycroft's at Woolston on the River Itchen in Southampton, to form the modern firm of Vosper-Thornycroft's.

The person in charge of running the fast boat division of John Samuel White's, having persuaded the directors that this should be the direction for the company, had a great idea for a hydrofoil boat. Austin could no longer remember his name, but he had built a man carrying model some sixteen feet in length. This was obviously complete with his design of hydrofoils and probably a Grey marine engine. However, the boat would not rise on her foils and some time was spent altering and fine tuning until this could be achieved. Eventually she rose and roared across the Solent and a visit by the Admiralty was duly arranged. They were impressed, as hoped, and the sought after order for a full size craft, of some sixty to seventy feet, in time arrived. This was to be powered by three Isotta engines from Italy. By the time the large boat was to be built Austin had left the firm, but he well remembered the trial craft buzzing up and down, viewed from the top floor window of the drawing office, and generally making a nuisance of itself in Cowes Week.

The full size craft was built at great expense in aluminium but wouldn't get up and never did. The designer had learnt the expensive lesson that there is a scale effect with hydrofoils. They do not scale up in a linear form. The craft never did succeed and was eventually broken up. By this time the war had started and Vosper's were very pleased to take the three engines for their MTBs, the supply from Italy having now dried up. All the early Vosper MTBs had been powered by Isotta engines with very little regard to the problems of supply should war break out.

The use of aluminium, or the then current material 'Birmabright', was offering new techniques for building. 'Birmabright' was a non-corroding, sea water resistant aluminium and therefore was ideal for boats. After the war, it was tried as a deck material for Firefly dinghies by the Fairey Marine Company. Austin's department designed a Director's yard launch for construction in 'Birmabright' that was highly powered, fast and successful.

He decided fairly quickly that it was not a particularly pleasant firm to work for at that time, it being noticeable that draftsmen came and went on a regular basis. Many workers found that alternating between firms could be beneficial to their wage packets. For instance, a person would work for Saunders-Roe across the river and then find that he could earn a little more at J.S. White's, whereupon he would move. Six months later Saunders-Roe would offer more and he would return to his former employer. This happened with some regularity. Austin recalls one draftsman who had been employed at Saunders-Roe, working on the detailed design of a large Flying-boat, one of the current projects, and possibly the A33 Monospar Cloud or the S 36 Lerwick, both in design at that time. He was working on a particular frame number for this flying boat when he changed employers to join J.S. White. A few months passed and Saunders-Roe offered him more money to return. This he duly did and returned to the same drawing board to work on the exact same project he had left some time before. It had remained untouched in his absence.

The final dissatisfaction came when Austin went to see a boat being built in the yard. Although this was not really allowed, the 'Drawing Office' being forbidden to go into the yard, Austin needed to see if a complicated steering design would work. Why the drawing office was forbidden to visit the building yard is not known, other than union demarcation is suspected. Austin was working on the steering gear of a 45ft Fast Motor Boat, a Customs boat or similar, twin engined and with a hard chine. The detailed work required a push pull rod system running along the side of the ship from two linked rudders to the actual steering gear which was a worm drive gear as made for a lorry. The installation space was tight, hence the inspection. Just behind the bridge was the heads and on paper the rods were run under the fold down washbasin and avoiding the heads pan which was mounted from the forward bulkhead. One lunch time, with great daring, Austin ventured down to the building yard and with some searching, having not been there before, located the boat.

On inspection he was somewhat concerned to find that the heads arrangement had been turned around with the heads pan now on the hull side and fixed precisely where the steering rods would have to run. The fold down wash basin was now on the bulkhead. He returned to the drawing office and reported these facts to the section leader, who was far more worried that Austin had ventured down to the yard floor. 'You haven't been down to the yard ... you shouldn't have done that, there'll be a hell of a row if anybody finds out..... I won't let on, but don't do it again.' Austin said, 'But look, they've 'messed' up the design, they've ignored the plan we've done with everything arranged and they can't now run the rods. The pan's installed, nothing will fit.' His reply was simply, 'Well, that's their worry, they'll have to work that one out, we can't.' Austin went away certain that that was that, and he did not want to spend his career in such a narrow-minded atmosphere. An opportunity would have to be watched for.

The opportunity was not long in coming when he received a phone call from a chap he had known at Dartmouth called Eric Synnott – whose family owned the 'Lady Blanch' they had used to tow the Dartmouth One Designs to Torbay. Synnott had gone to work for British Power Boats at Hythe and had in fact shown Austin over their works whilst Austin was still at Dartmouth. Austin was particularly self-conscious about receiving a phone call at work – a practice that was frowned on – but he told Austin that he had joined up with a yacht designer in London with himself doing the Yacht Brokerage, and that they needed a draftsman. Was there anybody in Austin's department that could draw a lines plan and work out construction and was interested in moving on? Austin admits considering each of his colleagues in turn with only one slight possibility, plus the obvious choice, himself. That decided he made plans to join Eric Synnott and the designer Robert Clark in London. A formal letter was promptly dispatched and a letter returned confirming the appointment.

Discussing it later, Austin said, 'Looking back on it, it's difficult to realise I was less than a year in Cowes. It seemed as though I packed in about three years worth of yachting.'

IT WAS DURING his time in Cowes that Austin was introduced to Offshore racing on a regular basis, often crewing for much of his time on 'DOLLY VARDEN', the yacht owned by Tom Ratsey and taken over by Chris Ratsey on his father's death.

On arrival in Cowes, Austin had been given an introduction to the Island Sailing Club by Alfred Mylne, the designer of all of Uncle Willy's boats. One evening Austin took himself down to the club, introduced himself and what he was doing, and explained that he wanted to get some sailing. He was immediately latched on to by Chris Ratsey who said something to the effect that 'You are remarkably brave to come in here like that and say that', and promptly signed him on. If not required aboard 'Dolly Varden', Austin would often crew for the Commodore, Jimmy Demant, who had a very old Six Metre which required bailing out around the course. Austin joined the Island Sailing Club and in fact remained a member until the early nineties when he resigned with great regret. The expense, however, of belonging to a club that he no longer visited required a common sense decision, despite being a member for over fifty years.

'Dolly Varden' was the works yacht for Ratsey and Lapthorn, the sailmaking partnership. It appeared however that there was some 'feeling' between the parties as a story about Tom Ratsey illustrates. Tom Ratsey was afloat in his launch during one Cowes Week, when he was hailed with a request to come and have a look at one of his new sails on a large yacht that did not seem to set correctly. 'Ah, Mr Ratsey, would you mind having a look at our mainsail? We don't think it's quite right.' Tom Ratsey duly boarded the yacht and briefly examined the mainsail, and with the words, 'Why, it's one of that man Lapthorn's sails,' he turned on his heels and stomped off.

'DOLLY VARDEN' was a large Itchen Ferry type boat, originally Gaff rigged, but converted to Bermudan under Chris Ratsey's ownership. She was often used to test new sails and ideas. It came as a bit of a shock to Austin to realise that the Ratsey family were not personally responsible for making the sails. They ran the business, but the foremen were the sailmakers. Chris Ratsey could set a sail beautifully but could not go into the loft and make one. It obviously paid therefore to look after your men, but inevitably there would be a number of men leave and there were several small sail lofts run by ex-Ratsey and Lapthorn foremen. Austin remembers one weekend racing when two sail bags arrived on board. They contained two Genoas which the Foreman wanted tried out having had a particular idea on their shape. They were both beautifully finished, but on hoisting the first one, it was awful and would not set at all. Chris Ratsey promptly gave the order to pull the clew out. He explained that he couldn't take it back and say it was awful so this was the easy way. The crew then winched the sail until the clew tore out and put it away in its bag. The second sail was nowhere near so bad and they raced with it. Not necessarily the best development methods. The winches on 'DOLLY VARDEN' were quite a new idea at that time and were American top action geared winches. Unfortunately for the crew, they were handed with the port and starboard turning in opposite directions. Despite large arrows painted on the deck the crew still often had the ropes put on in the wrong direction.

The races were organised by the local clubs and the Royal Ocean Racing Club. One exciting Channel race started off Cowes and headed East, through the Forts to round the mark off Selsey Bill. 'DOLLY' sailed like a large dinghy and it was a hairy ride down wind. The order from Chris Ratsey was, 'Only dinghy sailors on the helm'. The 'DOLLY VARDEN' sailed like a dinghy and needed nursing over the big seas. Only the finely tuned reactions of a dinghy helm would be able to anticipate the boat and ensure that she stayed square onto the bottom of the waves and did not broach. The homeward leg was a beat to windward which was less than comfortable. The boat was some forty feet long plus a fifteen foot bowsprit and, with the cutter rig and twin forestays, needed care with sail handling. Gybeing the spinnaker was always interesting and required twin spinnaker poles. Two poles can, however, allow extra tactics. One light weather race in the Solent found the 'DOLLY VARDEN' running dead down wind with the spinnaker set to port. Another yacht was closing and Chris Ratsey decided to luff her. He gave the order to send up the other spinnaker to starboard, set in stops. This done he luffed the other boat head to wind, stopping her in her tracks. As he did so the port set spinnaker was taken in and at the end of the luff he gybed and broke out the starboard spinnaker leaving the other yacht stationary. These spinnakers were the old single sided type set inside the forestay which are no longer used today.

Racing was the combination found today with a variety of cross channel races, races around the Island and shorter Solent races. Austin remembered one race that started and finished at Poole but raced right round the Island, something that seemed to happen more often then. The start was late evening and in the light breeze they found themselves close inshore under St Catherine's Point at dawn. The water was so clear Austin remembers they could look over the side and see the crabs walking along the bottom, and their keel getting closer and closer to the crabs. This was taken as a sign to tack. Saturday afternoons, however, usually found Austin crewing aboard Jimmy Demant's Six Metre, pumping out the old boat as they battled round the Solent club courses.

Austin continued his dinghy sailing by designing himself one of the new Twelve foot National class that had just been started in the autumn of 1935. The boat was sail number 150, named 'FIERY CROSS' – just beating Richard Roscoe to the name who had to settle for 'FLAMING ONION' –

FIERY CROSS

and was built at Lidstone's yard in Dartmouth for £25.0s.0d. She was not a success as 'she couldn't get out of her own way'. The class itself was a great success and remains so today. However, a trophy event was arranged for early September 1936 in Poole. It attracted 43 entries, but 'FIERY CROSS' was not to feature strongly. She arrived just in time for the last race of the event, her rigging being completed in Cowes the previous week. Unfortunately, she did not get as far as the first mark having been caught port and starboard soon after the start. There were no alternative penalties available then and the only option was to retire. The other four trophy races were not much more successful, and when in the autumn Austin moved to London and Robert Clark's, 'Fiery Cross' was transported to London, by Charles Currey, who he had first met at Poole, to race on the Thames at Ranelagh S.C. in their winter season. Charles had followed his father into the Navy, but was invalided out with lung trouble around this time and he went on to run the Burns Shipyard in Bosham followed by the Itchenor Shipyard where they built many of the new National Twelve class. He subsequently re-joined the Navy at the outbreak of war.

AUSTIN TELLS OF 'A 'Racer' on Passage', in an article for *Yachting World*, published on November 13th 1936:

"'FIERY CROSS' (N.150) was built to represent my idea of a twelve-footer fit to race in the fairly stormy seas met with in the Solent, and has turned out so 'tough' as to have

been likened to an Ocean Race.

Built by Lidstone at Dartmouth, she came up to Cowes to be rigged and was finished off amid feverish activity during 'Poole Week'. We actually went for our first sail at 11.20 p.m. on the Thursday night (September 3rd).

Those who were at Poole will remember how it blew all Friday so that racing was cancelled, but it quietened down in the evening and at 9 p.m. we set sail for Portsmouth, as a friend had very kindly offered to trail the boat down to Poole on Saturday if we could get her over to the mainland.

Lots of Fair Wind
I am afraid experienced navigators will regard us as a couple of young fools, setting off at night with no navigating instruments of any kind, or even a torch, but there was a moon just past full, which shone through rifts in the clouds and gave quite a lot of light. There was also a fair tide and lots of fair wind from the south-west.

Once clear of Cowes Roads, we set our course for the lights on Ryde Pier Head. This took us fairly close inshore, past the Peel Bank and Mother Bank buoys. Ryde Pier was reached at 10 p.m., having planed part of the way on a broad reach, but we did not quite relish a dead run across under full sail, so we hove-to, lowered the mainsail and blew across under jib. By the way, people say a dinghy won't heave-to; you just let everything flap, let the helm go right down, and she rides quite happily about a quarter-on to the wind and sea. Under such reduced sail it took another hour to reach Southsea, and it was just 11 o'clock when we landed on the beach through the surf. This was rather frightening – a dead lee shore. I had expected a sand or shingle beach, and it was rather a shock to find boulders bigger than my fist. I was so 'het up' that I was late unshipping the rudder, and tore off the lower pintle as we grounded. A crowd of amused spectators helped to carry the boat up the beach, and we loaded her on the trailer.

That 'Fiery Cross' did not distinguish herself at Poole was, I suppose, due to inexperience and complete lack of tuning, and anyway is nothing to do with passage making.

The other notable passage I have made in this 'Flimsy Racing Machine' was on Saturday, October 24th, from Cowes to Emsworth, as the first wet stage of bringing her up to London for the winter season at the Ranelagh S.C. This time, instead of my former and very inexperienced and rather frightened crew, I had Charles Currey, successful helmsman of 'MERMAID' N.109, who came over to Cowes with me to sail 'FIERY CROSS' over to the mainland and then trail her up to London.

A Day Passage
We collected her, all shiny varnish, and paddled along to the Island Sailing Club, where we spent the morning putting in Onozote buoyancy blocks, and rigging her up. The east going tide began at 11 a.m., but it was 11.45 before we set our sails and pushed off, dropping the centreboard into place as we punted into deeper water.

There was only a faint air from the west to give us steerage way. Although there had been fog early, this had quite cleared, and the sun blazed down with almost summer warmth from a cloudless sky. It even tempted Charles to shed some clothes. Gillkicker Point held no terrors for us today and we ran almost dead on port gybe. Later the wind veered slightly so that we had to gybe to get between the Dolphins which mark the gap in the line of bed-irons from Horse Sand Fort to the shore, gybing again the other side.

All this time the wind had been steadily freshening, and a jolly rolling sea with nice clean transparent waves had appeared to liven things up.

About this stage we were saying, 'Ah – we planed down that one – here comes another'. Later on it was, 'We're still planing – keep her going on the next wave,' and by the time we reached Chichester Bar we were planing continuously and were getting a little blasé.

We stood about two miles off shore on a broad reach, as it is so much more fun tacking to leeward than running dead-oh, and Charles had just announced that in a few more minutes we could gybe and run in, when there was a horrible 'ping' and the mast (a tent pole one) started to topple over the weather bow – the lee shroud had carried away. I instinctively put her into the wind, and by taking the strain in the forestay and weather shroud, it stayed put, swaying unpleasantly.

Charles, assuming it was coming down, went forward to ease its fall, but coining a new nautical command I said, 'Hold up the mast'. This he did while we lowered the mainsail, took the tail of the main halyard aft for a presenter and the jib halyard to the bottle screw for a shroud. We then proceeded under jib.

Going slowly like this we realised that there was now quite a fresh breeze and a lump of a sea, which we had not noticed while we had been skimming before them.

Charles noticed a kink in the wire part of the main halyard. Not wanting to damage it we cast off the tail from the rising aft, where it was doing duty as a backstay, and were horrified to see the mast topple forward again. The jib halyard was set up hard with the remains of the port shroud onto the bottle screw, and it was only now we realised the fallacy of this, as the mast could just run down the halyard as far as the head of the sail. In the general excitement the main halyard tail got adrift and was streaming out like a mast head pennant, so we had to get the boat round on the other gybe (the jib could not be lowered), and Charles supported the mast while I fished in mid-air for the main halyard. I had to hold the mast for a bit when Charles insisted on being sick (refusing to wait), but eventually we recaptured the halyard, took out the kink and made all fast again.

When we got into Chichester Harbour mouth out of the jump, we rigged the port diamond shroud as a main shroud and then re-set the mainsail, finally reaching Emsworth Sailing Club at about 4.45. The total distance is about 20 miles, and it was decided that a 4 knots average was quite good going.

We unrigged 'Fiery Cross' straight away before dark and then went to bed early, very tired and rather cramped in the legs. On Sunday morning we loaded her on the trailer and had a rousing drive to Putney, where I fear such a 'tough' ship will feel rather out of place amid all the smart 'town-bred- dinghies'."

Austin sailed the boat during that winter and early part of the following year, but the design was outclassed on the river and he sold the boat towards the end of 1937, as he became more and more involved with the 14ft International Class and decided his forte was crewing rather than helming.

One of the major characters in Cowes at this time was Uffa Fox and Austin first met him that summer of 1936. As Austin became more and more involved in International Fourteens from 1938 on, he came to know him very well. Uffa would sail anything that was available. Many stories abound about Uffa and his exploits, but Austin remembers one of his earlier encounters with the great man. One Saturday afternoon when Austin was sailing in the Six Metre he remembers Uffa and Bill Waite sailing 'BRYNHILD', the two man canoe. They were wearing the all-in-one waterproof sailing suits that had recently been developed, and were the forerunner of today's drysuits. As usual they seemed to be sailing through the waves rather than over them. When they arrived at the Island Sailing Club later and stripped off these suits, they had on normal suits underneath and were perfectly dry.

The world of yacht design was very different to that which we know today. A designer, unless he had a private income, was unlikely to be able to support himself and his business from the income of designs alone. Most yachts were one-off designs and the commission with regard to the amount of work needed would not pay the wages. Only a series run, as we see today, would bring in a suitable return. The amount of drawing work for each design was enormous and draftsmen were needed as well as the designer himself. Today it is easy to find just about any fitting we want straight out of the manufacturer's catalogue and off the shelf, and masts and rigging are supplied from specialist firms with their stock designs. Before the war, each yacht was individual and each mast fitting, deck fitting, deck plate had to be individually designed and drawn for that vessel. These would then be made by the local blacksmith and galvanised. As can be seen, this is a large amount of finely detailed work. However, to keep the business afloat most design houses were in partnership with a brokerage department, the trade in second hand craft being as strong then as it is today. Even great and familiar names such as Sparkman and Stephens were the same. Dave Sparkman was the broker and Olin Stephens was the designer. Robert Clark the designer had joined Eric Synnott the broker. When Austin joined he recalls that this was the start of a wonderful three years.

Strange as it may seem in these days of paper qualifications for everything, Robert Clark was entirely self taught. He had started life working in an insurance office but had been taken seriously ill and was bed-ridden for some six months or more. During his convalescence he had acquired all the yachting books he could find and studied well. He began designing whilst still in bed and completed the design for 'MYSTERY' during the convalescence period. This boat was an enormous success and put Clark on the map.

'MYSTERY' was a 10 tonner and had been designed for Francis Usborne who was to become secretary of the Yacht Racing Association in 1946. The boat was designed to Admiral Turner's Metacentric Shelf Theory for balance. This theory became well known with regard to Dr Harrison-Butler who modified several of his designs to conform. Austin recalls Harrison-Butler coming into the office from time to time to compare notes. One of the standing jokes in the office at that time, was that having re-worked one of his stock designs to the metacentric shelf theory he was able to say, 'The original design was a beautiful boat, perfectly balanced, and when I re-designed it, it was even more perfectly balanced.' The irony of this last statement was not lost on the Robert Clark design team.

In what could be termed his interview, Austin met Robert Clark for the first time and was taken for a sail on 'Mystery', whilst still working in Cowes, on a cold November, Saturday afternoon, to see for himself how good the boat really was. It was blowing hard and the boat was very tender, having been designed for a lead keel but being fitted with an iron one because Usborne could not afford the extra at the time. They thrashed down the Solent with the helm amidships and the coachroof in the water. There was no weight on the helm. This was very impressive and the appointment was confirmed with Austin to move as soon as possible.

"MYSTERY II"
Owner—
Mr. F. P. Usborne

Designer—
Mr. Robert Clark.

Builders—
A. H. Moody & Son Ltd.,
Bursledon

Finished with "RYLARD" Products.

MYSTERY

Austin found himself digs in West Cromwell Road in Earls Court and joined the team almost immediately, starting work in the Clark and Synnott offices in Lower Regent Street. An old school friend of Celia Farrar, Mabel Hills, lived in Nevern Square and although unable to take in Austin herself, she was able to recommend a house just around the corner offering Bed and Breakfast. This house in West Cromwell Road was demolished during one of the road widening projects in that area. Austin visited Mabel Hills, a concert harpist, regularly at her large house in Nevern Square.

The Clark office was about one hundred yards down from Piccadilly Circus and very handy for the Royal Ocean Racing Club at No. 2 Pall Mall. The R.O.R.C. building was destroyed during the war in November 1940, but there is a wonderful story that the following day when clearing out the building they managed to save a large quantity of bottles of spirits. These were loaded onto a stretcher and covered with a blanket. However, whilst being taken for safe keeping, passers by assumed the worst and would quietly raise their hats. Maybe the reverence was not totally misplaced. They worked long hours and with no evening meal available at the digs Austin would eat at the office or locally, often returning to work on after dinner.

The design being finished when Austin joined the firm was a small bilge keeler with shallow draft that looked almost the same as the later Uffa Fox designed Fairey

Buttercup

Buttercup sailing

Robert Clark

Atlanta. She was built at the Rowhedge Ironworks yard in Essex and was very advanced for that time with aerofoil keels. She was launched early in 1937 for Mr Foster and called 'BUTTERCUP OF COLCHESTER', sailed beautifully, and crossed the Atlantic after the war. (To see her photographs now, one could almost be looking at the original prototype of the post war Fairey Atlanta designed by Uffa Fox.) This yacht was followed quickly by 'ORTAC', a R.O.R.C. Class One offshore yacht that was to be one of the most successful racers of her day and included many innovations that we would now take for granted.

She was designed for Col King and built by Morgan-Giles. Austin was often required to go down to Teignmouth on the night train to check on progress, spend the day there and return to London on the next night train. During construction, she was planked all the way down and then the garboards were removed. The tanks and plumbing was then installed and when all the shavings and dust had been removed the garboards were replaced. This attention to detail ensured a clean well finished bilge. This same attention to detail was carried right through the yacht including the design of the fittings. As normal the yacht had twin forestays to allow easier headsail changing. However, if you have the sail on the leeward stay, the windward one will take the strain and the jib luff will sag away. Therefore each forestay had a lever to allow tension and this could be thrown off to ensure the stay with the jib on carried the load and did not sag away. 'ORTAC' was rigged to sail as either a sloop or a cutter and the inner forestay was set on a track and could be pulled away to allow the genoa to be set. Small winches were designed and made to tension the tacks of the headsails and a tension system for the inner forestay. As mentioned previously nothing was available off the shelf and every thing had to be designed in house. This included winches which were very new then although they are commonplace on every yacht today. The winches were designed in Clark's office and manufactured by a firm in Glasgow. They were probably the first ball bearing winches ever. They had sealed ball races on the main spindle for the assembly to turn on. Wanting to check their design, they were taken to the Naval Engineering Research Department in West London where a dynamometer was made available. However, the prototype winch was far too big and powerful for 'Ortac' and a scaled down model was then produced. The big winch was sold to MacAndrew for his Twelve metre and placed in the centre of the deck. For the first time ever it was possible to set and trim the genoa whilst sailing. Previously the technique had been to snatch in the sheet and cleat it quickly. To ensure the ideas worked, they often made 'mock-ups' of parts of the yacht in the office. 'Ortac' needed five of the bottom ratchet winches and they could not therefore be placed symmetrically. There were four main winches for the two headsails and one for the tweaker system on the permanent backstay. Using various chairs and tables they worked in the limited room of the cockpit 'mock-up'. They decided that as most people worked a bottom ratchet winch with their right hand, they would place the starboard winch close to the cabin with the handle on the aft side and the port winches off set aft by the distance of the long handle which would now be on the forward side. Although it drew odd comments, it worked impeccably. People do not realise that the position of the winch needs to be set for ease of use and it is the position of the turning blocks that affect the set of the sail.

Colonel King, owner of Ortac

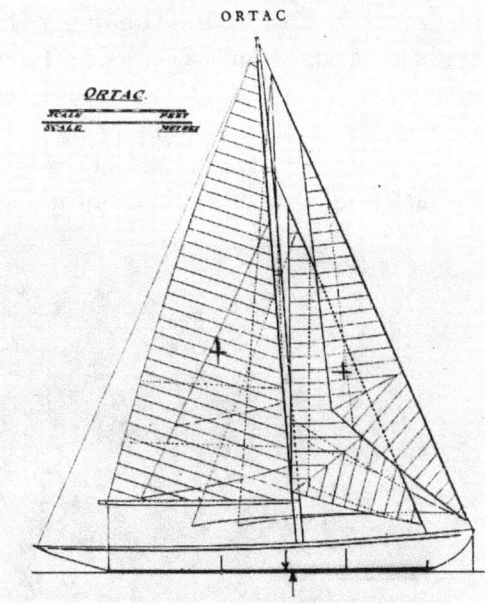

Ortac sail plan

Ortac **with the pulpit clearly visible**

There is one innovation, however, that all modern boats owe to 'Ortac' and Austin. Before 1937 very few yachts had lifelines, certainly none of the metre classes, and those that did exist finished at the stemhead, making the task of headsail changing a hazardous one. Construction had started on 'Ortac' and Austin was working on the detail of the deck arrangements. In the corner of his work sheet was a scribble or 'flash of inspiration' showing an arrangement of lifelines carried around the bow with two loops of steel tube. Col King looked in shortly after and spotted the 'doodle' on the corner of the drawing board. He cottoned on immediately and said he would have one on the yacht. Austin produced some working drawings and Col king took them with him on his next visit to Teignmouth. Morgan-Giles was outraged, 'I'm not going to put a monstrosity like that on my boat'. Col King's reply was to the point, 'It's not your boat – it's mine and you're going to put it on'. Once made, even Morgan-Giles agreed that the 'Pulpit', as the owner christened it, seemed to fit in with the rest of the boat. It stood quite upright on the stem, unlike the modern pulpit, so as not to be bent against a dockside. The top rail was shaped to fit the average human bottom, so that the sail changer could wedge himself in and be just the right distance from the forestay for hanking on a headsail. 'Ortac's' pulpit was strictly functional and the idea of styling was never considered. The modern artistically drawn, forward leaning ones found on nearly all modern boats, including motor cruisers, continuing the line of the stem, rather miss the point. Although with modern furling headsails the original task is required less often, the forestay is usually too far back from the pulpit to reach comfortably anyway. The over hang can be vulnerable in a dock and with the bow to mooring in marinas they create an obstacle course for heads as you walk down the main gangways.

The pulpit

'Ortac's' lifelines at the stern came down to finish on the rail like everybody else's, but F.B.R. (Buster) Brown, who used to crew regularly in her had a better idea. The following year he designed his own ocean racer, 'Mindy', and she had the rail carried round the stern as well – so, of course, it had to be called the 'Pushpit'. There were very few teething problems with 'Ortac' although one caused some consternation. When sailing it appeared that the forestay and backstay were stretching more than would be expected. On closer examination it was found that the masthead fitting was working its way down the mast. The masthead fitting was drawn to be bolted right through the mast, but Morgan-Giles thought that this would weaken it too much, so it was fastened with wood screws. The fitting was refitted this time with the bolts and all was well. 'Ortac' went on to a successful racing career and Austin joined her for the Cowes-Dinard race in 1937.

The Sussex Yacht Works at Shoreham became involved as one of the major companies building Robert Clark designs. They built several yachts to the 'Mystery' design and shortly after 'Ortac' the yard's owner, Jack Rawlings, had an ocean racer built to a Clark design called 'Erivale'. Although Jack Rawlings owned and ran the 'Sussex Yacht Works', he also had another large company in London – run by his father – doing electrical coil winding and had a financier's background. This ensured that the business was well managed.

'Erivale' was again an innovative and carefully thought out yacht, although somewhat larger than 'Ortac' with more drawn out ends. Robert Clark had drawn the lines and done all the basic work but left Austin with a fairly free hand with regard to the construction. Jack Rawlings was interested in new ideas and the boat developed several new techniques. The boat was built with teak planking and would normally have had grown frames. However, Austin designed a set of laminated frames. There were no glues as we have today and there were fewer laminations, but the frames were clench fastened and where appropriate the laminations continued right around to form the hanging knee of the deck beam. Once married up with the deck beam, a ring frame of immense strength had been formed. The frames were supported further with stringers and the resultant structure was equivalent to the space frames designed for hi-tech boats today. The space frame concept was confirmed fully with bronze tension strips bedded into the bulkheads from the chainplates down to the mast step. These bulkheads were each side of the mast. At the fore end of the coachroof the deck beam needed to be further forward to allow headroom down the companionway. This was not possible, so a deck beam was designed that curved in two planes. Although there was some head scratching in the workshop this was achieved and of course worked supremely well. Aluminium, or the material in use then, 'Birmabright', had been used to construct craft since 1927 when the Birmal Boat Building Company had been set up as a subsidiary of the British Aluminium Company. However, its use was still in its infancy but to save weight and construction complexities, 'Erivale' was fitted with a 'Birmabright' coachroof. A final problem to overcome was the steering. Abaft the coach roof was the main winch cockpit, then the mainsheet and then aft of this was the helmsman's cockpit. This meant that the helm was behind the rudder, whose stock came up in the main cockpit just forward of the mainsheet. The emergency tiller had to go on the rudder head, but used up the whole cockpit. They then designed a link gear that had a tiller growing off the main rudder stock under the cockpit floor off to one side, back ten feet and then back to the centre again to a tiller on a vertical shaft in the steering cockpit. The feel was excellent as proper bearings and ball joints were used where necessary and the helmsman had a clear view of his rig and no crew to trip over.

Robert Clark was a highly successful and prolific designer and the output of the office almost unceasing with the design team working long hours. The design team consisted of Robert Clark and Austin, with over the years a couple of lads on work experience. The lads tended to be very nine-to-five and once they had left the office, Austin and Robert would go out and get a meal and then return to the office to work until 10pm when the housekeeper would throw them out. One evening was different, when the housekeeper called them up onto the roof to see the Crystal Palace on fire some five miles away. Evening was when the real work was done. Robert rarely managed to get any serious work done during the day with the ever ringing telephone and a steady stream of visitors. Although they were long hours the work was very satisfying and highly enjoyable. Robert Clark would tend to produce the lines and the main layout drawings and basic specifications. Once the scantlings were decided Austin would do the construction drawings using a graded down scale of Lloyd's scantlings. Austin would detail the accommodation from initial sketches and fill in the sail plan and rigging detail also. There were an enormous number of drawings per yacht but Austin and Robert Clark worked very well together.

LIKE MOST DESIGNERS he had his favoured builders and although the Sussex Yacht Works completed many of the jobs, other orders were placed elsewhere depending on the requirements. The very large yachts were often too big to handle at Shoreham and Camper and Nicholson's would be used. However, if the costing had to be kept within tight budgets, Millers' of St Monance on the north side of the Firth of Forth would be given the job. Inspecting here meant the night train to Edinburgh and the local train at breakfast time with a short walk from the station. This Scottish yard built fishing boats as well as yachts and would turn out the same specification and quality as the south coast yards but at a fraction of the price. One such yacht was the eight ton 'INVERIE' which the office decided to deliver south themselves. The boat was finished early in 1938 and Austin was part of the crew that sailed the various stages

Peter Scott and John Winter getting the first bath

down the east coast. An account written by Austin for *Yachting World* was published in two parts on August 26th and September 2nd. The payment for these two articles, called '*Spring Delivery*' and '*On to Burnham*', purchased Uffa Fox's third and fourth books – and can be found in appendix 2.

One of the larger yachts built at Camper and Nicholson's was 'BENBOW', around fifty feet long and looking much like a scaled up 'Ortac'. She was built for a Mr Ted Gore-Lloyd who was head of Passing Cloud Cigarettes, a division of John Player. She was teak on steel frames and the owner had specified that he wanted an ocean racer on deck but a gentleman's yacht down below, with hot and cold running water to each cabin. This was of course achieved and on deck she was fitted with probably the first 'coffee-grinder' winch. The horizontal to vertical connection in the winch was made using parts from a Ford back axle. She was a beautiful yacht which reflected Gore-Lloyd's love of beauty in his home. He lived in a mansion at Hampton Court that backed onto Bushy Park. The house had been built for one of the mistresses of one of the Kings and on first seeing it she complained that the garden was not large enough. She was told that she could have as much of Bushy Park as the distance she could throw her shoe. This was done and the house had a garden that extended into Bushy Park a semicircle, the radius of the distance her shoe had been thrown. They were all invited to a party at the house to celebrate 'Benbow's' launch and Austin remembers that the basement housed a complete cinema. Gore-Lloyd had spent some time restoring the house and had removed the false ceiling in the hall to reveal the minstrels' gallery and the two large fire places both some fifteen feet high. When first restoring the hall he found that one of the fireplaces was missing. He set off to the West End to try and locate a suitable replacement but without much luck until one person remarked that there were some large pieces of marble out the back but they were too big for a fireplace. On closer examination they were found to be the actual missing fireplace that had been removed and sold by a previous owner. The size had meant that it was too large for any normal use and luck had prevented the pieces from being cut up.

The list went on with boats of all sizes. A stock design of around fifteen tons had at least four built and then there was 'CAYENNE', built for Dr Pepper and painted bright red. She was to be built by King's of Burnham-on-Crouch, who could quote only on Thames Tonnage. The design was drawn therefore with a snubbed bow because the bow was measured and a long counter because that was not measured. The order was given in good time but King's did not get on with her and various excuses were made as to why the work had not started. Eventually Dr Pepper and Robert Clark lost patience and decided to take the order elsewhere. Miller's of St Monance were asked to quote and they immediately questioned the ridiculously snubbed bow. They were given the explanation and said, 'But that's making it more expensive, we'll have a hell of a job to get round that bow.' 'Why can't we have a decent shape bow? It'll cost far less.' The plan was altered and a fine yacht produced, which is still on the East Coast today.

Yachts such as these are classics for all time and if well looked after will last indefinitely. They are often much better than our modern yachts and are well sought after. 'Cayenne' was being refitted on the River Orwell in the late 1980s for a trip around the world. 'Erivale' was eventually sold to the Greville family on the East Coast and spent many years cruising there and Austin saw 'Ortac' in Denmark in 1965 under the German flag and sailing for a German Army Academy. The only change seemed to be a new metal mast but everything else appeared the same, with her original cockpit, winches and pulpit.

With this sort of design workload, there was not a great deal of free time during the week. Occasionally, if a free evening, occurred Austin would go ice skating, or perhaps take in one of the many West End shows, or the cinema including the Marx Brothers who he loved ever since. However, every weekend was taken up with sailing, often sailing trials of one Robert Clark design or another, this of course was work and could occur mid week.

During the winter and spring of 1936/1937 the 'Fiery Cross', the twelve foot national, was raced – once in a snowstorm – at Ranelagh, but fared no better than on the Solent and Austin decided to sell her. He also decided that, although he was a competent helmsman and had learnt much about tidal stream and windshifts on the Putney stretch of the river, he was not cut out to be a racing helmsman. He always thought of the right tactic just too late. Therefore, it would be more enjoyable to be a first rate crew, and these are always in demand. Fortunately, Austin met an enthusiast who wanted to go dinghy cruising and he bought 'Fiery Cross'. The last he saw of them both, they were setting off from Burnham-on-Crouch loaded with camping gear and a Primus stove.

Towards the end of 1937 Austin agreed to crew an International Fourteen for the 1938 season at Itchenor with John Corry who had an Uffa Fox boat built in 1937 called 'Mikado' number 379. Unfortunately, early in the 1938 season, John Corry was posted to Australia by his employers to run their shipping base there. Austin was again without a sail but he was then introduced to Nora Chichester-Smith. She had been sailing with her husband, Colin, but they both enjoyed helming and decided to have a boat each for the prestigious championship trophy race, The Prince of Wales Cup (POW). With Colin's crew, Keith George – a Cambridge undergraduate – and their boat 'Mirage', they all set off in convoy for Falmouth with Nora trailing her boat, 'Shadow', behind her sporting Railton.

In Falmouth the well off owners stayed at the Greenbank Hotel, close to the Royal Cornwall Yacht Club, while several of the crews and some of the less well off owners stayed in a boarding house across the road known as 'The Monkey House'. Staying there were Peter Scott, then an aspiring young artist, who had won the POW the previous year in 'Thunder', and John Winter, who in 1934 had won in 'Lightning' and had been second the following three years. They had teamed up with a new boat, 'Thunder & Lightning'. Peter had lent 'Thunder' to his former crew, Charles Currey. Both boats were equipped with a new secret weapon – the Flying Trapeze – and they hoped for a good breeze on the main Cup day of Thursday, when its extra power could win the race.

The first two days saw racing inside the harbour, Monday up the Fal to Restronguet, going ashore for tea after the race, and Tuesday to St Mawes and the club there. Wednesday the fleet was out in the Bay in weather so calm that Austin dared take his camera afloat with him and managed to take some photographs. Thursday dawned with the hoped for breeze and Peter and John took turns at sailing the boat, so both wore a trapeze harness concealed in a zipped jacket until a few minutes after the start, when John Winter suddenly appeared standing horizontally on the gunwale. With this extra righting power, they soon worked out an unassailable lead and were nearly a minute ahead of Colin Ratsey in 'Hawk' at the end of the first round. After the second round, Peter and John changed over until the end of the race which they won by nearly five minutes. Colin Ratsey finished second and Stewart Morris was third. Charles Currey with Phil ('Percy') Gick trapezing in 'THUNDER' were in a fair way to be second, but they muffed the last gybe and capsized. In one of his books, Uffa Fox tells of this race and explained that Charles had tried to gybe when the boat was going down a wave and the shallow rudder did not grip when he bore away. Austin and Nora were not particularly heavy and had to work hard to keep 'SHADOW' upright, but managed a very creditable fourteenth out of 52 starters. Back at 'The Monkey House' after the race, Peter and John had the bath first by right of winning.

The following day several boats tried to rig up trapezes – which were banned by the class committee the following week. Aboard 'Shadow', not being able to manage a body harness, they lashed up a bell-rope with a length of old jib sheet attached to the wire shroud with three rolling hitches and a handle from the 'Monkey House' toilet to hang onto. They were going well until the rolling hitches slipped down and dumped Austin, towing him alongside by one hand with his head under water. The rush of adrenaline from this shock plus Nora's helping hand found Austin back in the cockpit, grabbed by the back of his jacket while she steered and held the mainsheet with the other hand. She encouraged another try, this time with five rolling hitches, but the performance was repeated and they decided to abandon their attempt.

The Committee were very much against the trapeze and gave Peter Scott the task of drafting the rule to prohibit it. In the end it was David Pollock, a lawyer, who produced the following gem: *'The use of any apparatus or contrivance outboard or extending outboard and attached to the hull, spars, rigging or crew, the purpose or effect of which is or may be to support or assist in supporting a member of the crew outboard or partially outboard is prohibited.'* The bell-rope or trapeze had been tried a little while before by Beecher Moore on his 'A' Rater on the Thames, but this was the first time it had been used in anger and was cause for great excitement. However, despite being a development class, it was banned and did not reappear in the Fourteens until 1969 after much discussion and argument, and long after most other high performance classes had adopted it.

Sailing a Fourteen Foot International was the premier dinghy. It certainly did not come any better and was the class that all small boat sailors aspired to. It was a physically demanding boat and as a development class with new designs each year could be expensive to remain competitive. People travelled to the centre of Fourteen sailing at Itchenor on Chichester Harbour and with much more difficulty than we do today with our own cars. Austin would have to take a train to Chichester and then a local bus to Itchenor.

There was one very sad episode whilst Austin worked for Robert Clark, and that was the death of Eric Synnott. Their secretary called Myrtle had 'hooked a lordling' and was engaged to be married. The Hon Highly-Bathurst offered to take the firm out to dinner, to celebrate the engagement, to Simpsons in the Strand. He, Myrtle, Robert, Austin and Eric settled down for dinner at Simpsons, and Austin was confronted with his first oyster. He tried one and decided it was awful, it tasted disgusting. He passed up on the rest of the plate and Eric kindly offered to finish them for him. The problem was that he developed typhoid and was dead within a week. This obviously caused a stir, although Austin was all right having only eaten the one. It took over a year, but the problem was eventually tracked down to West Mersea and contaminated sewage from one of the houseboats that had leached into the oyster pits. The person in the houseboat was a typhoid carrier although not suffering from it. Austin said naturally enough that he never touched another oyster, both because he did not like them but also as a mark of respect for Eric Synnott, when it could so easily have been Austin. The firm spent a little time without anyone else, but eventually they were joined by Harold Cluston who came in to run the brokerage and did so very effectively. This was an essential post to ensure that boats moved on allowing owners to build new boats.

By early 1939 war was looming, and Austin decided that work in a yacht design office would be little required in a time of hostility. He tried to join the RNVSR – the Royal Naval Volunteer Supplementary Reserve – later to become The RNVR, but was told that as a boat designer he would be better off designing or building the wooden craft that would surely be needed. He should therefore get himself a job in a boatyard. There was a choice of several yards that were building Robert Clark boats by that time, and Sussex Yacht Works were building the 'Mystery' design, this time with a lead keel. Whilst not a production line as we know it today, they had built a dozen or so and this certainly helped the yard and the designer's finances. Austin had been down to the yard several times to check on the boats being built and when he announced he was looking for a job, they offered him a position in charge of the drawing office which he joined during the spring of 1939. Initially the yard continued to build and finish yachts of around ten and twelve tons. As war was declared the yachts were laid up, being moved out or to one side to make more room for building. Some of the motor cruisers were re-launched in 1940 to take part in the Dunkirk evacuation. During the winter of 1939, it was decided to extend the building shed and make a new mould loft above. The builders arrived and dismantled the side of the existing building, but then the wind moved into the north east and it began to snow. The builders promptly disappeared for six weeks having not even rigged a tarpaulin. This was not a particularly pleasant time in the yard.

The yard was situated on the shingle spit that partly forms Shoreham harbour, launching into the river. The access was on an old rough road and shortly after the outbreak of war the whole area was mined and one had to be careful not to step off the road, although it did happen. With a vehicle one also had to be careful not only of the mines but also of the soft shingle which would swallow you axle deep instantly. Any vehicle that had been warned but still persisted in trying to turn round would be charged one or two gallons of petrol for the use of the yard slipway winch and snatch blocks to pull them out. On one occasion the Army, with a lorry mounted twelve pounder, sank in despite warnings that it was not wide enough to turn round. They requested to use the telephone, rejecting the offer of being pulled out for two gallons of petrol, saying someone would come and pull them out. Another Army lorry duly arrived and also got bogged down. With a captive clientele, they were eventually both pulled out by the yard for around ten gallons.

DURING THE WAR, Robert Clark was transferred to the Naval Construction Dept in Bath working on the design of the seventy-two foot H.D.M.L.s. Orders were given to several yards and Robert was farming out various parts of the design to the yards doing the building. With several boatyards in the group, one would be responsible for doing the design installation of each particular piece of equipment. Sussex Yacht Works had an order for two or three of these launches and Austin did the design work for the installation of the engines that they and a couple of other yards were using. Austin then did the steering gear for the whole group. The steering gear was fairly standard with rod and link steering that he had mastered at J. Samuel-White's and used with Robert Clark. Austin was not sure that Robert Clark ever knew of one small modification he made to the steering gear. The boats were twin screw and twin rudders and Austin used his experience to get the area and balance of the rudders right. He then recalled that he had seen a number of boats with a small hole in the rudder for drawing the propeller shaft out to save the need to fully dismantle the steering gear. The rudder would be turned ninety degrees and the plate removed. However, with twin rudders this was more complicated and Austin questioned why they had to be in line with the propellers. The answer is they do not and he decided to move the rudders two inches outboard. This caused no problems and in fact improved the turning circle as the rudder on the outside of the turn was getting more thrust from the propeller than the one on the inside. This design went ahead although Austin told no one. None of the drawings had the rudders and engine installations on the same sheet. No one at the main offices at Bath ever picked up this fact and when the overseers came to inspect it did not seem worth mentioning and they probably would not have understood anyway.

The Sussex Yacht Works built many boats and launches for the Admiralty including the H.D.M.L.s. Later during the war Austin was working for the Admiralty on Torpedo nets and whilst on the Clyde came across one of the H.D.M.L.s that they had built. During torpedo assessment on the Clyde, the main trials party was aboard a medium size Tanker. Austin had a bad wound on his hand that had gone sceptic and needed to get across to the Submarine depot ship where a doctor could dress the wound. Their H.D.M.L, allocated as their tender, was summoned to transport Austin across. Austin had to climb down the rope ladder and found that although not noticeable on the Tanker deck, there was quite a scend. It was now seven o'clock at night, dark, with the Submarine ship about a mile away off Rothsay. Austin took a leap and landed on the bridge deck, grabbed the handle and swung round into the bridge. As he was swinging round he remembered, 'Funny I put that handle there, it must be one of mine'. There had been no handle on the edge of the bridge deck in the original drawings and Austin had ordered one cut in, feeling that it was necessary for safety. This was a useful foresight as that night by the Tanker, with no handle he would have gone straight out the other side of the M.L.

Although war was imminent and Austin spent much of his free time in dinghies, there was still the opportunity for big boat racing in the 12-Metres.

IN THE LAST Cowes Week before war we find Austin aboard 'TRIVIA':

"In Cowes Week 1939 I was crewing in W.V. MacAndrew's 12-Metre 'TRIVIA', responsible for the runner backstays. Our opponents were Sir William Burton with 'JENETTA', T.O.M. Sopwith with 'TOMAHAWK', Hugh Paul with 'LITTLE ASTRA', Arthur Payne with 'VANITY V', Hugh Goodson with 'FLICA II' and Harold S. Vanderbilt with 'VIM'. A short diversion is necessary here to explain how she came to be racing in these waters.

The Americans had been slow to adopt the International Rule and the Metre Classes. The Rule was introduced in 1907 and several 12-Metres, as well as 23s, 19s, 15s, 10s, 8s, 6s and 5s were built in Europe but the USA had the Universal Rule, which produced the J-Class, roughly equivalent to the 23s, and the M-Class of about the same size as the 12s. Then in 1928, when the European Twelves were gradually changing over from gaff to Marconi rig, the American designers Burgess, Rigg and Morgan produced a 12-Metre design from which six boats were built by Abeking & Rasmussen in Germany and shipped out to the USA. The following year 'CANTITOE', a successful boat built in Norway, one of some twenty to Anker's design, was bought and shipped out, and also 'MOUETTE', built by Camper & Nicholson's for Sopwith in 1928 when she had the best record of any British Twelve. In 1929, after being sold to the USA, 'Mouette' dominated the American class and set designers there thinking about her great length.

Not much happened in the USA until 1935 when Clinton Crane designed 'SEVEN SEAS' and Herreshoff produced 'MITENA' which took length to the limit and was not a success. In 1937 Crane designed 'GLEAM' for himself. Using tank testing for the first time with her model against that of 'Seven Seas'.

Harold Vanderbilt, fresh from his America's Cup success in 1937 when he beat Sopwith's 'ENDEAVOUR II' with 'RANGER', was invited to sail 'SEVEN SEAS' in 1938. He was so pleased with her and the 12-Metre class in general that he commissioned the young and aspiring Olin Stephens who had teamed up with Burgess in 'RANGER's' design, to design 'VIM' for him, and in 1939 brought her over to Britain to race in the class here as Gerard Lambert had brought the J-Boat 'YANKEE' over in 1935. Olin's brother Rod was responsible for the rig and her duralumin mast which cost as much as a complete 12-Metre, and Rod was Vanderbilt's right hand man during the racing.

In those days the Rule required 12-Metres to have proper accommodation. The five paid hands lived in a spacious forecastle, while the saloon and aft cabins were well fitted out and usually finished in Honduras Cedar (lighter than mahogany) to save weight. Some owners and their afterguard lived on board, though the majority had the comforts of a motor yacht. When racing, the crew's pipe cots and bedding were often put into waterproof covers and left behind in the dinghy to keep the forecastle clear as a sail room. 'VIM's' accommodation was legal but somewhat spartan and it was obvious that no time or expense had been wasted on it. Everything below was painted spruce – as were the hatches and skylights. All the effort had been put into making her a successful racer.

'TRIVIA' was the most successful British Twelve at the time. Built in 1936 by Camper & Nicholson, MacAndrew had spent half her first season tuning her to his ideas and this had entailed several alterations to the rig and re-building the steering gear, which had so much friction that one could not 'feel' the boat at all. When 'VIM' appeared in 1939 'TRIVIA' was the only one which could really give her a race, and it was fascinating to watch her in action at close quarters.

One day during Cowes Week the course entailed a run down the Solent to Lymington Spit buoy and a beat back against the tide along the Hampshire shore. Most of the owners and skippers knew the Solent like the back of their hand and hardly needed a sounding lead but for Rod Stephens the chart was not enough and he had missed a party in Cowes the previous evening to carry out his own survey with a hand lead and line from a launch.

Most of the time during the race Rod would be standing close behind Vanderbilt, advising him and supervising the sail trim but as we approached the shore on each inshore tack he would be on the bow with his lead line in a box forward of the forestay and sounding continuously until he gave the lee-oh order and ran aft to help with the sheets.

On several of the inshore tacks 'TRIVIA' was on 'VIM's' weather quarter so we had to be ready to tack when she did. On one of these tacks I saw Rod, from his position near the wheel, glance up at the mainsail and noticed, as he had, that the bottom batten had worked loose – half way out of its pocket. Without a word he shinned up the six parts of the mainsheet, stood on the boom for a moment and then climbed the leech of the mainsail, gripping it between his knees, about 25 feet up to the batten pocket. Then, using both hands, he pushed the batten in and tied it into place, slid down the sloping sail, jumped from the boom to the deck and ran forward to pick up his lead line."

This was an amazing feat of strength and control and obviously impressed all that saw it, including Uffa Fox – who was not easily impressed – and who also recorded it in one of his books.

One job undertaken at Robert Clark's was particularly close to home, and that was the design of a new class for Austin's club, the Royal Harwich Yacht Club. The design was undertaken in the winter of 1936 as the third or fourth commission received and was well promoted by Sir William Burton who was keen to see a unified one-design on the river, particularly as the Orwell Corinthian One-Designs were now showing their age. The boat was to be about twenty feet overall and capable of racing around the Cork lightship outside Harwich Harbour, and be of a low price. Some requirements are never new.

Yachting World reported the design in an edition dated January 15th, 1937 and in an interview with the designer he described the boat:

"The maximum beam is disposed well up towards the deck. At length water line it is six feet so that the boat upright has the proportion, normal in this size of boat, of three lengths to one beam. By reason of the considerable dead rise, displacement is on the light side and the wetted surface in the upright position is low. A good performance in light airs may, therefore, be expected.

Displacement of 1.5 tons with a crew of two which allows an iron keel of 12cwt. Stability when pressed is good for the size of boat, for the shape of section has considerable reserve stability and, in addition, it will be remembered that the position of the crew when sitting on the side decks – without in any way leaning out to windward – is also very helpful. The 12 cwt of iron is sufficient to prevent the boat being knocked flat in normal conditions, but in the worst event, they are capable of floating on their sides with the cockpit clear of the water. The shape of the bow sections makes the boat dry when turning to windward in a slop."

"The available length water line fixed at 17 feet 6 inches does not leave very much overhang within the price aimed at, so the boat was drawn out forward rather than aft. For windward ability and those qualities of behaviour which are generally meant by the term good balance, it is essential that a boat should have four shoulders. In sailing in perfectly smooth water, these can be rounded into a blunt bow as in the Thames raters, but if the boat is to sail in any amount of a chop, the lines must be carried out normally which, of course, means some kind of bow overhang. The bow as drawn is considered as the shortest likely to be successful. No comparisons should be made with racing dinghy practice, which deals with unballasted boats that are intended to be sailed upright. Aft there is the inducement to carry out the lines in the form of a yacht style counter where price allows and in particular where the boat is to be sailed in open water. In this case, however, a square transom dinghy style is correct from the point of view of value for money. Besides this consideration of the dimensions of the hull alone, it should be noted that the bobbed stern lends itself to the use of a rudder hung outboard, as in a dinghy which in itself makes cheapness. The latter arrangement also goes with the short type of outside keel and gives a boat lively on the helm."

"The jib is of moderate proportions and may be expected to pass across the boat in stays with very little assistance. It is proposed that the helmsman would cast off the sheet in putting the helm down, and the forward hand, who can stand immediately by the mast, since the cockpit extends forward of it, would be able to see the clew clear of the shrouds as the boat is coming round, at the same time taking in the slack of the new sheet. The only skill called for is in the gathering in the slack quickly so that the clew can be hauled home while the boat is still paying off on its new tack. If this is done *correctly, no physical strength is required. The boom has been kept high to clear the heads of the crew when sitting on the side decks. Were the boom lower than this, it would add very little to the speed of the boat except when running dead. The boom droops to ensure effective use of the roller reefing as it is essential for the boom to be at right angles to the mast if the sail is to roll up far. A spinnaker of good size to assist the boat down wind is of the double luff type set outside the forestay with the jib doused. Set in this way, with the double-ended spinnaker boom it can be gybed easily and quickly."*

Austin and his brother sailing June in the late 1930s

AUSTIN WORKED WITH Robert on the rig design and they chose a new material – high tensile steel – which had already been used successfully in dinghies, to keep the jumper stays taught and eliminate the need for running backstays. Austin remembers that the yard in Sittingbourne were fairly stunned with this being used to much heavier plough steel wire.

Several firms tendered for the work of building the seven original boats and the Sittingbourne Shipbuilding Company was chosen on their price of £113.0s.0d plus a fee of six guineas per boat to the designer, totalling £119.6s.0d. per boat. They were ordered in November 1936 and the company committed themselves to a delivery

The RHOD June when first delivered to the River Orwell

date of Easter 1937 for seven completed boats. Whilst the specification called for best quality materials to be used throughout, including English Oak, Canadian Rock Elm and Mahogany planking with copper and brass fastenings, the yard itself had no previous experience of quality yachts and were more used to barge work. The final finish was very poor and each boat had to be upgraded by Harry King Boatbuilders at Pinmill, who recall the poor finish with a day's work sanding just to get them presentable. The sweet sheer was lost when the boats were removed from the moulds and everything seemed to sag a bit, which had to be resolved with the addition of shaped coamings and rubbing strakes. Austin recalls that they really wanted the boats built by King's of Burnham but the commissioning members of the RHYC had the attitude that anything above the lowest tender was mere profiteering, but as always you only get what you pay for. However, despite these initial troubles, the boats have stood the test of time and are still sailing, albeit with some restoration work. Their poor standard is noticed at the start of every season, when they need a couple of tides to swell the planks again and stop the leaks.

Six of the boats were towed round from Sittingbourne by a launch but 'MIRANDA' No. 4 was sailed round by Robert Clark and Austin. They left King's Ferry early to catch the tide, 'MIRANDA' having been brought down the creek from Sittingbourne itself the previous day, with Robert and Austin spending the night at the ferryman's house. Dawn saw very little wind but the first of the ebb took them down the Swale and out into Whitstable Bay clear of the Isle of Sheppey where they found a nice breeze to take them across the estuary, skirting the Maplin sands on the last of the ebb and taking the new young tide up the Crouch, gaining tacking practice with the wind against them. Here they found the local Burnham and Corinthian One Designs having their Saturday afternoon races and they quickly realised that they had quite a fast boat.

The boat was left on moorings for the week and the journey continued the next weekend but without Austin. Robert Clark recalled that it was a different sail with the weather quite nasty and rough in the Wallet, such that they sheltered in Brightlingsea for some time. However, the boat duly arrived at Pinmill and was handed over to her new owner, Frank Tempest, with pride. When the others arrived there was an almost family outing with all the boats sailing but not seriously racing. That would follow with trophies fought hard over. For Austin it was a real family affair, with No. 2 'JUNE' owned by his brother Norman, No. 1 'SANDPIPER' owned by his uncle, Walter Packard and No. 6 'HALCYON' owned by another relation, A. Packard. Austin continued his long association with the class by making sails for them in the late 1960s and after his brother died and the boat returned from the Walton Backwaters he again saw it race in the class until he sold it in the late 1980s.

The final part of the story is that several years after the first seven boats, another one was built at the yard but did not join the fleet; in fact it was built with a cabin. Although not originally ordered from the club, in about 1960 she was purchased by George and Lizzie Ditton and brought back from the Medway. Modified to fit the class rules, she was renamed 'Queen Bee' and raced with the rest of the fleet, although the starboard locker of her cabin days can still be seen. The fleet still races and can be seen at their various moorings around the site of the RHYC at Woolverstone.

Unfortunately, Austin lost contact with Robert Clark during the early part of the war after joining the Admiralty, and did not see him for many years. One day a Royal Harwich Yacht Club member was walking through Harley Street, London in the 1960s and spied the name on a brass plate. Passing this information on to Austin, he contacted Robert and they resumed a close friendship until Robert's death in the late 1980s.

CHAPTER 4
THE WAR YEARS

By the time war was declared in September 1939, Austin was fully installed at the Sussex Yacht Works. They were soon at work moving things around to move the laid up yachts out of the way and to make space for the Admiralty orders. The yard was busy building MLs and it was an interesting time.

In April 1941, Churchill summoned Captain C.N.E. Currey – Charles's father – to give him a review of the Actaeon Net Defence trials. Churchill said, 'Tell me about your nets again, you have 20 minutes.' Two hours later, Churchill gave the go-ahead with the instructions, 'Use any facilities and personnel you need – if you can save one ship you will have paid for the whole job.'

Austin's work at Shoreham continued until the summer of 1941 when Captain C.N.E. Currey came to 'drag' Austin out of Sussex Yacht Works and up to London to work for him at the Admiralty Old Building, on the Torpedo Nets Project. This was to be his job for the remainder of the war. Captain Currey was in charge of the project until he went to the USA in late 1941 to start work on a similar project. As the project developed, a head of the design office was appointed – Captain H.P. Wilson – with whom Austin worked very closely. Although Austin could have had a uniform position, Captain Currey said, 'He could be of more use in civilian clothes, as he could then say no to Admirals.' This was to prove useful on a number of occasions. The Battle of the Atlantic was raging and the losses were very high. Churchill knew the ships needed more protection and the project found itself in the pleasant position of nearly being able to have anything or anyone it wanted. However, Rear Admiral W.B. Mackenzie joined the department as Chairman of the Actaeon Net Defence Committee and he was never popular with his staff and could sometimes make working conditions unpleasant.

Although based in London, Austin moved around a lot and spent much of his time at the National Physics Laboratory Testing Tank at Teddington, tank testing the various projects. He in fact lodged in Teddington at the old Clarence Hotel. He divided his time between here and London, commuting as necessary but always living in Teddington. There were periods in other places, however, and at one point Austin was moved to Portsmouth to re-establish the experimental net making works. This had been in use before the war but abandoned. They had taken over Lennox Garage in Southsea to make the early experimental nets in 1939 but when the project

Splines, proportional dividers, planimeter and batten weights in use

was dropped in 1940 the place remained unused except as a store. It was not handed back. By late 1941 Austin needed to re-establish the net making and he spent some time drilling the concrete floor and grouting in tubes into which metal rods could be dropped to provide the weaving matrix.

One lunchtime Austin ventured upstairs to find a deserted drawing office over the showroom that had been abandoned when the Navy pulled out previously. Not wanting to see things go to waste, he quickly annexed the drawing office and all the equipment that had been left in it. There he found beautiful six foot lancewood Splines, a six foot wooden Straight-edge with Ebony edges, Batten Weights, and a pair of Harling's Proportional dividers. These items lasted Austin throughout his life, although the Straight-edge was eventually damaged beyond use, but long after the war. The remaining items are still in use by me today.

He returned to London for a while and then found himself in Southampton to establish the Net making factory there. This was in 105 Shed which still stands today. On a visit to Southampton in the early 90s Austin revisited the shed to find the weaving peg holes still in the floor from its war time use. The size of this project can be imagined when one realises the size of the shed, some 700 ft long and 80 ft wide. The first job was to lay out the grid for drilling the peg holes. Needing a right angle in the corner to start from, Austin had brought a brand new tape measure with him from Portsmouth Dockyard Stores, a so called metallic tape. Using the 3-4-5 triangle method, he laid his lines in the corner to find that they did not fit. Something was obviously seriously wrong. He checked himself and then decided to check the tape. It was a one hundred foot tape and running it out round a peg and back it returned to a different place. Something funny was going on. Austin now marched into town and finding an ironmonger's in Southampton, purchased a one hundred foot steel tape. He eventually received his money back. Returning to the shed he laid it along side the metallic one to find 9 inches difference in one hundred feet, the metallic tape being short. Austin took the tape back to Portsmouth Dockyard saying, 'Here's a duff tape.' The reply was a little disconcerting, 'Oh they're all like that. It's to allow for stretch.'

The Navy tradition for oddities was continued when Austin needed a shackle for the net rigging and for the kites. Despite the 20-ton load, an ordinary shackle would vibrate undone and release. The answer would be pin and forelock shackles and Austin duly went to the stores to enquire. Looking them up in the rate book the storeman said, 'Yes, here they are. ' Shackles, pin and forelock for bowsprit shrouds.' Well they're only a hundred years out of date, they're still in stock.' No doubt even today there are dusty corners of Naval stores that hold hidden treasures.

Nets were made at Southampton throughout the war, with two RNVR Officers running the operation with a lot of civilian workers. Austin was mainly there to do the technical parts not known to the officers and to set up the works and get it into production. At this point he returned to London, although there was to-ing and fro-ing until D-day in 1944.

They had been working on research into how to catch torpedoes using a model torpedo and a model string net. They were beginning to catch the torpedoes but they did not know exactly how they were catching them. Whilst they could launch the torpedo directly at the net, they could not simulate the fact that both torpedo and net would be moving and the torpedo would therefore hit the net at an angle. To solve this they estimated the angles and fired the torpedo at an oblique angle into a stationary net. To fire the torpedo, however, it needed to be mounted to run on a track. From a yacht design background, it was an obvious choice to select mast track and Austin set off to Davey & Co in West India Dock Road to procure the necessary track. This, Austin recalls, as D-Day itself. Having moved out of the Admiralty Building, a tube and bus journey began from the new offices at Queen Anne's Mansions. The new Home Office is now built on the site. Queen Anne's Mansions was a nine floor Victorian block of flats built entirely of brick and before the age of steel framed buildings. It had unfortunately been slightly bombed and the occupants had been moved out as it had been declared unfit for human habitation, and the Admiralty had been moved in. A bomb that did not explode had entered the building vertically and carved a shaft one flat in area and nine floors high, embedding itself at the bottom. There was a locked door at one end of Austin's office with nothing but air the other side. They were based in Queen Anne's Mansions for some time, and had generally finished the initial design work and organisation, so the whole project was being slimmed down slightly. They were moved from Queen Anne's Mansions and relocated to a private house in Chelsea where the drawing office was situated in the maids' bedroom, where at lunchtime they would sit on the roof and watch the doodlebugs coming over. If they were to the left when they cut out then they would tip down to starboard and there would be no worry. The other side, however, needed watching and might require a slide down the roof into the gully and a rush below. Strangely very few caused this as the main track was always to port.

Whilst they were in Queen Anne's, John Powell joined Austin. Austin first got to know John Powell at Sussex Yacht Works, where he was a boat builder apprentice. Here Austin needed someone to help him in the drawing office with all of the Admiralty drawings for the boats they were building. They had tried to get an assistant and had several unlikely candidates for the job, eventually deciding to take one of the lads out of the yard. The brightest of them was Johnny Powell and he joined Austin in the drawing office. Although really wanting to be a boat builder, having left school and moved straight into the apprenticeship, Austin discovered that he was in fact a Public schoolboy and therefore better educated than many. This grounding meant he took to the work 'like a duck to water'. Austin soon had him drawing lines plans and he proved to have a flair for the job. Austin moved to the Admiralty and Johnny Powell took his place at the Sussex Yacht Works. About a year later Johnny was 'conned' into the Admiralty by one of the boat building inspectors who came round to the yards. He was told that they were very much in need of naval architects and designers in Bath. This seemed a good way of pressing on with his career so he moved to Bath, where instead of doing something exciting and useful such as designing Battleships or the like, he found himself designing the allocation of ammunition stowage in landing craft. Whilst necessary it was certainly not exciting and after a few months he telephoned Austin to explain his predicament. 'Get me out of here, I'm going mad.' The only way out was for Austin's department to apply to have him transferred to them. After a while and no doubt the right representations this was achieved and John Powell joined Austin's department. At this point being very like minded, they 'got up to all sort of tricks'. The frantic pace of war meant little time for settling in and John left DNC Bath on the morning train to London and Queen Anne's Mansions to meet Captain Wilson. He was greeted with, 'Hello and you're booked on the night train to Hebden on Tyne with Austin to see a ship being netted.' They caught that evening's 11.15pm sleeper and were met by a WREN driver who took them straight to the ship and the Lieutenant in charge.

One lunchtime in Queen Anne's Mansions they took the lift down to the basement to see what went on and discovered a beautifully appointed workshop to maintain the building. The workshop was fully equipped and had a splendid Chief Engine Room Artificer in charge. He may have been there before the war, but Austin suspects he was a war time appointment with the Admiralty. The discovery was fortuitous as they needed bits and pieces made for the experimental nets project and this could not be better. In particular they needed a plug and socket to join two lengths of electric cable together under load – electrical plus mechanical load and of course under water. This was for the magnetic arming cable around the net to deal with magnetic torpedoes, to set them off under the net.

The Germans knew we had the nets but they did not know how they worked. They had decided that the best way to beat the nets was to fire a torpedo under the net with a magnetic pistol to detonate the main charge. At this time we knew the Germans had the weapon, some having been captured with a supply ship, but it does not seem that they had started to use them. The threat of magnetic torpedoes

With the booms out in position to support the net

had been known about since the very beginning of the project and Charles Currey had addressed the problem when working under his father Captain Currey at the beginning of the war. To deal with magnetic mines, they had discovered that a cable towed behind a ship with a pulse current put through it would set up a magnetic field and detonate the mines on the bottom. They rigged up one of these cables across the road at Eastney Barracks, driven by the generator that they had used for Magnetic Mines. Charles Currey drove a truck underneath with a German captured torpedo in the back. The magnetic pistol was intact although the detonator and charge had been removed. A couple of wires had been attached to the magnetic pistol which would give a ping in a pair of earphones. A seaman sat astride the torpedo on the back of the truck while it was driven back and forth under the cable at 20 knots, 25 knots, 30 knots etc., listening for the ping which would indicate that the torpedo would have exploded. The Germans were not using the magnetic torpedoes, although we knew they had them, and the project was put away until re-started by Austin when the Germans were aware of our nets and began to research other methods.

Austin needed junctions for the different sections of the net so that they could be coupled up. The Department of Electrical Engineering had designed a junction-plug and socket, which was 8 inches diameter, 18 inches long and was made from solid brass and weighed around 50 lbs. 'And heaven knows how much it would cost to make'. The team decided they could not have a hulking great thing like that on the net, being concerned not about the weight but the bulk and drag.

Having found this workshop in the basement of Queen Anne's Mansions, Austin and Johnny Powell set to, to make their own plug and socket with the help of the Chief E.R.A.

The workshop was complete with a lathe and welding gear and the unit was

The boom end just visible the start of the net

constructed out of bits of 1½ inch water pipe. This became the outer casing and was cut and welded to form a taper at either end, and screwed together with a left and right-handed thread. A piece of discarded curtain rod was used in the centre for the conductor to pass through and the whole sealed with run in lead once the wires had been brought through. Rubber discs were used in the centre and, as the unit was screwed together, the rubber was compacted to form both a water tight and good electrical join. The unit was smaller, neater and cost only a few shillings in materials, but now needed testing. At Portsmouth, the prototype with a length of cable in it was taken to a department with spare submarine batteries and coupled up to give the required 300 amp hours at 2 volts. This test passed, they continued to H.M.S. Dolphin, the Navy Submarine, base to test the water integrity in the escape tank at the required 30 feet. Finally, they returned to Portsmouth and the Chain Cable Test House and instructions to 'please break this'. The cable being used had a nominal breaking load of 12 tons and they would need about 8 tons maximum at the socket to be able to pass the requirements. The cable eventually broke at 12½ tons clear of the socket just before the entering the taper. As can be imagined Austin and Johnny Powell were delighted.

By the summer or 1944, with the flying bombs becoming a menace and the horror of the V2 suspected but not known in detail, an order was given that any government department that did not have to be in London, was to be moved out. So it was that over the August bank holiday Austin and his department moved to Scotland. Austin recalls that there was a skeleton staff on for the bank holiday weekend, with three of them doing one day each. Austin had the Saturday off and he went down to the Royal Canoe Club to put a coat of varnish on his 10 sq. metre canoe, 'Valiant'. This was the last time he saw the boat for some years. He rang the office that evening to check, 'OK to come in tomorrow? Nothing going on is there?' to be told, 'Yes there is, everybody has got to come in tomorrow.' Following Sunday's train journey from Teddington, he arrived to find complete chaos and a full exodus begun. The entire office was to leave Monday morning for Scotland in six 3 ton trucks. Everyone lent a hand with the packing, even the Officers with their sleeves rolled up. John Powell recalls that the Army trucks were pulled straight off the production line at Luton and arrived freshly painted and with no number plates. When the work was finished it was decided to celebrate with a beer just around the corner. As was not unusual in those days the pub had run out of beer but had some cider. Considering the hot day, cool cider was very welcome, but very quickly the whole party was feeling a little worse for wear

Valiant at the Royal Canoe Club Teddington

and they adjourned to Cadogan Gardens to sleep off the effects.

Austin was to travel up with his immediate boss, Captain Wilson. Johnny Powell and Rita Tester were sent off on leave until the department was settled. Austin travelled in Captain Wilson's car with all the Top Secret documents and plans, and Austin's treasured drawing instruments, including the lead Batten Weights in the rear foot well. The six 3 ton trucks left early on the Monday for a long trip to Scotland, there being no motorways such as we have today.

Austin, Rita Tester, Capt H Wilson and John Powell

Nothing was left behind bar the chairs and a table; all was in the trucks. The entire department was in fact vast by this time, controlling hundreds of people all over the world with fitting depots everywhere. The design office was by now a very small part of the organisation and was in fact winding down in some parts because most of the design work had been done in the earlier stages. Once things were in full production the design team were not required and were now spending their time researching the finer detailed points of torpedo catching. As Captain Wilson said, 'There is no point in hurrying. It will be Wednesday before the trucks get there. I've always wanted to have a look at the Lake District. Let's go there.' They duly set off in Captain Wilson's Morris 12 and spent the first night in Derby. After finding a hotel, the car was driven to the Police station yard and the request made, 'Armed guard please'. With the importance of the contents of the car, no chances could be taken. This was repeated the next night in Kendal.

They moved on the next day to Glasgow, and the small office already established there to service the fitting depots on the Clyde, one at Greenock and one across the Clyde at Helensburgh. In anticipation, the Scottish office had requisitioned a building in the slums in Annisland on the north bank of the Clyde, the office in Glasgow being two rooms in an office block with no spare capacity. The building in Annisland had been part of some W.R.E.N.S accommodation for a nearby training unit and was a very old stone built building, quite out of place in the slums, probably an old doctor's house and ghastly. On arriving for a look they found the Admiral ensconced in the best room in the house on the ground floor. This was all very convenient for the Admiral as he lived just down the road in a village called Gartocharn on the lower edge of Loch Lomond and was collected for work by a service car. The Admiral's room on the left was complete with a carpet, and Captain Wilson was to have the other ground floor room on the right, but with no carpet. There was no plumbing to speak of and, as was the case at that time, the privy was down the garden. However, the only way to reach the privy was through Captain Wilson's office, up three steps to the window sill, out through French windows and off down the garden. Needless to say, Captain Wilson did not think this a very good idea. Although it was still August, winter was not that far away. He also noticed that the fireplace was as normal under the chimney, but that the chimney was on the outside of the walls and the walls were four feet thick. This meant that the fire, when lit, lurked down a tunnel four feet away and would do little for heating the room – Captain Wilson had a gammy leg, walked with a stick and found stairs difficult. This was following an injury when blown up in Portland Harbour in a dive-bombing raid whilst in command of a Cruiser. The ship was sunk and there was considerable loss of life. He had subsequently been given a shore job, being unable to return to sea. Austin therefore went up three flights of stairs to see where the drawing office was to be and found they had been allocated what had been a maid's bedroom. Unlike Chelsea, this room was in the pitch of the roof, ridiculously small for three people and the top of the window barely reached knee height. It was very unsatisfactory. Austin returned to Captain Wilson who said, 'Just as I expected'. He then told Austin that, as the civilian, he was the only one qualified to go and say 'No' to Admiral Mackenzie, a local man who wanted to live near home. With some trepidation Austin did so, which as he says was not very pleasant. He was a very obnoxious Admiral and a very nasty piece of work. He ranted and raved but could do very little, certainly not sack Austin although no doubt he wished to. Eventually he took the line that if they could find anywhere else they had better go there. Austin departed his presence as quickly as possible.

Captain Wilson and Austin returned to the car and decided to first try the depot at Helensburgh some twenty miles down the Clyde. They asked the Lieutenant Chaffin R.N.R. who was in charge if they had a spare room. There were some twenty ratings in Nissan huts in the garden of the main building of the unit, which was an old house adjoining the hotel. They had possibly been one and the same at one time. They were told that they could have the room upstairs for a drawing office, although it was supposed to be the sailors' recreation room. However, to use it meant getting the stove going and one was already alight in their mess room so they saw little point in using another room. There was also another little room alongside that Captain Wilson could have as his own office. They were taken upstairs to find that this room had been an artist's studio some 30 feet long and 15 feet wide, with plate glass windows 10 feet high all along one side and across one end, overlooking the Clyde.

This could not be more perfect and they moved in immediately. They asked the Police where billets were to be found and were told that the Seaview boarding house across the road already had a number of naval personnel and this would be the best place, with Mrs Bell the landlady. This house had been a holiday boarding house before the war and was literally just across the road. Austin shared a room with Johnny Powell, who eventually arrived at Helensburgh station at about 11.30 pm one evening with his bicycle and was collected by Captain Wilson, and although rationing was in existence it did not seem that noticeable and the food was first class. Captain Wilson took a room in the Queens Hotel – to be joined later by Mrs Wilson – and the team settled in until the end of the war. Mrs Bell was a lovely person and knew their problems. She was most helpful if meals were needed at odd times. She also knew Admiral Mackenzie, as she came from Gartocharn village and had been 'in service' at the Big House as a girl. On one occasion they were due to join a ship in the early evening for torpedo trials, and it was arranged that Captain Wilson would join them at Seaview for high tea as he would miss dinner time at the hotel. Mrs Bell rose to the occasion: 'Fresh Salmon, Mrs Bell! What a treat! Wherever did it come from?' 'Shush! Out of the burn at Gartocharn!' Apparently he was not liked by the locals either.

Greenock and the Clyde were interesting places and used by Austin's department for torpedo trials, so he had been up several times to Customs House Quay. On these occasions he stayed in a Bed and Breakfast in Gourock, at the home of Mr Black of 'Black's Sailmakers'. There were always shipping movements and Austin remembers both the Queens and the Mauritania, all on troop duties.

On one occasion a ship had left to do some sea trials which Austin was not permitted to join, the trials being outside the Clyde. Whilst waiting for her return, over one of Mrs Black's excellent breakfasts the next morning, from their picture windows he saw the 'QUEEN MARY' entering the Clyde with a large notch out of her stem. He later found out that she had cut the Cruiser 'CURACO' in half. This tragedy had occurred out in the Atlantic when the 'CURACO', following an Asdic contact, failed to notice the 'QUEEN MARY' coming up on her at around 40 knots. The 'QUEEN MARY' cut straight through the 'CURACO' leaving nothing more than a notch in her stem at the level of the 'CURACO's' deck. The 'QUEEN MARY' had been speeded up during the war. On launching, only two of her funnels smoked, the middle being dummy with accommodation and storage. However the space was available down below for more boilers and these were duly fitted making the middle funnel smoke. This took her from her original design requirement of 32 knots to a new top speed of around 40 knots. The 'QUEEN ELIZABETH' was a little faster still and these speeds made them such excellent and safe troop ships.

The net project had been a resounding success and at the final count some 800 allied ships and the same number of American vessels had been fitted with nets. After starting the project here, Captain Currey spent most of the rest of the war in America supervising the fitting of nets to the American vessels and Liberty Ships. With these latter ships being launched at the rate of around one a week with nets from new, this was a major undertaking in itself. All new British ships were fitted with nets, freighters and tankers.

AT THE WAR'S end, Austin was not immediately released, being retained to compile the full history of the project until February 1946. He then returned home to Suffolk to start the next projects. John Powell, who had worked so closely with Austin, had been transferred in 1945 to HMS 'VERNON' at Port Edgar where he spent eighteen months working on mines and mine clearance. Back in Civvy Street he then worked for the designer Arthur Robb on various boats and also then built boats in Emsworth, including the 'MOUSE OF MALHAM' for the famous offshore racer Captain

Illingworth, about whom his accountant said, 'Do you think you can find a hobby that doesn't cost you £20,000 per year.' He then went on to form his own company, John Powell Spars, building masts in Nissen huts in a disused gravel pit in Emsworth. The longer the mast, the more sections of Nissen hut were added on. Austin stayed in close touch with him on various projects as he became one of the leading specialist mast makers and in fact fitted a metal mast to 'Gulvain' long before Proctor's were in production

During the 1930s and up to the 1960s yachting magazines often ran design competitions. This practice faded away and has only recently been revived in Britain by the magazine '*Classic Boat*'. Austin had entered some in 1933/34 but without success and admits it was a little heavy going. However, during the war, *Yachting World* ran a competition for a Twenty Ton Ocean Racer to be built after the end of the war. This was while they were in Scotland and, between them, Austin and John designed the boat. It had to be original drawings with no copies and to show alternatively with and without a paid hand. The two accommodation plans with deck, sail and a full set of lines were duly produced and sent in. They were acknowledged but then nothing more was heard. The publication date arrived and, scanning the magazine, they saw that the first prize was very mediocre and the second more so. For third prize the magazine had to apologise for the poor quality of the drawings. Things were busy and time was not found to follow up their query until six months later when the drawings were returned without comment. Normally they would be covered with the judges' markings in 4B pencil, but they were completely clean and had obviously been lost or mislaid and never looked at. Come the end of the war, Austin wrote to Haylock, the editor, saying he was coming back south and hoped to look in on him. On his arrival at the office the secretary informed Austin that, 'Sorry, the editor's very busy, he can't see you. What was the name again? Oh, weren't you in the design competition? You were unlucky, weren't you?' 'Yes, we were unlucky!' The poor girl had been given the editor's dirty work to do and Austin realised that Haylock would never come out of his office to face him, probably because he knew just what Austin was likely to do.

Wartime sailing was limited but possible. In 1938 Austin and Charles Currey had decided that they needed a cheap knock-about sailing dinghy to explore the many shallow creeks in Chichester Harbour when not racing. Austin had seen some 11ft Pram dinghies in use by the youngsters at Felixstowe Ferry, which had been designed by a local artist in Suffolk, Kaye 'Corky' Edmunds. These were lug rigged, but with a new rig would be just the thing. Some interest was shown at the Itchenor Club, and Austin and Charles ordered six from Mitchell at Brightlingsea. Pulling dinghies then cost a pound a foot and the agreed price was £15, built in Parana pine, for a complete hull with oars, rowlocks, daggerboard and rudder but no rig. Austin and Charles designed a new gunter rig with an up-and-down yard and a Bermuda cut mainsail. Charles was working at the Itchenor shipyard where the solid mast and grooved yard and boom were made, and Lucas agreed to make the sails. The boats were put on the train to Liverpool Street Station in London and Austin and Charles collected them

from there and took them south

Austin retained a boat for himself and the Curreys and the others were sold on, the first to Cyril Clarke. This was named 'Hops' after his favourite drink. Austin and Charles decided that this could lower the tone of the class and Austin quickly named his 'Skips' to be followed by 'Jumps'. The next two followed suit with 'Leaps' and 'Bounds'. Much enjoyment was had exploring Chichester Harbour, and when war broke out Austin took the boat on a trailer to Shoreham to sail on the river there. A little later they added a jib, which improved performance and did not upset the balance.

All opportunities to sail had to be taken and part of Austin's job at Shoreham was to source and find timber. John Powell often accompanied Austin

Skips sailing in Scotland

as part of his training, and on one trip to Emsworth for oak the dinghy was taken on a trailer behind the car. Having finished business, the two of them took the boat to where the Chichester Marina now is to sail. Early in the war they were not allowed on the harbour, but there was a large meadow flooded for defence to a depth of four feet or more and made an excellent sailing lake. Enjoyment finished, the boat was reloaded and returned to Shoreham. Later in the war, when restrictions were eased slightly, the 'Skips' was issued with a fishing licence and a number painted on her side and she was able to sail on the main harbour. By this time Austin was working in London and 'Skips' was looked after by Charles Currey at Bosham, although Austin would take a weekend down to Chichester Harbour whenever he could.

Even during the war there was the opportunity for boat acquisition, although Austin's Int. Canoe, 'Valiant', was not sailed until after the war. Austin acquired 'Valiant' through a sailing friend John Aumonier. For some years and whilst Austin was at Shoreham, John Aumonier had been teaching Biology at hospitals, but now had switched training to become a doctor. Austin saw John Aumonier occasionally whilst they were both in London and knew he was concerned about the fate of the boats. John owned another canoe called 'Wake', on which he had been the pioneer of fully battened sails in this country, and together with 'Valiant' and all the other British canoes they were kept in a barn at Hayling Island. At the outbreak of war, all the canoes had been stored in Hayling Island Sailing Club's clubhouse, but this had been requisitioned to be used as the training base for the Cockleshell Heroes. The canoes had been hastily moved to a barn but this was only one hundred yards from an Ack-Ack battery and therefore very vulnerable. One incendiary could have wiped out the whole British canoe fleet, this was some twenty boats. John Aumonier reckoned that now the worst of the blitz was over it would be better if he could get 'Wake' away from Hayling and bring her up to the Royal Canoe Club at Teddington.

Austin and John travelled down to Hayling one weekend by train, taking bicycles to get around the island and staying aboard John's family houseboat in Mengham Rythe. They contacted the farmer whose barn held the canoes and planned 'Wake's' removal. When showing them round, he happened to mention that 'Valiant' was for sale. She had been Roger de Quincy's boat when he and Uffa Fox (aboard 'East Anglian') had successfully challenged for the International Canoe Trophy in America in 1933. Now ten years old and a little outclassed by the finer lined and beamier newer boats, she was still in good condition and at £50.0s.0d. the price was right both for purchase and the fact that it would cost very little more to transport two canoes in the same railway truck. Austin completed the purchase and the following weekend Charles Currey was enlisted to help with a car and a trailer to transport the boats to Havant Railway station where they were packed in sacks of straw and Southern Railways duly parked the truck in the goods yard of Teddington Station a few days later. With plenty of help from members of the Royal Canoe Club, the two boats were trundled through the streets on hand trolleys and ferried across to the club's island home. Once in London, Austin was able to do a little maintenance on her. However, an International Canoe on the river at Teddington can be very exciting. Just as the fitting out was completed, the orders came through to move to Scotland so Austin never sailed the boat until well after the war.

THE CLYDE IS a beautiful place to sail and was an opportunity not to be missed, as Austin told in March 1992:

> *"Shortly after D-Day my admiralty department was moved to the Clyde, so 'SKIPS' was loaded onto a railway truck full of large shackles, and duly arrived at Greenock where we had a depot. On a bright Saturday afternoon John Powell – my wartime assistant before he took up spar making – joined me on a ferry trip to Greenock. At Greenock a five ton crane lowered 'Skips' into the water and we rigged her and sailed the four miles across the Clyde to our base at Helensburgh. Compared to Chichester Harbour, the Clyde seemed like open ocean.*
>
> *The Clyde yachtsmen seemed to wait for a 'nice day' to go sailing but, with 'SKIPS' on the beach and able to be rigged and afloat at 20 minutes notice, we would grab a nice evening after work and have a splendid sail after tea. With double summertime we could stay out till 9 pm if there was any wind. We probably got in more hours sailing than the rest of Helensburgh put together.*
>
> *The Clyde tends to produce too much wind or too little, and one can sympathise with the big ketches with the 'Clyde rig' of jib, mizzen and engine. But, having had to row home a few times, we decided that 'SKIPS' needed a spinnaker. We started looking at photographs to see how to shape one. In our design office we used to get large drawings sent from the USA, usually in the form of tracing prints on a cotton based backing.*

When these became out of date and were replaced we had to destroy them (officially). However, we found that boiling them in the old kitchen copper would remove the drawing and leave the cotton backing which was equivalent to handkerchief material, and got used for just that by Rita Tester, who had been a dressmaker before joining the Admiralty. Some of the drawings were as much as 20ft long, so with careful washing to remove the TOP SECRET part there was enough for a spinnaker. Based on a Beken photograph of 'THUNDER' with her cotton spinnaker off Cowes, our first effort might not have satisfied Mr Ratsey, but it took 'SKIPS' along nicely.

After the defeat of Hitler, VE Day was celebrated by the first post-war regatta on the Clyde, organised by the McGruer family from their boatyard at Clynder. Rita and I sailed 'SKIPS' round into the Gareloch and collected our sailing instructions from the end of Clynder Pier. The course for the dinghy handicap class (most of which were yachts' tenders) was up the Gareloch and round a large mooring buoy off Faslane. When we reached the buoy in the lead we found a huge steamer moored to it so rounded the steamer as well. However, the youngest competitor, a junior McGruer, managed to squeeze his 9ft pram between the buoy and the steamer's stem and came out with a commanding lead. We were second on handicap."

CHAPTER 5
WOOLVERSTONE SHIPYARD

Having returned home to Suffolk from Scotland in 1946, Austin found himself without work but intending to find a position in a shipyard. However, with the end of the war, men were being laid off and things did not look promising. He returned to the house in Stutton which his mother had bought in around 1944 to move out of Felixstowe and to move closer to Austin's uncle, Walter Packard, who already lived in Stutton. Austin continued to live in that very pleasant house until his death.

About this time the Royal Harwich Yacht Club were considering moving from Harwich itself where they never actually had premises, meeting in the Pier Hotel, to take a lease on the foreshore of Woolverstone Park for a new clubhouse. Woolverstone House was a large country house, one of several in the area, on the banks of the river Orwell some seven miles upstream of Harwich. It was suggested that the club would be looking for someone to run the adjacent boatyard. Before the war it had been arranged that the Royal Harwich Yacht Club would move to Pin Mill some two miles downstream of Woolverstone and take over the site with Gus King's Boatyard. However, during the war, plans went awry and the site ended up in the hands of Gus King's son who had no intention of parting with it to anyone, least of all the Royal Harwich Yacht Club. They then learnt that the former Naval base at Woolverstone was to become available with Nissan Huts and slipways. This had been a Landing Craft base constructed by the Navy during the war. Prior to the war there had been only the estate hard used for landing coal from Barges. At this time redundant Tank Landing Craft were moored all along the beach. The club really only wanted a club house but they wanted the facilities for their boats to be looked after and Austin offered his services to run the boatyard for them, sub-letting from their main leases. As is often the way with club committees they took an age to

The Royal Harwich Yacht Club stands today in the background

make a decision and eventually the estate people, who could not get any answer out of the club, suggested that Austin should take the main lease and sub-let to the club. Austin comments that, 'like a fool I said yes!' and in the autumn of 1946 the business was started and a few yachts laid up for winter.

He admits that he had nowhere near enough capital to run things properly and started the yard on a shoe string which is how it continued. The club eventually leased and moved into the two Nissen huts that stood where the new club stands today, with the rubbish dump in front. This was eventually straightened out and the present lawn laid.

The hard at Woolverstone with the cathouse in the background

There were no facilities as one sees today, only the pier and a concrete foreshore made up of the concrete chocolate blocks. Behind this was a smooth concrete strip and the road leading up as it is today. The Navy had laid all the concrete strong enough to take tanks and their transporters and, as Austin remarked, it must have been pretty good stuff as he did not think anything had ever been done to it since. This had been built in 1943/44 ready for embarking tanks heading for France. A little down river, off Pin Mill, a flotilla of dummy landing craft were moored 'for the enemy to come and bomb' as a distraction.

The first job was to lay up boats for the winter of 1946/47. This had never been done before at Woolverstone and the method was sorted out as they went along. There was no method of moving the boats up into the higher areas and they were hauled out and chocked high on the foreshore. They had a winch driven by an old tractor engine that had come from the other end of the park by Freston Hill where it had been used at 'Slumpy Hard. There was a slip with rails and a trolley and the winch driven by a Fordson tractor engine. Austin bought the lot quite cheaply and moved them down to Woolverstone. They never did install the rails because the ground was not suitable, but the winch is still in operation today, although now driven by an electric motor. The yachts were floated into cradles and with a system of snatch blocks pulled up ways until they were above the tide line. That winter was the big freeze starting on the last day of January 1947 and they didn't see the grass until the end of March. The hard was a glacier with water seeping out of the cliff and freezing. They would put ashes down but over night they would be covered and the ice built up to some two feet thick. This was not the best conditions in which to try and start a business.

Austin had an awful job getting the business going. He had a boatbuilder, Geoff Quantrill, who started working in the barn at Austin's house in Stutton before they had a suitable building at Woolverstone. General repairs to dinghies were the first jobs there. Eventually during the first winter they moved to Woolverstone and

Woolverstone before the big sheds and the corner of the cottage before thatching

planned for the spring. Austin took on more staff and set about laying moorings. This involved buying second hand anchors and chains and all the paraphernalia needed for a boatyard. He says, 'I don't know how we did it quite honestly' and it was a very stressful time. For 'a bit of light relief' they took on some boatbuilding. They had two Nissen huts parallel to the shore as workshops of a sort. These became a mess hut or work room and the varnish shop. The latter was cleaned and tidied and became the yard's main varnish and painting shop. The main building was on the top of the hill and still survives today. This had started life as a First World War portable church. Austin bought this from Henry Fox who had the yard where Fox's Marina now stands in Ipswich and who no longer had a use for it. They dismantled it and moved it to Woolverstone and it became their main boat building shed for all the time Austin was there. There was also the big oil fuel tank left by the Navy which was cut into and used as a store. Finally there was the Nissen hut office on top of the hill and, according to the planning people, on the skyline. This could not be accepted in peace time. Austin offered to camouflage it and though they were not sure, they did not specifically say no. They returned to the yard and built a timber framework over the hut and thatched it. He says it looked like something out of Snow White. About a year later he saw one of the planning people and asked about his hut on the skyline. 'What hut?' came the reply.

One gain from the Navy was fuel found when clearing up and cutting into old fuel tanks. This was carefully siphoned into drums and lasted the yard launch for years. The launch was an excellent ex-RN Naval Cable Cutter, bought from disposals at Plymouth where it had been used in the harbour for under-running mine cables. It was about twenty-five feet long and had no engine although there were signs of a Stuart Turner 8HP. The yard fitted a Kelvin petrol paraffin engine and the launch did years of work, proving a good sea boat quite capable of doing a trip to

Boats at Woolverstone looking up to the Nissen hut cottage

the Walton Backwaters and back towing a yacht and did the work on the moorings with a roller on the bow. After Austin had left the yard, Judy Cracknell who was running the yard, contacted Austin to design a replacement as the original boat was now getting a little tired. Austin took the existing proven lines and modified minor points with a little more flair in the bow for example and a little longer. It was built in house and was the largest new built boat so far at the yard. This boat, we believe, is still in use today.

Austin checking the canoe VALHALLA with Percy Lipsett

Care had to be taken on the acceptance of jobs and the 'Just' jobs could be dangerous to costings. Austin remembers one local farmer who had a sixteen foot or there about clinker dinghy that, like many farmers' equipment, had been stored outside with no cover. He came in to ask if they could 'JUST' scrape and varnish the inside. Austin, remembering the very long and painful hours restoring his Dart Dinghy, asked the farmer what he thought the boat was worth. 'About £200,' was the reply. 'Well, if you want us to completely strip the inside and re-varnish it, the job will cost you £400'. Considering the amount of work involved, this was a fair price but the farmer declined.

If boatbuilding was to be Austin's business, then one had to be involved with boats at all times if orders were to be found. Whilst there was the every day maintenance and laying up of yachts which would be the 'bread and butter' for the yard, the orders for new craft had to be sought and would give the yard prestige. Austin plunged straight back into the racing scene in the spring of 1946 with the Fourteen Foot International Class. Even before the yard was established he began to do a little work from his barn in Stutton.

The first task that year was to prepare the Fourteen's 'THUNDER' AND 'THUNDER & LIGHTNING' for the coming season. 'Thunder' had been stored at Peter Scott's home in Norfolk and 'Thunder & Lightning' in a garage in Itchenor. During the war years little had been done to them and they needed stripping right back to bare wood and re-finishing. Both boats showed signs of being nail tired, being very black around some of the nail heads. The boats were stripped and bleached with Oxalic acid to restore the colour, but they were concerned with the blackened nail heads.

Expert advice was sought which confirmed that electrolysis had taken place. This was unusual as copper nails in mahogany should have been fine and not all nails were affected. Further examination located the aluminium jib sheet tracks let in to the gunwale and the nails affected were the ones that had bent very slightly on insertion and the sea water had completed the circuit. Although the track could only be replaced by more of the same, all was well sealed and the boats prepared for the season and the 1946 Prince of Wales Trophy in Torbay at the Brixham Yacht Club. This was subsequently won by 'THUNDER & LIGHTNING', sailed by Peter Scott and John Winter.

To be commercially successful in a class usually means that one has to be actively involved on the racing circuit, meeting and competing against your potential customers. Over the years, the older classes such as the International Fourteen and National Twelve have acquired some magnificent trophies and they are fought over as hard today as when first given.

AUSTIN RACED REGULARLY in the fourteen Class before and after the war and was fortunate to win some of the trophies including the 'Itchenor Gallon' as he tells here:

"One of the highlights of dinghy racing in Chichester Harbour is the Itchenor Gallon, and the huge silver tankard has traditionally been presented filled with beer with a hop floating on top, and is passed round as a loving cup so that everyone in the fleet gets a drink.

While I was crewing regularly with Charles Currey we made a speciality of the Gallon, winning it in 1948 in 'THUNDER' in survival conditions. The committee apologised afterwards for starting the race, not realising from their sheltered position on shore that it was blowing Force 8 out in the harbour. Charles remarked before the start that if we could survive we should win – and this we did – largely because most of the fleet capsized. Our mainsail was well reefed, and we were using a small jib.

On the long beat down to the entrance of the harbour we were taking a lot of water aboard, there were no self-bailers in those days, so I was using a long-handled bailer – a saucepan on a broomstick – from a sitting out position. It was not necessary to bale the water over the side. I just scooped it up from the bilge and poured it out in mid-air when it blew away to leeward. The broad reach up the Emsworth Channel and the close reach down again were fast and very wet, and then we had a dead run up the main channel to the finish with three gybes at bends in the channel.

Some boats elected to tack round rather than gybe, but that was nearly as dangerous because of the risk of missing stays. We should have liked to take the jib down as it was not safe to sheet it in because it made the boat roll badly, but I dared not go forward, so we had to leave it flapping madly with the sheets free, and it nearly beat itself to pieces before we finished.

Peter Leckie in 'ELAN' was next behind us, but he turned away short of the finishing line. He had been caught port and starboard at the start, but had elected to sail on round. However, there was no way of knowing that he was not racing, and he was severely criticised for not going home, as he had put several boats at risk, and some had capsized in trying to keep ahead of him. (Unlike today's racing rules, there were no alternative penalty turns for rule infringements at that time and if caught in a situation the only choice was to retire).

We won again in 1949 in 'SUNRISE', one of the first of the Uffa Fox designed Fourteens built by Fairey Marine; and again in 1951, 1952 and 1953. In 1950 we were second to Mike Ellison in 'THOR', and only by a bit of fast thinking managed to finish ahead of Stewart Morris in 'MARTLET'.

It was a light weather race with an easterly wind which meant a long beat up the Itchenor Channel against the tidal stream to the finish, with short tacks out into the tide and longer ones along the edge of the mud. Stewart was ahead of us, and had just made his last tack out into the stream so that he could lay the finish line in enough water for his centreboard, when Charles and I realised simultaneously that we could cross the line on the tack we were on if we did not mind going hard aground in the process. 'Shall we?' 'Yes.' We didn't need to discuss the matter. Charles gave her a good full and I pulled the centreboard up as we slid up the mud and took the second gun with our bow about a foot over the line and the boat practically high and dry, stopped by the rudder. Stewart was still out in the tide.

A few yards away in a boat moored tight on the transit to observe finishers on the line (the limit mark was high on the bank) was Charles' father, Captain Currey, who had been my wartime boss in the Admiralty. 'Do you boys realise,' he said, 'that although you have finished and got your gun, you are still under racing rules until you are clear of the line?' This meant we could not get out and push 'Thunder' clear, and we might have to wait there until the tide came up again.

I went and sat on the bow to take some weight off the stern, while Charles managed to unship the tiller and then used it as a lever to pull the rudder up out of the mud. We then backed the mainsail, first on one side and then the other while we rocked gently, and the boat slowly slid back down her groove until Captain Currey announced that we were clear of the finish line. Then we paddled her astern until we could ship the rudder again and sailed across the stream to the club slipway and a hose pipe to get rid of the mud."

DURING 1947, AUSTIN embarked on a new technique of cold moulding which was to make him the first and leading exponent of this method. The other key player in this scenario was Frank Priest who was the Technical Service Manager for Aero Research (now Ciba) of Duxford. This company produced the Aerolite Urea Formaldehyde glues for the building of the Mosquito aircraft and were keen to find further uses for the product. Frank Priest was a keen Merlin Rocket sailor and appreciated the possibility of a boom in sailing dinghies and small yachts, whilst Austin needed to find projects to keep the yard employed. The Aerolite glue was a mixture of syrup-like liquid and acid hardener. The piece to be assembled would be coated on one surface with glue and the other with hardener (accelerator) before assembly. It was, however, possible to assemble the joint and wipe it with hardener which would also set off the curing process and the Fourteens were coated in diluted Aerolite prior to varnishing.

Cold moulded boats with mechanical fastenings had been around for many years going right back to Sam Saunders' 'CONSUTA' in the early years of the century. However, moulding with cold setting glue was a new technique which Austin realised would simplify the whole process. The Americans had experimented some years earlier and Austin had read an article in an American magazine in 1940, but little was known of the method in Britain. There, the process produced waterproof plywood using Phenol Formaldehyde resin developed in the 1930s but still needing heat and pressure to cure it. This plywood was used for bulkheads and frames in the pre-fabricated Fairmile MLs and thin Birch plywood for aircraft. In 1940 the Skaneateles Boat Company in the USA produced an eight foot dinghy, designed for them by Sparkman & Stephens, whose shell consisted of three skins of 1/16 inch Mahogany veneers laid diagonally with each skin at right angles to the next. The planks were coated with the glue in liquid form and allowed to dry. They were then laid up cold on a solid mould with a few staples to hold them in place, extra veneers being added in way of the keel and gunwales. The whole was then placed in a rubber bag which was sealed and the air sucked out under vacuum pressure. This unit was put into an autoclave (a giant pressure cooker oven) and the glue was reactivated and cured at a temperature of 300° F with a steam pressure of 85lbs/sq in.

It was a variant of the Skaneateles hot moulded method that was first tried successfully in Britain by the Fairey Aviation Company who had finished the war with similar equipment to the USA firm. The big autoclaves at Hamble had been used to build the troop carrying Horsa Gliders used during the war, and they had a huge stock of thin Birch plywood. Sir Richard Fairey, the company chairman, was keen to find new work for his factories and so Fairey Marine at Hamble was born and the range of hot moulded dinghies that included the Firefly, Swordfish, Albacore, International Fourteen and the cruiser, The Atlanta. These were all designed by Uffa Fox. The earliest of these was the Firefly which was built in hundreds and early in its career was the single handed class at the 1948 Olympics in Torbay.

THE NEED FOR autoclaves tended to limit the possibilities of hot moulding and Austin searched for a simpler moulding process. It hinged round the discovery of Aerolite, a cold setting glue. It was frowned upon by some purists as it would not pass the boiling water test but, since only lunatics actually boil their boats, it has proved perfectly satisfactory in boats, some now over forty years old. After the war, timber was in short supply but Austin found the local timber merchant importing huge quantities of plywood, mainly Birch, for the building trade. It came packed in crates protected by layers of Birch veneer off cuts used in the original manufacturing process. It was normally swept into a heap and burnt, so they were more than happy to let Austin have a trailer load to experiment with. Much of it was scrap anyway with knots and badly warped panels but enough was salvaged to try and build a boat.

The simplest type of boat would be an eight foot pram, which if successful could be used as a yacht's tender. There were several clinker-built prams around, and they chose a traditional beamy type with a flat bottom and a firm bilge to copy for a mould. The mould was a simple affair with frames about two feet apart covered with three-quarter inch square battens and the whole structure covered in polythene to prevent sticking. The battens were about an inch apart at amidships, coming together at the bow and stern. The American Skaneateles and Luders boats were laid up with several skins of mahogany veneer on opposite 45 degree diagonals, so each was at right angles to the next as in conventional plywood. However, there seemed to be a case for some longitudinal strength with a fore-and-aft skin sandwiched between two opposite diagonals and, since it would not be seen, the veneers need not go full length as long as a reasonable shift of butts was observed and the planks could be allowed to lie where they wanted with stealers as necessary. (Stealers are shaped planks to fill in odd shaped gaps). Another point in favour of having adjacent veneers at 45 degrees instead of 90 degrees was that there would be less strain on the glue line when the wood swelled with moisture.

Austin made a model with thick plane shavings as planks running diagonally across the bottom and up the other side. They were held in with domestic pins to a solid block mould while the glue set, but when released it twisted like a potato crisp with the two diagonals pulling in opposite directions. This proved that the planking had to be symmetrical on either side to cancel out the pulls. A four inch by half inch Spruce keelson was set into the mould and the diagonal veneers butted on the centreline, held down by using enough staples from the office stapler to hold all the inner skin in place while the middle one was fitted. Then, lifting one side at a time, this was glued with yet more staples, removing the inner skin ones as they went.

To ensure that the skins remained attached to the mould, a dummy inwale above the proper one had been made, to which all the skins were fastened and which was sawn off along the sheer after everything was complete. When the glue had set but not completely cured, the staples were removed and the surface cleaned up to remove any excess glue and the outer skin carefully fitted, and glued and stapled into place.

An external keel was glued over the centreline join in the planking and screwed to the keelson. When released from the mould, the shell sprung outwards a little, but not as much as it would have had the centre veneer not been there. The shell was then pulled in to fit the transoms and the gunwales, risers and thwarts were fitted. The first efforts of veneer planking were not particularly attractive, so the boat was painted which made the staple holes much easier to fill. She weighed about half the weight of the clinker built version, rowed well and would carry four people.

This experimental boat went to Martin Beale, whose sister Joan was working in the yard, to use as a tender to his small cruiser and to give it a proper test. It certainly received this as we shall see shortly. However, one problem was quickly evident. Birch is a very close grained timber and did not take the Aerolite glue very well. A search was on for another alternative timber. Austin obtained a list of veneer suppliers from Aero Research and started working through it. Austin was not alone in experimenting with cold moulding as a process. John Chamier, of Tormentor Yachts at Warsash, used two skins of marine plywood cut into thin planks and glued on opposite diagonals with Aerolite. He built many Flying Fifteens and Flying Dutchman dinghies by this method, but it seems that Austin was the only person using veneers for cold moulding.

The search for better veneers became more urgent as problems arose in the next job. Early in 1948, the yard had an order from the Royal Canoe Club for a pair of

The first stages of cold moulding

The shell of the cold moulded Canadian canoe for the Olympics

The Canadian canoe at the Royal Canoe Club

Canadian type paddling canoes for the British team in the Olympic Games. The design came from Canada and was a very unstable racing shape for a single paddle, used in the kneeling position and most unlike the shape used for lazy afternoons on the river. The traditional construction of these canoes was thin, carvel Western Red Cedar planking nailed to wide thin Birch timbers, and the whole covered with canvas and painted. Austin decided to spread the timbers even wider so that they became a transverse Birch Veneer inner skin and to glue the whole thing together. The appearance of the varnished canoe with no nails was much admired, but the Cedar was not as dry as it should have been and did not glue well to the Birch and there were de-laminating problems which would require both canoes to be re-built.

Fairey Marine were nearly at the end of their stock of Birch aircraft ply and were also searching for alternatives. Their future plans included building Fourteen Foot Internationals as well as their successful Firefly and Swordfish. Charles Currey, Fairey's Sales Manager, had also started working through a list of veneer suppliers. Most of those on Austin's list only supplied decorative veneers, or else only rotary cut for plywood making in eight foot lengths. Austin now understood more and more about veneers and was looking for those sliced cut in long lengths. Unlike rotary cut, this will lie flat and not try to curl. As the list of dead ends grew, Austin eventually fetched up at John Wright Veneers in the East of London where he was greeted with, 'That's funny, we had a Mr Currey in here yesterday with the same question.' Not only that, but they had the answer: Agba (Tola Branca).

Agba was a little known Portuguese West African tree, brought out with several others not normally exported when the forests were being cleared for the ill-fated Ground Nut Scheme. It is light, strong, and durable and takes synthetic glues well. Fairey's quantity requirements were obviously many times that required by Austin, so they came to a friendly arrangement. John Wright's would cut up a whole log at a time, up to sixteen feet long in their huge 'bacon slicer' – the largest veneer machine in the country – and the majority would go to Fairey's with a little put on one side for Austin at the same price.

The Canadian canoes were re-built with two diagonal skins and gave no more trouble, though they were still well admired and Austin even learnt to paddle one without falling over, but the British team did not distinguish

The first stapler for cold moulding

themselves. Austin had also learnt that the mould needed to be far more substantial than had been the case so far and that the stapling machines needed improvement. Inserting and removing thousands of staples was a tedious process and left holes and often bruises in the wood where the bridge of the staples had been, and over the years many methods were tried to improve this problem. The office stapler was not strong enough and hard on the hand and most of the label tackers on the market were designed to nip the fold of skin between thumb and forefinger and could not press down on the work at the front because the lever hinged down at the back. Eventually he found the 'Primo Tacker' which was designed ergonomically and was strong enough for continuous use with veneers up to 2mm thick. For heavier work, there were no machines available and Austin designed and built from scratch a pump-action stapler which took ⅝ inch bookbinding staples and would fire them into hardwood and hold 3mm veneer for gluing.

One of the cold moulded Skipper pram dinghies

The next project was a re-working of the clinker built dinghy 'Skips' that Austin had had all through the war. Again, built in cold moulding, the weight

Rigging Skipper at the Festival of Britain

Skipper prams on route to Rugby School

went down and it sailed very well, if a little tender. A proper, much stronger mould was made and several 'Skipper' dinghies were built. Solid crooks were difficult to buy, so the quarter knees were laminated, as was the centre thwart which curved up to make its own knees at the gunwale at either end. As said, it was a little tender and could perhaps have been improved by a few more inches beam for stability, but was popular with sea-scouts as a trainer and a fleet of six were sold to Rugby School sailing club, three complete and the others in kit form to be finished off in the school's workshops. Later, one was exhibited at the Festival of Britain in 1951, and during the boat show at Earls Court in January, they would plank a boat up on the stand during the day. However, during the night it was dismantled for the operation to be done again the next day. Austin made a point of attending the British boatshows as this was an important showcase for the yard.

THE FIRST IN-HOUSE designed and built International Fourteen started as a discussion at the 1948 Olympics in Torbay. Martin Beale was there with his small cruiser 'NEPEMTHE', supporting his Fourteen Foot International helm, Stewart Morris who, with David Bond as crew, was winning the Gold medal in the Swallow Class. One evening after racing, a group had gathered in the cabin of Martin Beale's yacht to discuss many things including boat shapes and that of the Fourteen Foot International in particular. Bruce Banks was at this time considering replacing his Uffa Fox designed and built boat 'WINDSTAR' K469, and asked Austin if he would knock his ideas into shape along with his own and build him a new boat. The answer was of course yes, and the path was set for one of the most complicated and yet most successful Fourteens ever. At some time during the evening disaster struck and they ran out of beer. Martin Beale volunteered to row ashore and get some more. He was a big chap and heavy, as befitted a Fourteen Footer crew, and took a flying leap into the dinghy from the deck of the yacht. It is easy to be wise after the event, but as the prototype moulded pram dinghy had no frames or floor timbers – the planking finished on either side of the centreline – there was nothing to hold the two sides together except for the plank keel. This keel split down the middle with his weight and Martin went down between the two halves which closed on him like a man trap. By the time he had been extracted everybody was soaked and the planning meeting was adjourned. The dinghy was salvaged and returned to Woolverstone for rebuilding. This time, the replacement boat in Agba had the keel as a strip of ⅜" plywood and the diagonal skins crossed the keel at 45 degrees and met their opposite numbers at right angles. This meant that there was a herringbone arrangement connecting the two halves of the boat and no further trouble occurred.

The discussions and research for Bruce Banks' new boat continued over the summer and autumn of 1948. It was decided that they could not produce what they wanted for the 1949 season and Bruce bought 'Fairwind' K544 to tide him over. This boat was the first of the hot moulded Fairey Marine Fourteens built to an Uffa Fox design similar to 'Martlet' K507, in which Stewart Morris and Martin Beale won the P.O.W. cup in 1947, 1948 and 1949 (Bruce Banks finished fifth in 'Fairwind'). Austin, with Charles Currey, had taken the lines off 'Thunder' K388, the 1937 Uffa Fox built boat and winner of the P.O.W. that year, sailed by Peter Scott and Charles Currey. They believed that this was one of the fastest Fourteens of the Uffa Fox boats, having sailed it together – loaned to Charles by Peter Scott. In 1938 Peter Scott teamed up with John Winter to race 'Thunder & Lightning' K409. By 1939 Peter Scott decided that 'Thunder' was the faster boat and asked for it back, loaning Charles and Austin 'Thunder & Lightning' instead. The comparison was rather upset when Charles and Austin beat Peter Scott and John Winter into 6th place. On the slip however, it appeared that 'Thunder' was slightly finer and had more hollow in her waterlines than 'Thunder & Lightning', which Austin thinks gave her more of a 'bite' to windward. It is not possible to check this however, as if you refer to Uffa's drawings, both show straight waterlines. In common with other famous designers such as G.L. Watson with Britannia, the published lines were slightly faked to protect against copies.

Later in 1947/48 when Fairey's decided to follow the Firefly with a Fourteen, they naturally went to Uffa for the design. Austin has always wondered whether Uffa was looking at his published plans when he drew the Fairey Fourteen as it had straighter waterlines forward than the boats he was building himself. Either this was self-defence or possibly he was hoist with his own petard. It is not uncommon for designs published in books and magazines to differ slightly from the real thing, as this allows the designer to protect himself and his ideas from straight copies on which he may find it difficult to collect royalties. Indeed, when the magazine *Yachting World* asked to publish a set of Austin's Fourteen lines, Austin prepared a set that whilst very similar to his boats and of a perfectly competent design, were not exactly what was being built. Some months after the design was published, he received a letter passed on from the magazine and requesting a reply. A furious reader had scaled up the design to eighteen feet and stated it would not sail, was very tender and wanted to know why they should allow this to happen. Austin had an enjoyable time writing the reply, pointing out that the Fourteen at fourteen feet long is balanced with a beam and sail area for people standing six feet high. If the design was scaled up to eighteen feet, then they would need to scale the crew up to nine feet six inches to achieve the same sailing performance. No wonder it was not a success.

Austin crewed for Charles in 1949 in 'Sunrise', the second of the Fairey Fourteens, finishing second to Stewart Morris in 'Martlett'. At the championship cold moulding was as usual under discussion, particularly as it had now had most

WINDSPRITE the International 14 for Bruce Banks

of the problems ironed out. However, Bruce Banks was not entirely happy with the diagonal planking and utilitarian finish of his Fairey boat. Against the legendary 'grand piano' finish of some of the Uffa Fox boats, it lacked a certain style. The bow shape of 'WINDSPRITE' K583 Austin unashamedly admits was inspired by 'Thunder', but the stern was much wider than any of Uffa's boats to give a bigger planing area without squatting, and once seen to work, the later boats were wider still.

Bruce was very keen that his new boat should have an outer skin of proper Honduras Mahogany, laid fore and aft over two inner diagonal skins of Agba. This was proving a big problem in that the forests in British Honduras (now Belize) had been worked out and the timber was very rare. It did not affect Fairey's as they only used the Agba in short lengths and Uffa was still building his planked Fourteens using Brazilian Mahogany. Whilst this was basically the same tree, it was grown in different soil at a different latitude and had therefore a somewhat different grain structure.

Then one day Austin's contact at John Wright Veneer phoned to say that they were demolishing an old veneer store which had been badly bombed, burnt and abandoned. Under heaps of rubble some pre-war veneer had survived including some boards of 'Grand Rim Mahogany'. Austin asked, 'What on earth's that?' thinking of some exotic plantation in the Caribbean. 'Well,' came the reply, 'if you imagine yourself seated at a grand piano, the vertical side leaves the treble end of the keyboard by your right hand, sweeps round in a series of curves to do with the acoustics and comes back to your left hand at the bass end. It's sixteen feet long, and a foot wide and sawn 3/16 inch thick.' There was just enough, and planing it down to ⅛ inch got rid of the soot and stains from the wrecked building. Geoff Quantrill managed to book match the planks. Port and starboard were mirror images and each twelve inch board yielded three planks, kept in their original position so that when they had been spiled and shaped together the grain matched up again and it looked like one wide plank, repeated four times on each side of the boat, and with each board turned over so that they matched each other like the pages of a book. The transom posed a problem until Austin was able to acquire the solid Honduras lid of a 'cottage piano' from a local restorer, who had scrapped the piano to use parts to restore the action of a newer one. They managed to obtain some Honduras faced ply for the buoyancy tanks and nine coats of varnish were used to finish the boat. She was indeed beautiful, and when people said she 'looked like a grand piano', they little realised how close she had been to becoming one.

The Fourteen Foot class had a minimum amount of buoyancy that was required and most boats had only the minimum. This could make the boats very difficult to bail out after a capsize. In 1935, Stewart Morris with 'ALARM' K347 had a huge bow buoyancy tank which ingeniously drained spray into the centreboard case. This was frowned on as self-bailing was forbidden, and later boats had only a small bow tank or none at all to save weight. Austin argued that the weight of the bow tank was better than having several gallons of water slopping about forward of the mast and 'WINDSPRITE' had a tank the regulation 6 inches below the gunwale and extending back to the mast, which it helped to support. This was done with a laminated bracket instead of the normal mast thwart which allowed the crew to reach forward when setting the spinnaker. The large bow tank kept the bow up when swamped and made it possible to sail on with the water running out of the restricted transom drains. This was still not ideal, however, as 'WINDSPRITE' still had her transom submerged after a capsize and later boats added more buoyancy in the transom.

The interior of WINDSPRITE

Bruce Banks began his career as a civil engineer and when Austin first met him he was Assistant County surveyor for Wiltshire, and living in Salisbury. He was a very talented engineer and made many fittings for his boats in the workshop at his home. Dinghy fittings off the shelf were still some years away. As the boat idea with Austin developed, Bruce would make the patterns, Austin would arrange the castings and Bruce would do the final machining. This was some time before Bruce established the famous and successful sail loft, although he had started to make his own spinnakers fairly early on using Ivor Williams as a supplier of cloth. Ivor Williams made ladies underwear and was using very suitable cloth for spinnakers and Austin would use him at a later date when he had his sailmaking business.

'WINDSPRITE' was not just a thing of beauty, she was also a marvel of ingenuity. Her centreboard was pulled up and down by an endless rope via gearing – no pulley blocks. The upper end of the board had a semi-circle of gear teeth machined from Tufnol turned by a Tufnol pinion on a shaft driven outside the plate case by bicycle chain and sprockets led back beneath the thwart to a vee pulley and rope which emerged through two bullseye fairleads in the thwart. The arrangement

WINDSPRITE wining the 1950 POW

was so sensitive that if the centreboard touched the bottom and swung back, the 'up' rope would shoot up from its fairlead like a mini Indian rope trick. The centreboard also had a pair of rollers set through its thickness which allowed it when fully down to 'gybe' or rock a few degrees on a vertical axis to give tactical lift to windward. This effect could be cancelled by pulling the board up a few degrees, when the lateral rollers ran up wedges either side, centring it in the fore and aft plane. 'Gybing' boards were to become very popular, but not for another twenty years.

For the centreboard arrangement, Bruce gave Austin the broad outline of what was required and left him to design the Tufnol and bicycle gearing in detail and get it machined. However, for the reefing gear, he built practically everything himself, making the patterns and machining the castings. The whole gear mounted inside a square section of the mast between its support against the forward buoyancy tank and the gooseneck. The main halyard winch handle went into a fore and aft socket in the aft side of the mast below the gooseneck and hoisted the sail, when by means of two clutches it could be connected to the gooseneck spindle. The diameters of the full halyard winch and the circular boom were such that by turning the handle the main could be lowered and the sail rolled round the boom, at first going slack and then tightening after two turns. This was sufficient for most situations and meant that two reefs could be taken in very quickly at the start of a beat and shaken out again for the reaches. In really heavy weather, by manipulating the clutches, the reefs could be taken to four turns and shaken out to two, but the gearing did not allow compensation, nor did it need to do so. It must be remembered that, whilst with modern rigs and sail cloth, reefing no longer plays a part in the modern racing dinghy, at that time it was a fundamental technique and the ability to do this at will was a substantial advantage over your competitors. 'Windsprite' is still the only boat to have won the P.O.W. four times and established Austin as a design force to be reckoned with and, in the times before mass production of a particular design, set him on the path to being one of the most successful International Fourteen Foot designers ever.

There was also repair and modification work and one major job involved a Fairey boat – when they had eventually realised what was wrong. In 1949 De Forest (Shorty) Trimingham of Bermuda had ordered 'BARILEA' K555, one of the first batch of Fairey Fourteens. In 1950 he collected it from Fairey's in time for the P.O.W. at Hunstanton in Norfolk, where he finished third behind Bruce Banks in 'WINDSPRITE' and Stewart Morris in 'MARTLET' K507. After this she was shipped back to Bermuda for the rest of the season. In 1951 the boat returned and Austin crewed for him in P.O.W. at Plymouth. Austin collected 'BARILEA' on his trailer from Itchenor Sailing Club and took her to Devon behind 'Bumble' the Bentley. They were sharing a hotel with Charles Currey and his wife Bobbie in the village of Newton Ferrers, overlooking the river Yealm, while the dinghies were based at the RAF Seaplane station at Mountbatten on the eastern side of Plymouth Sound.

On route to Plymouth, Austin and 'Shorty' sailed together for the first time, with several other boats, at a meeting at Exmouth, the base for several West Country Fourteens. Not being used to each other's routines, they capsized rounding one of the gybe marks and this problem persisted in the practice race at Plymouth. This was not acceptable, so having righted the boat they retired from the race, returned ashore for dry clothes and then went back out to practice, approaching the Melampus buoy from many different angles to gybe round it until after a dozen or so attempts it was smooth and proved no further trouble. It always takes time to get used to a new crew and Austin was used to Charles Currey's techniques. The almost perfect conditions in Bermuda had allowed 'Shorty' to become a master of getting a dinghy onto the plane and keeping her there. This required constant attention to detail, as it does today, and needed adjustment to course, mainsheet, jibsheet and centreboard. The centreboard was adjusted by a bight of rope that fell naturally to the crew's hand, forward for down – aft for up. After the gybeing practice they planed back across the harbour with Austin having one hand adjusting the jib sheet and the other on the centreboard rope, while 'Shorty' played the mainsheet and steered the course for every wave met.

During the regular races of the week they managed to keep out of trouble and perform consistently, winning the points cup for the week. However the main trophy is always the Prince of Wales Cup itself and the big race on Thursday dawned with a drifting match. Bruce Banks with 'Windsprite', having won the previous year in a good breeze, was now showing how fast she could drift. After the start, they saw Bruce edging over towards Jennycliff Bay on the East Shore, where a high cliff is topped by a shooting range wall that had been known in the past to deflect the wind below. Deciding that there was no point sitting becalmed in deep water they slowly followed 'Windsprite' inshore, watching Bruce's crew Keith Shackleton standing in the bow conning her between the rocks visible in the clear water. 'Shorty' produced a small bottle of rum and sprinkled a libation in the bottom of the boat. 'Sweetens the bilge,' he said, and presently they could see what Bruce was aiming for. The wind was basically a light Easterly and most of it blowing horizontally off the top of the cliff, leaving the sound below becalmed. However, a little breath was doing a 'reverse thermal' down the cool shady cliff face and fanning out on the water at the bottom. 'Windsprite' caught this breeze first and set off with a ripple at the bow towards the mark buoy at the west end of the breakwater. Austin and 'Shorty' followed as soon as they felt the breeze, but 'Barilea' felt sluggish in the light winds, despite the offering and aroma of rum. 'Windsprite' had a handsome lead and, try as they might, Austin and 'Shorty' could not hold on and were eventually unplaced.

The sluggishness was attributed to weight and at the end of the week the measurer's scales showed her to be some twenty pounds over weight with no correctors to take out. Something odd must have happened when she was built, as the rest of her batch seemed quite normal. 'Shorty' asked Austin to take the boat back with him and do whatever was necessary to get rid of the extra weight, then race her to make sure all was well before shipping her back to Bermuda. The drive back was also an experience as the short comings of older technology made themselves felt. Whilst driving an open car such as the Bentley by moonlight is easier than an enclosed saloon, the dynamo proved its notorious reputation for not being able to keep pace with the load of the headlamps, and as they became dimmer and dimmer, they were forced to stop somewhere on Salisbury Plain and sleep till dawn. Austin dropped 'Shorty' off at Stewart Morris's flat in Chelsea in time for breakfast and pressed on through London before the rush hour, back to the workshops at Woolverstone.

The boat was examined carefully and there was nothing extra that could be removed, leaving no option but the hull itself. The standard Fairey Fourteen was built with three skins of 2.5mm Agba veneer, diagonal outer and inner with a middle fore and aft. The only way to get rid of ten percent of her total weight was to remove the outer skin completely. A tool known as a 'Hag's tooth' – a sharpened steel spike protruding, in this case, 2mm through a block of wood – was made and the hull was scored all over to this depth. It was then planed by hand until the score marks had been removed. By this time the glue line was beginning to be exposed, and the hull was now sanded until the glue line showed evenly all over. The hull was then primed and repainted. Dinghies in Bermuda were always painted, as the intense sunlight wreaks havoc with varnish, and 'Shorty's' boats were a distinctive blue/green. To describe this process is short and sounds very easy, but the amount of work involved is long and hard, requiring many hours of endless planing and sanding to achieve the final result.

The boat refitted, she was re-measured and weighed at 225lbs including a few correctors. Austin then followed the orders to race her, to check everything was functioning all right. They took her for an initial sail on the river Orwell by the yard and she felt completely different and so decided to race her in the August Regatta circuit. Needing a good helm, Austin signed on Sam Waters from North Norfolk who was selling K557 'FLYING FOX' before getting a new boat. The first race was to have been in the sea at Lowestoft for the Sir John Beale Trophy, but it was blowing too hard and the Committee at the Royal Norfolk & Suffolk Yacht Club moved the whole affair onto Oulton Broad. Sam made a good start, but half way up the beat Austin realised that 'BARILEA' was feeling sluggish and unlike on the river Orwell. It was just a 'seat-of-the-pants' feel and difficult to define. 'Sam, there's something wrong – she feels as if she's sailing in treacle.' 'Don't worry,' said Sam, 'just take a look over your shoulder.' Austin looked back to find they were leading and it was not until after they had won the race that he worked out what had happened. Austin had never sailed a Fourteen in fresh water before, and this allowed the boat to float deeper in the water – equivalent to some twenty pounds more displacement. They had a wonderful week racing at the different clubs round the Norfolk Coast doing well in

K635 THUNDERBOLT launching off Hunstanton

several of the trophies including a second in the Wash Bowl. After this, 'BARILEA' was crated up and taken to London Docks to be shipped to Bermuda, from where a while later came the cable – 'Thank you for making my boat go so fast'.

MAKING BOATS GO fast and then even faster is the main purpose of the designer and in 1953 Austin went radical:

The pump staple gun on WARRIGAL'S first layers

"There must be a subconscious quirk which affects boat designers, and which makes them stick close to a rule limit – large or small – as if there were a big advantage just the other side of the limit. The Fourteens, from their earliest days as a National Class had had a rule: 'Beam – Minimum to outside of skin. 4 ft 8 ins.' So generations of Fourteens were built with a beam of 4 ft 9 ins without stopping to wonder why the rule was there in the first place. It was probably to prevent narrow gutted river boats which would have been un-seaworthy in open waters.

In 1953, after six – shall we say conventional – designed Fourteens, I had a request from Jack Blundell, a colourful character, for something out of the ordinary and I took this as a licence to experiment within the rules. Having crewed for years in minimum beam boats, and tasted the joys of trapezing, I decided to use the freedom which cold moulding gave to the builder, and roll the topsides horizontally, so that helmsman and crew with the back of their knees against a comfortable radius were sitting more than nine inches further outboard before leaning out at all. The building mould which had been used for 'WARRIGAL' was modified, the roll-out radius being what the diagonal veneer skins would accept without trouble. The total beam was now 6 ft 6 ins, so the leverage was increased about 40%.

For the 1953 Prince of Wales Cup week at Lowestoft, Jack Blundell, knowing his own limitations as a helmsman, recruited Jack Knights, who had done well in several different classes, to sail the boat while he crewed. During the early part of the week they were finding out how to sail 'THUNDERBOLT', as her enormous beam caused certain problems, such as scooping in water over the lee quarter if she was allowed to heel. For Thursday's big race it was blowing enough for most of the fleet to be reefed or sailing with a small or

WARRIGAL at POW Lowestoft 1953

Warrigal on Bumble

no jib. 'WINDSPRITE' used her reefing gear to roll the mainsail down to the bottom batten for the start and each beat down the coast, shaking out to full sail for the offshore reaching legs. I don't remember seeing any spinnakers. A photograph from the committee boat soon after the start shows 'Windsprite' in the foreground, 'Warrigal' on her weather quarter with a reef she had to stick with and heeling. I was crewing 'Sunburn' with Charles Currey, also reefed and heeling, and just out of the picture, and there was 'THUNDERBOLT' way out to windward with full main and genoa and bolt upright. She was undoubtedly leading at this time but shortly afterwards made a base navigational error by tacking inshore out of the favourable tide, and came out fifth at the weather mark.

On the first reach out to sea, and the second back to the starting line near the pier head, 'Windsprite's' ability to shake out her reefs allowed Bruce Banks to increase his lead. At some stage we got ahead of Stewart Morris in 'WILDFIRE', and 'THUNDERBOLT' was working her way through the fleet. During the third beat I looked over my shoulder and saw 'THUNDERBOLT' close astern and about to go steaming through to windward, when there was an almighty crack and her mast collapsed in a heap of splinters with the sail going over the side. This was entirely my fault as designer, as I had not appreciated that her much greater stability would throw greater compression loading onto the mast, and she had the same type of single spreader wooden mast as 'WARRIGAL' and the others.

The Royal Norfolk and Suffolk's rescue boats were fully occupied dealing with capsizes, and one boat drifted ashore on the concrete blocks north of the harbour entrance and was written off. 'THUNDERBOLT' – with her crew – was left to drift as she was in no danger, and wind and tide must have almost cancelled out as we saw her on the fourth and fifth rounds a little closer to the harbour mouth. After we had finished, second to Bruce Banks and ahead of Stewart Morris, we found ourselves not far from the drifting 'THUNDERBOLT' so we went back, passed her a line, and towed her under sail into the harbour. Seeing her insurance underwriter on the pierhead as we went past – 'How's this for a bit of salvage?' – got a great wave.

The two Jacks cannot have enjoyed their afternoon together much and they never sailed together again. Jack Blundell, now as helmsman, used to have difficulty finding a crew as he acquired such a reputation for capsizing, even in moderate conditions. I went with him once thinking I could help, but he dunked me by scooping the boat full of water when tacking, and over we went. Although I believe she never won a race for Jack Blundell before eventually being sold to the USA, it was obvious that 'THUNDERBOLT' had such potential that she was a menace to the class as it then was. The class committee, headed by Stewart Morris, soon brought in a new rule limiting the maximum beam to 5 ft 6 ins. In the meantime I had received a cabled order from Rowe Spurling in

Bermuda, who had been going to have a conventional boat, to build him a replica of 'THUNDERBOLT' instead. It was obvious that had I done so she would not have been given a certificate; so it was arranged with Rowe Spurling that we would keep to the new maximum beam by rolling the topsides right over through a semi-circle so that the gunwale was looking downwards. This entailed more alteration to the mould and we had to steam the veneers to get them round. The result – 'ILYS II' – complied with the rule and was very comfortable to sail, although without the power of the full beam, but it was so difficult to achieve that we never built any more similar, and made a new mould to a different and more rational design which produced 'Bolero' for Stewart Morris and several more like her."

Start of race at POW Lowestoft 1953. K572 FIRETAIL, K597 WINDRUSH, K394 FAFNIR and K583 WINDSPRITE

AT THE 1953 P.O.W. in Lowestoft, K572 'FIRETAIL' – a Fairey boat – was written off by the insurance company after drifting ashore and losing her rig and being badly holed on the concrete blocks north of the harbour entrance. As it happens, the Underwriter for Navigators & General Insurance – who was himself a Fourteen Footer sailor – was watching the race from ashore and after assuring the owner that his boat was covered for total loss, bought the wreck to rebuild for his own use.

At Woolverstone, having the skills and the Agba veneer, they were used to repairing cold moulded boats with a steady stream of Fireflies to repair. Often Bert Lamb, the local Navigators & General agent, would ring up on a Monday morning to say there was a damaged Firefly at Felixstowe Ferry with a hole the size of a dinner plate – this was how they calculated the damage – and would they please collect it and have it repaired for the following weekend. Therefore when 'FIRETAIL' arrived the project was not totally daunting, though her mast, sails and rig were scrap, the transom badly damaged, the thwart broken, two large holes close together in the bottom starboard quarter and two smaller ones near the port bow. Fortunately, none of the holes had punctured the buoyancy tanks and the gunwale and centreboard case were intact.

It was decided that she was repairable and that a little surgery here and there could bring her up to date, considering the Fairey's had made modifications to their mould since they built her. The holes in the hull were repaired first, patching and cutting in veneers as necessary. The transom was then cut carefully away and shores sprung between the gunwales amidships and aft. There was a bit of creaking and groaning but the hoped for movement took place. A new transom was made and fitted and new thwart stylishly made to arch across the boat onto the side tanks, which they now angled downhill.

Doing the buoyancy test on Bolero

The extra beam was not at first noticeable but when 'Good News', as she was now called, made her appearance at Hayling Island the curved thwart and downward splayed tanks did cause some comment. She showed an excellent turn of speed and Austin found himself approached by Colin Chichester-Smith – the head of Fairey Marine – who asked 'What have you been doing to that boat? She's right up among the leaders.'

Austin's reputation as a Fourteen designer and builder grew continuously and in 1956 they built 'Bolero' for Stewart Morris, the very successful Fourteen Helm and Gold Medallist at the 1948 Olympics. Stewart made a very unusual stipulation when he ordered the boat. The minimum stripped hull weight was 225 pounds and it is normal to build the hulls a little light and use corrector weights, which can be removed as the boat is re-weighed after soaking up. All boats gain a little weight, even fibreglass and there is always a little weight which will never be lost. Stewart did not want this and quoted the rule which said: 'If boats, when new, are found to be underweight owing to any error in building, correctors, not exceeding 10lb, may be added above the waterline.' He said there should not be any error and that he wanted the boat the right weight without correctors. Austin,

The top part of Bee's Wing, before being covered

tongue in cheek, failed to convince him that if a boat were built underweight deliberately (i.e. on purpose and not in error) then strictly within the letter of the rule she would not have to have correctors.

Building to an exact weight poses many problems when working with natural materials which may not all be identical. The boat was to have two diagonal skins of 2.5mm Agba and an outer skin of 3mm Mahogany, all matched planks similar to 'Windsprite'. Eventually they used an outer skin of 2mm Khaya which is another form of Mahogany and resembles Honduras Mahogany. It is, however, a little heavier and would not soak up as much water as a lighter variant. Great care was taken at every stage and there were several weighings in the building shed as the boat neared completion as fittings were added and several coats of varnish applied. She was then loaded onto the trailer and taken to be measured by Eric Willis at his house in Esher and to have her buoyancy test completed at Thames SC.

Eric had borrowed a steelyard from his butcher for the weighing. This was brand new, kept in reserve and stamped by the Weights & Measures inspector, and far more sensitive than the normally used spring balance scales. 'BOLERO' was slung level for weighing, then lowered back onto the trailer to weigh the slings. Eric did his calculations and then did them again. 'Stewart's not going to believe this,' he said. 'She's half an ounce over weight.' Austin breathed a sigh of relief. 'BOLERO' was again a very successful P.O.W. winner and is still sailing in the classic division of the Fourteen Foot class today. 'WINDSPRITE' and 'BOLERO' were the only two boats built to have matched fore and aft planks, the others had standard diagonal veneers, until the five boats built by John Fisk at Canvey Island which were built of two skins of 2-ply and showed transverse grain.

Applying dope to Bee's Wing

'Bee's Wing' on the canoe DEFIANT

As WE HAVE already seen, as a development class, the Fourteen was a strange mixture of development and prohibition. The banning of the trapeze in 1938 put the class behind for many years and, as always with these things, set people looking for alternatives as Austin describes:

"One of the duties of a yacht designer in a development class, apart from designing a fast boat, is to find a loophole in the rules as written and drive a horse and cart through it. Any talk of 'evading the spirit of the rule' is only an admission by the rule makers that they have got it wrong. A rule is a legal document and does not have a spirit.

It took a little while to find the weak spot in the rule banning the trapeze – which was designed to make the crew's job as hard and muscular as possible – and reflected the thinking of the helmsmen without reference to the Crew's Union. It turned on taking the converse of the wording: that if a contrivance did NOT itself extend outboard, then it could legally support a member of the crew outboard.

From this, what was needed was a structure, vertical on the gunwale and unable to lean outboard, from which the crew could hang and take some of the load off his leg and tummy muscles. Some head scratching produced the 'Donkey' for help in crewing

Charles Currey in K545 'SUNRISE', one of the new Fairey 'Mouldies' in 1949.

The 'Donkey' consisted of 18 inches of light alloy tube with a foot which hooked into the gunwale track for the jib sheet fairlead, and a wire stay from half height to an anchorage on the centre thwart of such a length that the tube could be pulled upright but not outboard. When released for tacking, the foot tripped out of the track and the whole thing fell across the boat ready for use on the other gunwale.

In use, the 'Donkey' stood between the crew's legs as he sat out. He could either hang out a limited distance from the top in some comfort, or further out from half way down with more effort. The length of the human arm was the limiting factor, and a crew with arms the length of a gorilla's would have had a distinct advantage.

A modification for MkII the following season was a jamming cleat on the side of the tube at a third of its height for the jib sheet. The last couple of inches of jib sheet had to be the most difficult to pull in and then hold, and if the sheet was led to this cleat and jammed while the 'Donkey' was still leaning inboard a little, then a pull on the hand grip gave a three to one advantage.

Bruce Banks and Keith Shackleton with 'WINDSPRITE' came up with a variant with their 'Donkey' hinged on the centre thwart so that it could swing to either side or lay flat on the thwart when not in use. It had a half-cleat on the side at a ⅓ of the height and the sheet was led under this and then over a notch in the top of the crew's hand. It gave a three to one advantage, and because it could lean to windward still inside the boat it could be used to trim the jib sheet in or out when sailing.

We considered leading our sheet over a notch in the end of the 'Donkey' for the crew to hang out further on that but decided that the outboard part of the jib sheet could be considered a 'contrivance' and so illegal.

The prototype had a red rubber bicycle handlebar grip which gave it a decidedly rude appearance. Before the new Fairey dinghies went to Canada with the British team, which had small central anchorage lugs built in to attach the donkey – taken as a secret weapon, ours was tied round and under the thwart with a rope strop. When coming ashore after a race the strop would be undone and the 'Donkey' stowed away in a bag marked 'Sail Battens'. Although our competitors could see we had something useful we managed to keep its detail secret for most of the 1949 season. So much so that after one race Bruce Wolfe, who we had beaten, ran the length of the slipway at Itchenor to examine 'Sunrise' closely before remarking 'That's the first time I have known a gadget which when removed leaves no trace.'"

The method of 'Donkey Riding' became no longer necessary when the trapeze was allowed some years later. The Author is not aware of its general use in any other class, but it is interesting that the technique has great merit, in that it is still used by Glen Foster, a top Fourteen sailor from the early 1960s, who uses one on his International 5.5 Metre Class keelboat to help him hike from the helming position.

Austin was now at last able to try his International Canoe 'VALIANT' on the Orwell river, but found the tree lined shores made the wind uncertain and the boat very difficult to sail. He admitted that, despite several years of trying, he never really mastered the International Canoe. The class also sailed at Aldeburgh on the East Coast as well as Hayling Island, and the open flat marshes made the boat much easier there. Roger de Quincy who, with Uffa Fox, had successfully challenged for the International Canoe Trophy in America in 1933, lived in the area as did 'Bee' Mackinnon, another stalwart of the class. Austin eventually despaired of mastering 'Valiant' – although it has to be said that a river with gusty wind from behind trees is not the best place to master a canoe – and sold the boat to Billy de Quincy, Roger's brother who had been the original owner and used the boat in America. Billy de Quincy kept this famous boat for a few years and she was then sold onto Tony Rutherford who returned her to Hayling Island via the Canoe Club in Teddington. Some years later, by the side of the old A12, Austin saw a Canoe parked in a cafe and Austin pulled in to investigate.

Recognising 'Valiant' as he approached, he found Tony Rutherford inside, who he had not met before. The usual greeting of 'Dr Livingstone, I presume,' forged a long friendship. Tony Rutherford subsequently restored the boat and renewed the deck with a new modern spoon deck. He worked for the distribution department of M.G.M and, although not trained with his hands, the workmanship was superb. This workmanship was repeated again in 1953 when he ordered a Canoe shell off the same mould as 'Eastwind' from Austin and finished it himself. A complete hull was also built for Jack Blundell of Fourteen fame. Considering his record for capsizing in the Fourteen, a canoe was not perhaps the wisest choice. A story tells of a canoe meeting at Hayling Island with Jack Blundell's wife sitting on the club balcony. Someone remarked that there was a canoe capsized and they wondered who it could be. The weary, dry reply came, 'Who do you think?'

In 1949 Bee Makinnon (a maths master at Eton) asked Austin to build him a wing sail for his Canoe 'Defiant'. This was Austin's first experiment with wing sails and its lessons would serve well for his later very successful rigs 'C' Class Catamaran rigs in 1964. This was probably the first specifically constructed wing sail for a boat. Until then the other experiments had actually used wings borrowed from aircraft.

Austin writes of this in an anecdote in 1991:

"Lord Brabazon was probably the first person to try putting a wing on a boat. He was a great experimenter, and used his Bembridge Redwing One-Design as a test bed for several of his ideas. The Redwing class had a splendid rule which allowed any sort of rig or sail up to 200 sq ft of measured area, and at some time in the early 1930s he mounted an aeroplane's wing vertically on a turntable on the deck. It cannot have been very efficient, as he did not keep it very long, and even Beken cannot trace a photograph of it in action. There is photographic evidence, however, of its successor, an autogyro rotor mounted on edge that drove the boat along once it started spinning, and which caused chaos off Cowes as it flailed its way through the anchorage.

Uffa Fox also tried an aeroplane's wing in the mid 1930s, this time on an International

Fourteen dinghy. He used a wing from a small biplane which had wings of symmetrical section, four identical half-wings. This must have been very inefficient in flight, but was designed for aerobatics, so that it could fly equally badly upside down or right way up. Uffa found the symmetrical section half-wing allowed him to point high, but it had very little drive. The ailerons must have been able to turn both ways, so would have been some use as trailing edge flaps. It was short of area for the dinghy, but a larger one would have been too heavy to hold up.

My first experience with a wing sail was in 1949, when P.V. (Bee) Mackinnon asked me as a boatbuilder to make a rigid wing for his 10-sq Metre Canoe 'DEFIANT'. It had to be symmetrical, though we both knew it would be more efficient with a hinged flap to give some camber, but this would have added quiet a lot to the weight, and also to the cost, which was the ruling factor. The NACA 0018 section is used today for keels of yachts and wings of aerobatic model aircraft. It has a very good lift/drag ratio, but this was not enough. A boat has the drag of the hull through the water to add to that of the sails, so a high lift sail is needed to overcome the total drag, even though it means the sail having more drag itself.

Building 'Bees Wing' was not like boat building at all – more like a glider's wing. The ribs and cross bracing were all in ¼ inch square spruce with corner brackets of 1mm birch plywood, and 1mm ply was wrapped round the leading edge as far back as the main spar. It stood 19ft high, with the top 5ft removable for transport, and turned with ball and roller bearings on a 6ft internal pylon, a tripod bolted to the hull. It weighed 20lb complete, so no compression loading.

As with a glider's wing, it was fabric covered and doped. Available spinnaker cotton was too heavy and regular aircraft fabric even heavier. Nylon was in existence for parachutes, but not for sails until several years later, but I managed to get hold of enough handkerchief material in its raw state – un-bleached Egyptian cotton – and had it seamed into a large panel. This was stretched over the frame and pinned together along the trailing edge, back to the sewing machine for a seam, and then pulled over the frame like a sock.

The job of aircraft dope is to shrink and tighten the fabric, but the shrinking force is considerable, and I had memories of a beautiful model aeroplane built by a boy at school whose father was in the RAF and sent him some dope for it. As it dried it shrank, and shrivelled the model into a screwed-up ball. It reduced the normally stoical boy to tears. I consulted Jimmy Ledwith, a Merlin Rocket helmsman and chief chemist at Cellon (who made Cerrux varnish, but whose main line was aircraft dope). He experimented with sample panels, and sent a gallon can of model aircraft dope which was exactly right.

Even with the reduced shrinkage of model dope, great care was needed, and it had to be applied to both sides of the wing at once or it would have warped. Here I was ably assisted by Johnny Ford, a young sea scout who was camping with his troop in the park, had been out sailing in my pram dinghy, and wanted to do something useful.

We had 'DEFIANT' on her trailer for fitting the tripod and setting everything up, and mounted the chocks used for assembly onto the trailer alongside the hull for a travelling cradle. The trailer and load was then hitched behind the venerable Bumble and we *set off for Hayling Island, Johnny came along for the ride. On the road I was concerned that the wing, which stowed on its leading edge, stood about eight feet above the ground, would tend to lurch sideways on corners. I need not have bothered – the wing acted as a tail fin, and the trailer banked inwards.*

Assembled on the beach and launched into Chichester Harbour only a light cord was needed as a mainsheet, as the wing was almost balanced, and Bee set off to try the new rig against the other Canoes. As had been expected, 'DEFIANT' would point very high, and this could be a tactical advantage; but she lacked drive compared with the soft and fully battened sails of the others. On shore again we soon found out that a wingsail cannot be left to weathercock, but starts to hunt from side to side, and would capsize the canoe unless the whole affair was laid on its side.

Ever since then I have managed to have wing sails with camber, adjustable if possible, and tried to persuade others that a symmetrical section 'with a very good lift/drag ratio' cannot be expected to win races."

CONQUEST **the hard chine canoe by Jack Holt**

UNFORTUNATELY THESE LESSONS have not always been heeded as can be seen from some of the later wing rig designs.

In 1952, there came the first post war challenge for the International Canoe Trophy from Lou Whitman of the USA. The Royal Canoe Club decided that new boats would be needed to select a defender. Jack Holt designed and built 'CONQUEST', a hard chine canoe, and with the cold moulding technique perfected, Austin built 'EASTWIND'. 'EASTWIND' was framed to take all the stresses in torsion and therefore the skin was light and not under strain. It was still thicker than necessary, however, to reach the minimum weight required under the class rules.

This method of building is now common place in small lightweight boats and some offshore racers. 'EASTWIND' and 'CONQUEST' had identical sail plans, each boat having her own soft mainsail, while they shared a fully battened one at first, later having one each. The fully battened rig had first been pioneered by Manfred Currey in Germany in the 1920s and developed on the canoe 'WAKE', by John Aumonier in the 1930s.

It was known as the 'Chinese' rig because of its junk like look and proved very successful. In light weather the sail remained in an aerofoil, waiting for the next puff of wind instead of stalling about, and in strong winds the boat could be made to point higher in the gusts and the top of the mainsail twisted off to de-power the rig. Despite its advantages, sailors were generally conservative or had class rules that limited batten

Eastwind **showing the curved seat**

length so until after the war very few other rigs were made with full length battens. Both boats had maximum length sliding seats, although 'Eastwind's' was certainly an innovation. Initially both canoes had similar straight line speed, but Austin developed a self tacking jib including a leech line, on a counterbalance (similar to that used on radio controlled boats) and this worked very well, giving 'Eastwind' a definite advantage in tacking speed.

Austin had found that when sailing 'Valiant' as a novice, it was very difficult to sail a canoe upright because the helmsman's bottom on the sliding seat was only a very few inches above the water and would dig into the smallest wave. Arguing that if the end of the seat was higher, the boat could be sailed more upright without the helmsman being washed off the seat, a new design was built which was curved and dipped into the scooped out cockpit. Sailing 'Eastwind' with this design of seat proved a great success, although Austin still found it difficult psychologically to keep the boat upright, as it felt as if it was falling over to windward. The experts mastered it with no problem and the seat was eventually developed into the ladder rack type used today, where the helmsman can push himself right out to the end and even hang over the end of the seat.

The selection trials were held in Chichester Harbour, with Peter Griffiths sailing 'Conquest' and Graham Goodson sailing 'Eastwind'. Sometimes the whole canoe fleet would sail with these two and at other times they simply match raced each other. Graham Goodson was tall, had very long legs and sailed with the mainsheet and tiller extension in hand, his feet on the gunwale, but not using the full length of the slide. Lou Whitman's canoe, although beamier than the early American designs, was relatively narrow aft with the rudder hung on the stern post, linked to a T-shaped yoke post close abaft the sliding seat, and through which the pole tiller slid transversely, the end moving fore-and-aft to steer the boat. Lou, who had relatively short legs and a compact body would cleat the main and

Austin sailing Eastwind

jib sheets, and retire to the end of the seat where he curled up and sailed the boat with only the tiller for control. Tacking took time and if it became overpowered his only choice was to capsize and start again. The venue for the challenge was to be Aldeburgh in Suffolk, which was Graham's home waters, with the racing to be either on the sea if the weather was fine or behind the shingle bank on the river Alde at Slaughden if not. Graham thought that his boat speed was good enough, but that if he could lure Lou into a tacking match, with his superior speed through the tacks he was bound to win.

The actual challenge was an anti-climax and a great disappointment, as a few days before the racing was due to start, Graham went down with pleurisy, and although he was soon on his feet, he was too weak to actually sail. Peter Griffiths found himself as defending helmsman with no experience of 'Eastwind', and very little of sailing on the river Alde as the weather was not suitable for the open sea. The racing was early in the morning before the wind got up, and Peter opted for the soft mainsail. Unfortunately for the defenders, Lou Whitman managed to get the better start twice and pulled away to win the International Challenge Trophy in two straight races.

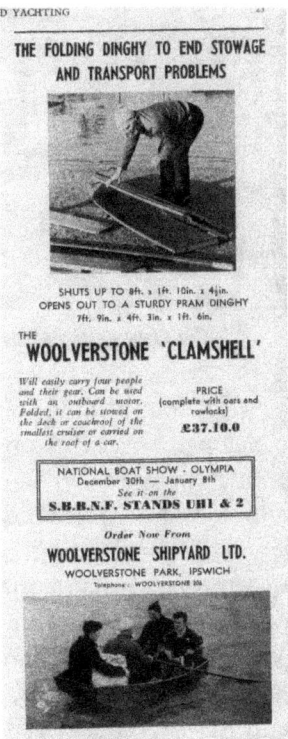

Advert for Clamshell

All types of work were considered and the yard finished off hulls from other builders. They completed a Fairey 505 hull and a Flying Dutchman hull from Tormentor Yachts. This Flying Dutchman was the fastest one around, and Austin kept the speeding ticket from the Police to prove it. Most of the building work was, however, racing dinghy orientated as this was the area in which Austin's reputation had grown. He never stopped considering improvements or innovations that might be made. One 505 was finished from a Fairey hull which had unfortunately sprung when taken off the mould and was now the wrong shape. They had to build a new female jig to put the hull into and it then took a half a ton of ballast to hold it down into the right shape before the decks could be put on. It was however, a good boat, but not sailed a great deal as the owner found it a bit much to handle.

December 1954 saw the folding dinghy, the 'Woolverstone Clamshell', on sale for £37.10s.0d at the boat show at Olympia. Austin developed this boat to service the growing yacht tender market and made many cardboard models to get the panel shape right. It was a good winter filler and the yard sold quite a number. It is still

A Woolverstone Clamshell

The Clamshell on a Boatshow stand

produced today in a very similar form called the 'SANDHOPPER'. In 1956 the magazines reported that Woolverstone Shipyard had launched three new versions of their 'CLAMSHELL' folding dinghy. The first was a special eight foot version for Ocean Racers, with inflatable buoyant thwarts. These were self erecting in an emergency, by means of a gas bottle. This model, along with the one at six foot, were pram dinghies and there was to be a twelve foot folding stem dinghy for sailing, rowing or use with an outboard. Also developed was a fifteen foot folding speedboat to take a larger outboard and fast enough to tow water skiers. Unfortunately, the latter two never went into production, although the card models still exist.

Austin had become a respected authority on small boats and was giving lectures on various subjects at many venues including the '*Build Your Own Dinghy Conference*' of 1956 organised by the Central Council for Physical Recreation. Opened by Stewart Morris at the Duke of York's Headquarters it featured a miniature boat show with designers and builders, and lectures by Austin Farrar, John Westall, Roland Prout and F.B. Priest of Aero Research, who gave two lectures on gluing techniques. The expansion in the choice of dinghies was evident when one sees the list of exhibitors. It included the 505, National 12, International 14, G.P.14, Moth and a Simpleton Pram. Today this conference continues under the guise of '*The Dinghy Sailing Show*', organised by the Royal Yachting Association. This allows classes to display their boats with the help of class builders, and has lectures by well known sailors.

During this time the East Anglian Offshore Racing Association was formed with a meeting at Woolverstone. A show was put on for all those interested in sailing and clubs were invited to bring along their one-designs. It was well attended and a great success. This could have been one of the first boat shows, and certainly the first one on the East Coast.

In 1953 the East Coast was devastated by the North Sea surge and the floods that ensued. At that time boats were laid up on the hard along the foreshore, pulled up above the high water mark. The backwash of the surge returning down the River Orwell did the most damage. As with a normal tide, the surge followed the north bank up the river and returned down by the south bank. This wall of water some ten feet high – higher than the pier – swept through the yachts leaving them in a heap at the Cat House

The 1953 floods at Woolverstone

end. There was seaweed on the top of the pier rails, two boats were written off and substantial repairs had to be made to several others. One of the written off yachts, the 'BONNIE JEAN', was a lightly built cruiser built unusually of Beech and folded flat in half after the deck came off. The owner was philosophical saying, 'I would be the chap who hadn't renewed his insurance. I run an Insurance company.' Mr Frank Hussy's 'SAPPHIRE' was carried up into Woolverstone Park and came to rest a quarter of a mile from the river. 'Sapphire' was originally a Royal Burnham One Design which Austin had purchased as a wreck from a mooring at the RAF station at Felixstowe – presumably she had belonged to an RAF Officer. She had carried away her mooring and ended up impaled on two posts on a nearby groyne. The insurance company had offered her to Austin as a wreck and with a bit of work with bags and oil drums they managed to float her off and tow her back to Woolverstone. She was rebuilt and given a rig, a near copy of the Royal Harwich One Design, her rig having gone. Sold to Frank Hussy, she gave years of enjoyment and service.

Austin had been a member of the Royal Harwich Yacht Club since about 1936 and with his deep involvement in racing it was only natural that he should be 'dragged' into committee work and organising race meetings. As always with these things, despite a committee, Austin remembers doing the vast amount single-handed and when things went right nothing would be said, but if not then it would somehow be his fault regardless of the reason. Trying to organise an open meeting and sail in it yourself – as he did with the Swordfish and Firefly – always provided an extra challenge. For the Swordfish meeting the club was very advanced, borrowing radio sets from Pye's of Cambridge to help with communication on the course. They were not the small sets used today, being more like the size of a small suitcase. The batteries needed charging every night at 12 amps for 12 hours. The first night the shop in Harwich could not believe that small batteries could take this and charged them at one amp. The next day the batteries did not last, but it did not happen the next time.

The 1953 floods at Woolverstone

Burton Cup fleet in front of a Sunderland flying boat

The Burton Cup fleet leaving Felixstowe

Leaving the dock. N527 Goblin, N462 Mimulus - Ian Proctor

Open meetings and regular travelling was a very new thing after the war with the advent of more cars and easier transport. Before the war people would travel to their dinghies, not move the boats, and it would only be the National Championship which would see a mass movement of boats.

There were really only two major classes before the war, the Fourteen Foot International and the Twelve Foot Nationals. It was the latter that for the first post-war championship in 1946 gathered at the Felixstowe RAF Flying Boat Station under the burgee of the RHYC to race for the Sir William Burton Cup. The RAF had only recently moved back from their wartime base on the Clyde, so as well as a Sunderland on the apron and another in one of the hangers, the next hanger was full of gunboats from wartime duties as HMS 'Beehive'. Austin gained the euphemistic title 'Organising Secretary' to the RHYC Committee which had members from supporting clubs: Harwich & Dovercourt SC, Felixstowe Ferry SC, Waldringfield SC, Orford SC and Aldeburgh YC. This meant that the committee would decide what needed to be done and Austin would get on and do it.

The duties included liaising with the RAF to get permission to use their facilities, clearing course areas with the Harbour Master, getting flag officers from the clubs to be Officers-of-the-day to run the races, producing course cards and programmes and persuading local firms to pay for advertisements in the programme. The RAF was keen to help and set aside their fire floats as rescue boats – these could pump out a dinghy in thirty seconds. They cleared a large space on the apron and one of the slipways. However, although today all dinghies have trailers and launching trolleys, this was not the case then and, without trolleys, it was easier to leave the dinghies ranged along the edge of the apron and launch straight down the beach when the tide served.

There were some snags which inevitably caused complaints from some of the competitors. Beecher Moore was particularly keen to point out that it was a day's hike to the toilets in the officers' mess and the pub was even further. However, Austin, on a tip-off from one of the RAF sergeants, found that at one point in the heavy steel fencing which enclosed the base there was a loose panel near the head of the slipway which, when a loose bolt was removed, allowed easy access across to the old Felixstowe Dock Station toilets and a short cut to the Little Ships Pub. Apparently this exit had been used for years, and was tacitly approved by the authorities.

The RAF's meteorological station was in a hut on the apron near the slipway and the met officer – keen to help – would issue frequent bulletins. However, they tended to go into detail about the winds at 10,000 feet but had little idea of what was happening at ground level, which for the first three days was enough to prevent any racing. He took a long time to live down one incident, when he came rushing out with a forecast sheet, saying the race should be stopped because there was going to be a terrible storm. The fleet had gone afloat and with no radios there was nothing they could do except wait and cross their fingers. No doubt at 10,000 feet there was a storm, but in the harbour the fleet sat becalmed for some time. Of the thirty seven entries, some still had their wartime permit numbers painted on, while some of the helmsmen were still in uniform including Flt. Lt. Ian Proctor with N462 'MIMULUS' who was third, and Air Commodore (later Air Marshall) Sir Arthur McDonald with N23' FARANDOLE' who won the following year. The winners of the Sir William Burton Cup for 1946 were Jack Holt and Beecher Moore with N493 'LAUGHTER', and in second place was Michael Goffe with N504 'WANTON'. Like the International Fourteen with the Prince of Wales Cup, the National Twelves still race for the Burton Cup today.

By 1954 Austin had started to think about the future and the realisation that there was very little money in boatbuilding. By this time the entire Woolverstone estate on Shotley Peninsular had been sold up piecemeal, mainly to tenants, and Austin had managed to buy the freehold of the boatyard. At the same time the Royal Harwich had bought theirs. Austin's package included the famous Cat House which meant that he could have someone living on the site. The Cat House is famous in the area as a haunt for smugglers in days past. Here a figure of a cat would be placed in a lighted window to let the smugglers know that, for the time being, all was well and it was safe to land. Jeff Quantrill settled in with his family until they moved to Ipswich. Percy Lipsett then took over.

It now appeared that sailmaking would prove a more profitable occupation and Seahorse Sails was born at Hadleigh in Suffolk. Austin started making sails whilst still running the Boatyard and the two overlapped for a time until he finally sold the yard in 1959 to Mr David. He employed Mr Debbage, an ex-pattern maker, as yard manager, who latter started the boat transport company which still operates from New Cut East in Ipswich Docks. Cash flow had always been a problem and, though there were some excellent times, Austin was not sorry to leave the financial worries behind.

CHAPTER 6
SAILMAKING. SEAHORSE SAILS, SEAHORSE OFFSHORE AND AUSTIN FARRAR SAILMAKERS

S EAHORSE SAILS WAS established with Leslie Widdicombe, who owned the clothing factory in Hadleigh in Suffolk. The factory had been a full clothing production unit for wartime government contracts, except for a small part which made coir mats, weaving them by hand. Leslie Widdicombe had taken over the factory from his father-in-law, J.H. Price & Co., and expanded the mat production into carpet production. He had bought some carpet looms and was producing narrow width carpets that could be joined up to form larger areas. The business did quite well. However, when he had the idea of moving into broadloom, (whilst sailmaking had already started), the machinery investment alone of some £60,000 plus warping machines, etc. proved a costly burden. The broadloom set never did work properly and did not last for long, although the narrow loom carpets continued for some time. The clothing contracts from the war had finished. Meanwhile, Austin had taken this area over for the sailmaking loft. The area was gradually transformed with benches and a plywood floor. At this time, power was still produced by a big old diesel engine and the machines were driven by shafts and belts. When the mains power came on line and the engine was removed, it left room for another table large enough for dinghy mainsails. Leslie Widdicombe ran the firm and over saw production while Austin did the technical input and retrained some of the girls from clothing to sails, using most of the original machines.

Austin had met Leslie at Woolverstone where Leslie was sailing his 505. He had taken an interest when Austin was finishing a 505 from a Fairey shell and had then bought one from Jeremy Rodgers. He had built it with his brother whilst still at school and it was a very beautiful boat. Jeremy Rodgers eventually had his own yard which became famous for its offshore boats, including the 'Contessa' range. Leslie Widdicombe sailed the 505 at Woolverstone in the handicap fleet, but was never happy with the Elvstrøm sails that had come with the boat. He knew that Austin had experience with sails and asked him if he would like to have a go at making new sails for the 505. Austin was happy to do so and Leslie obtained a roll of Terylene from a supplier in London whom he knew. The first sails were not bad and the next suit even better. Leslie, who had been looking for something to utilize his factory now

Government contracts were finishing, asked Austin if he would like to team up and make sails properly. Austin said yes, as he was fed up losing money at the boatyard, and Leslie replied that they were in business. One of the countries most innovative sailmakers started in business as simply as that.

Receiving a regular salary for the first time in many years was very pleasant, but Austin feels that much of his success in sailmaking was due to not having to unlearn the techniques of cotton cloth. He came in at the beginning of the development of Terylene and could focus all his development skills on this product without any outmoded and ingrained practices. He worked on some of the most important sail developments in the fifties and sixties, and certainly left a legacy that is still in use today. Austin was entirely self taught in the art of sailmaking and must be the only successful sailmaker who did not serve any sort of apprenticeship. Although many new sailmaking firms started up in the 1960s, most had some training. Bruce Banks worked for Lucas until the son joined the firm and Bruce realised that he would only ever progress so far, and would be better with his own company. Austin even ended up with his own language to start with; broadseams to the trade were called closures by Austin. However, unfettered by any previous training, it allowed him to think freely through problems and requirements.

Seahorse Sails gave a start to some of this country's leading sailors and sailmakers, including Peter Bateman, Andy Cassell (now of 'Ratsey and Lapthorn'), Eddie Warden-Owen of 'Bruce Banks' and Eddie Hyde, who went on to found the famous firm of 'Musto & Hyde' with Keith Musto, who represented Britain in the Flying Dutchman Class at the 1964 Olympics in Tokyo winning the Silver medal. Subsequently, with the firm producing both sails and clothing, they divided the company to form 'Hyde Sails' and 'Musto Clothing'. Andy Cassell is one of the gentlemen of the sport and a superb sailor, particularly as he was born without legs. Sailing dinghies such as Hornets and Flying Dutchman, he was known to snub the mainsheet on a cleat screwed through his trousers to his false leg.

The Seahorse Sails logo

After a year or so, Seahorse had its one and only brush with cotton. A client ordered a suit of sails for an 'Enterprise' dinghy and at first agreed to have them in white terylene. The class then informed him that the only colour allowed was blue which was not yet produced in terylene. This left no choice but cotton, and it required much persuasion from the client that Austin should make the sails in cotton. The client was told he would have to pay for a full roll of cloth, to which he agreed and, with great trepidation, Austin set to work. Austin was never really sure but the customer was delighted and said they set beautifully. The rest of the roll was now surplus and

A Seahorse Sails sticker

Working on a cruising spinnaker at Seahorse Offshore

the brilliant idea was shirts.

The leading machinist was the redoubtable Mrs Marsh who had been the expert at shirt making for the government contracts. She found her plywood templates from under the bench and some twenty minutes later there was a finished shirt. All the loft had these blue cotton shirts and many are still going strong today. A short time after this, Austin was due to be presented to the Duke of Edinburgh at dinner during the IYRU annual conference. On checking his boiled dress shirt he found that it had gone home and was no longer serviceable. It was then that Mrs Marsh made him a boiled shirt in terylene. The body was made from some reject material that was too porous for sails, and the front and the collar were made from some very close woven, very smooth and quite shiny cloth. It was made that afternoon, worn that evening and worked perfectly, looking and sounding just like a real cotton boiled shirt.

As time went on, Leslie Widdicombe became convinced that the only money was in dinghy sails whilst Austin wanted to concentrate on big boat sails and the growth of amateur offshore racing. Eventually the relationship soured and split, as Austin realised that he needed to expand on his own. Around this time, Jim Welland and Tony Brierly entered the scene and they formed a separate partnership which was initially called 'Seahorse Offshore'. These two never worked for the original Seahorse, Austin had met them through ocean racing. Austin was still at Hadleigh and in 1960 was involved in making sails for the Twelve Metre 'KURREWA', but by 1961/62 Austin had moved to Martlesham with the new company 'Seahorse Offshore' in the old gymnasium of the now closed RAF base. About two thirds to start with, they eventually took over the whole building. Development plans for the new A12 road through Martlesham Heath meant the building had to be demolished and the company moved into a new building, unfortunately smaller and of course more expensive. This building was just up the road from the old gymnasium. Austin recalls that the firm was quite happy there but needed more space and, as it was confusing with two companies called Seahorse, they reformed the company as 'Austin Farrar Sailmakers', moving across the road into a building twice the size and of course (in the name of progress) four times as expensive. Austin was never

The Austin Farrar Sailmakers team

fully happy with this name as he felt that a company was better without one person's name attached to it. The company was successful but the hours were long and for over ten years, work continued late into each evening, with the main evening decision being whose turn it was to go and get the fish and chips. This seemed the staple diet for a long time. 'Austin Farrar Sailmakers' concentrated solely on big boat sails and did not venture into the dinghy market at all.

Leslie Widdicombe retained ownership of the original 'Seahorse Sails' and was helped in the management by Mike Richardson who ran the works, as Leslie Widdicombe moved towards retirement. Mike Richardson had no training as a sailmaker but was a very good OK sailor and a salesman. Pete White was also there and they were joined by Adrian Jardine. They concentrated on dinghy sails and sailing but, due to a lack of orders and cash flow problems; this eventually led to its demise in the mid seventies. Leslie Widdicombe retained the ownership of the buildings and today the spar firm Z-Spars is in one part run by Dave White – Pete White's brother – and the rest of the building is given over to a new company producing tarpaulins and tilt covers for lorries.

'Austin Farrar Sailmakers' continued in business until 1981 when, with a full order book and having agreed an overdraft to bulk purchase cloth to fulfil those orders, the bank changed their mind, called in the debt and sent in the receivers and a locksmith on the same day. By 1982 the remains of the company had been bought by John Young who moved the firm from Martlesham down to Whitmore's loft in Ipswich Docks – Joe Whitmore having decided to retire – and, with John Young who had already bought the remains of Starbury Boatbuilders, the Multihull specialists selling mainly to the French, formed the 'Ipswich Boatbuilding Partnership'. With the sail loft established, the boatbuilding moved into one of the Maltings on the other side of New Cut East. The firm at that time had the contract to build 'British Airways', the big catamaran for Robin Knox-Johnston. There were various problems with the project, with design specifications being changed after building had started. Lack of co-operation and the lack of marketing of the new sail loft spelled eventual disaster for the whole 'Partnership'. Austin, who had remained with the company, decided to hang up his sailmaking, gather his personal bits and pieces, and work from home as an independent consultant and designer.

Whilst still at Hadleigh he received excellent feedback from Adrian Jardine on the development of spinnakers for his Flying Dutchman. The loft gained an enviable reputation for spinnakers and Austin was probably one of the first people to apply science and maths as well as feel to the job. He had experimented in the early days with coated terylene sailcloth, applying resins to see the reaction. At first, a small jib would be made and set for a week in a local quarry to flog. This was superseded by a machine to do the same research. Cloth was rated on porosity and most standard cloths were not very good. The meter used was made by Gurley but a new simple porosity meter cost some £50.0s.0d. This was far too expensive, but Austin knew of a shop in Soho which sold ex-military surplus and, calling in, found a Gurley porosity meter on the shelf behind the man's head. At thirty bob, and the same for one behind it, Austin bought both. They used them on a stand at the boat show. One machine was set up with standard porous cloth and one with a coated cloth which stayed hard all through the show, impressing even cloth manufacturers. However, the big manufacturers had also been working on new cloths and they now became available on the market. This approach continued into spinnakers. The Jardines' continual trials combined with their many photographs of their own and competitors' spinnakers enabled many developments to take place and be applied with enormous success to many classes. As the sails and their panel layouts became more complicated, Austin eventually worked out his own Spherical Trigonometry programmes to give himself total control on shape.

However, the first problem was to find a suitable cloth, as the main spinnaker cloth then was parachute nylon – old silk, woven porous. Parachutes needed a pressure escape hole, or they would wobble about on a bubble of air and be unstable. Whilst some spinnakers had been made this way it was not satisfactory and Austin developed his own coating on cotton and nylon. They had been producing versions of the ordinary cotton type cut spinnakers. These were two halves with a centre seam and, although you could change the angle of the centre seam, the sail relied on the bias stretch of the material to get its shape.

THE AMERICANS HAD developed resin filled nylon which was more or less airtight, although it soon broke up under use. However, with this cloth the Americans had been able to successfully produce what was called the spherical spinnaker, which is one with many shaped panels. Adrian Jardine had bought one of these spinnakers for testing and examination and it was looked at in great detail. When looking at it sailing, it became apparent that they had constructed it by joining a curved panel to a straight panel. This is normal sailmaking practice, to shape one edge only but in this case, because one side still had the selvage on it, it caused wrinkles along every seam. The first thing to do was to put half the shape on each panel and mitre them together. This seemed so obvious that it was a puzzle why no one had tried it. Whilst this obviously improved the sail no end, the cloth was still not right.

The porosity meter

Austin purchased his nylon from a firm in Great Yarmouth. They were nominally silk weavers but had spent the war making parachute material, and now produced nylon for ladies' underwear, which was also supplied to Austin for spinnakers. Ivor Williams supplied a similar material to Bruce Banks. Austin had taken quite a quantity of this nylon for doing the ordinary spinnakers and on one visit he got talking with the new manager. He had taken over from his father and was quite a go ahead person. They discussed the parachute material and how it had to meet certain porosity. They had meters to check that the cloth was between the set limits and if outside these limits it was rejected as scrap. He had a roll of cloth that had been rejected by the inspectors as not being porous enough and, knowing that Austin was trying to get an airtight material, offered the roll to him to experiment with. This was received gratefully and Austin set to with ideas to fully air proof the cloth, including varnish.

A Fireball mainsail at Seahorse Sails

Whilst this was very good for porosity it did tend to leave the cloth a little rigid. He then thought about raincoats. These were, of course, fully waterproof and air tight but still flexible. Austin found a manufacturer of raincoat material in Surrey and took the roll of cloth down to them. He asked for a very thin layer of

The monster International 14 spinnaker

their waterproof coating to be put on to the cloth and this turned out to be a flexible polyurethane.

When the cloth was returned to Suffolk it was perfect. Completely airtight and still flexible enough to make sails from. Austin started making spinnakers with fully fashioned seams immediately and it produced a magnificent sail. By the time of the 1960 Naples Olympics, 75% of the Flying Dutchman class had Seahorse spinnakers, including the Gold and Bronze medal positions. Seahorse had the run of the material for about a year before anyone else caught up with them, including the Americans but, unfortunately, it was reckoned to be un-patentable. They say that imitation is the sincerest form of flattery but a while later they found an advert in an American yachting magazine for 'Seahorse Type Spinnakers'.

The only sore point was that they were twice the price that Austin was charging and they were selling them. They nearly put an advert in themselves, saying 'Real Seahorse Spinnakers, Half Price'. Eddie Hyde was working for Seahorse at this time and left shortly afterwards to found 'Musto & Hyde'. It shows how good Austin's design was when you realise that Eddie Hyde was still making spinnakers close to the Seahorse pattern thirty-three years later and with only the minutest of modifications until the class changed the rules on spinnaker sizes in the early 1990s. The Hyde spinnaker was a standard for the class and very few top boats would sail without at least one in their sail wardrobe. It took some time for the new construction and design methods to be applied to all classes because so many classes, such as the Dragon and Flying Junior, had rules calling for specific things which would not be acceptable with the new methods. The Fourteen Foot International, however, soon realised that the new techniques would provide new opportunities, as we shall see later. Today, with the number of different materials available for sail cloth and the vast number of weaves and constructions, it is easy to forget that these only started to become available from the late 1950s onwards. Before that it was still cotton and flax.

While there was no spare time to design new boats for the Fourteen Foot class – though he did act as consultant to the last of his designs built by John Fisk – Austin still remained involved over the years making sails and in particular spinnakers as he describes here:

"The International Fourteens of today have spinnakers unrestricted in area but in the days of Fourteen Foot 'I' measurement (a left over from when the spars had to stow inside the boat), when I was crewing in them, building them and making sails for them, the only restrictions on spinnakers were the skill and daring of the crews who had to set them.

When Charles Currey and I were sailing 'Thunder' we had a cotton spinnaker which was considered very large – 14 feet leeches and 14 feet on the foot. However, with the coming of stable nylon, half the weight of cotton, it became possible to have larger ones, and an arms race ensued. With less porous material used for ladies' underwear, Bruce Banks, who was making his own spinnakers long before he took up professional sailmaking, had a splendid flesh coloured one for 'Windsprite', known as the Pink Perfection. It was still a bit porous but set the future.

After several spinnakers for the Flying Dutchman class, just in time to sweep the board in the 1960 Olympics, Stewart Morris had one for 'Lucilla' K747 early in 1961. It was now possible to make bigger sails set and Stewart's had 15ft 9in leeches, a maximum girth of 15ft 1in and a foot of 14ft 8in. It cost £23.10s.0d. During the season, Stewart sold the boat to Barry Perry, who renamed her 'Scandalus'. However, he kept the spinnaker (which carried his racing flag emblem of a four leafed clover) and used it in 'Gossip' K767 to win the Prince of Wales' Cup at Whitstable in 1961, re-sailed after being abandoned for a gale on the Thursday.

Jon Allen, who had 'Polyester' K728, asked me how big a spinnaker was now possible. As a result we produced his Monster, yellow and turquoise horizontal stripes, with leeches of 16ft 7in, maximum girth 17ft 4in and a foot of 15ft.

This produced a phone call from Stewart Morris: 'That's a very large spinnaker you've made for Jon Allen. Make me a bigger one'. So Stewart had the 'Pumpkin', bright yellow (hence its name), leeches 16ft 10in, maximum girth 19ft 6in and a foot 17ft 3in. It set well, looked like its namesake from in front, but if the wind let up, it was long enough to get under the stem and stop the boat.

Jon Allen got to hear about the 'Pumpkin' and asked for an even bigger sail – 'But keep it the same colours, so Stewart won't know.' Jon's Super Monster had 17ft 0in leeches, 21ft 8in maximum girth and a foot 19ft 6in. It was quite difficult to set, even on the land rig as shown in the photograph, without a mainsail or a pole. I don't know how often it was used in a race, but it was probably the largest Fourteen spinnaker ever made, before the change of rules allowed masthead sails."

The sails had become so large as to be of little use except on a dead run and even then were difficult to set, so common sense prevailed and better all round shapes were developed.

After the 1958 defeat, a decision was made to challenge again for the Americas Cup then sailed in Twelve Metres. Two identical boats were built in Scotland to the design of David Boyd for the challenge of 1964. The eventual challenger was 'Sovereign', with her tuning partner 'KURREWA V'. In the event, let down by poor sails and technique in the Newport conditions, 'Sovereign' was soundly trounced losing by the largest margins ever, fifteen and twenty minutes. Interestingly, both 'Sovereign' and the winner 'CONSTELLATION' were sold to the French as a preliminary for their own challenge, and a series of races was arranged between the two boats with Bob Bavier – 'CONSTELLATIONS' skipper in the cup races – steering both boats at one time or another. It was reported back to David Boyd that if both boats had Hood sails there was very little difference between the two.

AUSTIN BECAME INVOLVED with the 'KURREWA V' syndicate early in 1960 and began work on sail development for them. However, as so often with British campaigns, internal politics and egos made it fairly fraught most of the time. 'KURREWA V' was being managed by Owen Aisher for the Livingstone brothers who owned her. They were Australian sheep farmers who seemed only to sign the cheques. At this time Owen Aisher was also running Ratsey & Lapthorn's, the sailmakers, and not surprisingly they were the main sailmakers for the syndicate. However, Austin had done a lot of work for 'STUG' Perry on spinnakers for his International 5.5 Metre, 'Vision' and, as helmsman of 'KURREWA', wanted Austin to again work on spinnakers for 'KURREWA'. 'STUG' Perry had taken the Silver medal in the 1956 Melbourne Olympics in the International 5.5 Metre class. This class, like so many, had no cross width measurements and had seen a lot of sail development from its inception with sailmakers trying to get as much nylon as possible in the measured wire perimeter of leeches and foot.

In France, Jean Jacques Herbulot made spinnakers cut well oversize, in which the straight panels lay diagonally from leeches up to the centre seam. A loose hem was put on and the sail left to float on the margin wires. When the sail was set, the head would go up but there would be folds of nylon lying on the deck until it filled, when the loose cloth would climb up the wires until the whole sail evened itself out as a near hemisphere, relying on the nylon's softness and stretch to take its shape. Austin also remembers a Russian 5.5-Metre spinnaker which was substantially bigger than a hemisphere – for use only on a dead run. Seen from astern, one could see the circle of the leech and foot measurement wires, and the sail standing out beyond them

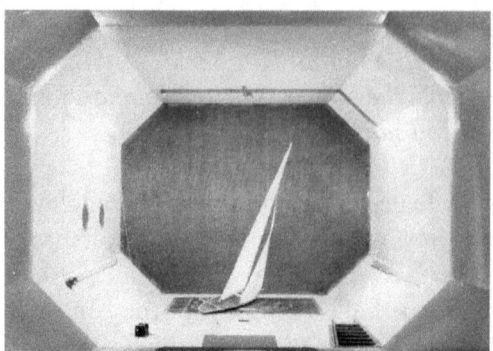
The wind tunnel with a 12 Metre model

Testing a spinnaker for KURREWA

like a half opened mushroom. It looked marvellous, as if it had more effective area for the wind to work on, but it probably only set because the Russian nylon was a bit porous and the most telling point is that the boat was no faster than the others. Size, as they say, is not everything.

ALTHOUGH MOSTLY PRO-RATSEY'S, Owen Aisher did – a little grudgingly – agree that Seahorse were making some very useful sails and the development began. Austin quickly realised that an enormous amount of development would have to be done to be competitive with the Americans and asked for time in the Southampton wind tunnel. This was agreed and provided Austin with a chance to renew his acquaintance with Southampton, where he had been involved with the staff there through his work on the college small craft committee. This committee helped with work for the wind tunnel and reviewed potential student projects. It also had Owen Aisher and Tom Thornycroft as members. Rather than just student projects, 'KURREWA's' sails were to be a commercial project.

They then set to and built a 1:9 scale model, consisting of the rig, deck and backbone. This was mounted on trunions on the turntable so that it could be set at any angle from upright to 20° of heel, using small screw adjusters to lock the positions. The mast was complete with a luff groove and all the rigging was wire and to scale. Seahorse Sails were to research spinnakers and genoas, and Ratsey & Lapthorn were to develop the mainsails. (The Seahorse loft was too small to cope with Twelve metre mainsails). Austin made a model mainsail for use in the tunnel and it remained constant whilst they tried various genoas. Part of the development was checking different materials. Two identical genoas were made, one in a porous material and one in a totally non porous material. The differences were measured and found to be substantial. At other times development concentrated on various Genoa shapes.

Austin's experience of 12-Metre spinnakers pre-war had very little bearing on the more modern sail. Then, races were won on the windward legs, and a good long spinnaker run was a signal for the lunch basket to appear rather than any serious racing. They were, of course, Egyptian cotton and because it was impossible to weave any lighter, there was very little difference in the cloth for a 12-Metre or a Fourteen Foot International. The sail consisted of two flat halves joined on a curved centre seam. The cloths in some sails were near enough straight, while the more ambitious ones met at a small angle, which also increased the bias angle at the centre seam and helped feed the shape into the body of the sail. The formula for the leeches gave a length similar to the forestay and, amazingly for our eyes today, there were no restrictions on foot or cross measurements. In fact, they were not even mentioned in the rules.

A cruiser spinnaker under test

IN MANY WAYS these measurement were self regulating in that any sailmaker making a sail wider than the accepted optimum would find that the extra material would not feed into the sail and it would end up with a roman nose which would then not set. The sails were not used as they are today. They were usually set to windward of the forestay, seldom taken round it and were of very little use for reaching. Some had vent holes down the centre seam, borrowed from the aviator's parachute, which at that time, not being deliberately porous, needed a hole in the middle for stability. They were known as Tom Ratsey's Peep Holes. After the war, and with new materials, spinnakers began to play the part we know today and much more development work went into them generally.

The work on spinnakers involved great attention to shape and size, and the latter caused some friction between Austin and the crew. The crew wanted to have the biggest spinnakers possible, which was unfortunate really because if they had bothered to consider the total failure of the large spinnakers on the unsuccessful 'SCEPTRE' challenge of 1958. Austin was against this, having spent a considerable time studying photographs of American spinnakers. The aerial shots showed quite clearly that very few of them subtend more than a right angle in plan. Despite the fact that the Americans seemed to have settled on relatively small spinnakers and, with the amount of research that they did it must be for very good reasons, Austin could not convince the crew away from wanting the maximum size possible.

Austin made four model spinnakers for wind tunnel testing and, across the different conditions, the one with a ninety degree head proved to be the best. The monster looked like it might be a good running spinnaker but turned out to not even be good at that and certainly would not reach. Despite the problems, the research was immensely interesting and Austin learnt a vast amount about the behaviour and workings of spinnakers. The wind tunnel model was set upright and, using the four little electric winches from outside the tunnel to control the mainsheet, spinnaker sheet, foreguy and pole downhaul, one could watch the lift and drag meters while making adjustments. Standing in the tunnel clear of the model, with a streamer on a long stick, it was also possible to trace the actual flow of wind round and over the sail. It showed that the spinnaker is not a lifting sail as such and the higher it is set the less work it does.

One point learnt early on was that a spinnaker will not work without a mainsail as it will just stall, because the spinnaker and the mainsail work together as an aerofoil. All the air goes sideways across the spinnaker, none comes out the bottom and you can fly a spinnaker as high as you like and the air will still not come out of the bottom. If you fly the spinnaker too high though, the top is horizontal and therefore useless. The sail must be kept down and, even running, the air flow is across the sail behind the main, i.e. horizontal and is still like this a couple of boat lengths clear away. This means that when you pass another boat to weather, you can collapse their spinnaker from at least two boat lengths away, the wind flow being at right angles to your course. The width of the spinnaker decides how hooked it is behind the mainsail and reaches a point where it is no good as a forward pulling aerofoil. This was highly instructive and the sails were the same format as the Fourteen Foot International and Flying Dutchman spinnakers. The photos of two red and white spinnakers, one from the Twelve Metre and the other from the Fourteen set at the same angle, illustrate the scaling down of the shape. Unfortunately, most of the knowledge fell on deaf ears. Stug Perry took it in but was out-voted against the cry for maximum spinnakers.

The best design sail was made, and then began a fight to get the crew to set it correctly. This was an uphill struggle. The crew would insist on setting the sail sky high to get the lift. Austin obviously knew that this wouldn't work but faced a barrage of questions and comments. 'We need it high to get lift.' 'No, you don't.' 'It's very small.' 'It's the right size. Look at the pictures of the American ones; you will see that they've all got spinnakers about this size.' 'Why can't we have a big one? We want the biggest one possible.' Eventually Ratsey's made a quite enormous green thing that when eventually set had the biggest Roman nose ever seen. Ratsey's only way of making a spinnaker this size was to make it in two halves and then tailor the centre front seam until it looked right. This they would do by hanging it up in the loft and then go round pinning false seams in until they were happy. This still did not mean it would set in the wind. The Roman nose was gradually paired down until the sail set after a fashion. Meanwhile, Bruce Banks was making the large blue star cut for use on 'Sceptre'. This sail looked marvellous but did not really drive the boat along and, when tried against Austin's red and white spinnaker, set correctly, 'Kurrewa' was able to sail straight past with no effort.

Austin had the considerable uphill struggle to get the crew to set the sail right and eventually took the skipper into the support boat with him and went ahead to view the spinnaker from off the boat. From a couple of boat lengths ahead, with a loud hailer, Austin set the sail from the launch at the angle he was used to looking at it in the wind tunnel. The pole, guy and sheet were adjusted until Austin was happy and the skipper immediately remarked that it looked a completely different sail. That was how the sail was to be set, but if Austin was not there the crew would not follow the right settings. They were caught on photograph and the crew would insist on setting the sail with the top of the sail horizontal and the base level with the spreaders and enough room underneath to drive a double-decker bus across the foredeck. It is very sad that this sort of attitude has blighted so many of the British campaigns over the years.

The skipper was so pro-Ratsey that he was determined to kill the Seahorse involvement, whatever the cost. On one occasion, with Austin on board, 'STUG' Perry called for the red and white Seahorse spinnaker, only to be told that it was not on board. When questioning why, the answer was that they had been clearing out the sails and decided to have fewer on board. When they returned to the dock in Gosport, Austin and Stug found the Seahorse sail hidden under the cockpit. Whilst there is very little satisfaction in it, 'Kurrewa' could not compete against 'Sovereign' and 'Sovereign' was soundly thrashed in the actual cup races. The inability of so many of our sailors to listen to ideas outside their own personal tunnel vision has cost us many regatta successes. Unfortunately, this situation still exists today.

Austin at the sewing machine

The same situation existed with the genoas. At that time, all genoas were mitre cut, as cloth capable of taking cross cutting having not yet been developed. There was an awful problem getting good material of the right weight to stand the forces and much skill was needed to cut the centre seam right. Hood's in the U.S.A. had made stretch luff sails and Austin used this technique to make the sails here. Once again the crew would not control the sail as needed. The Hood genoas were shackled at the tack and stretched entirely upwards on the halyard which meant it was made substantially short to allow it to take up its shape. Austin did not see why you should start with any smaller sail than necessary and designed his sails to be tensioned by a tack cunningham. This would require a winch on the foredeck and although he cannot remember the reason, it was made clear that this would not be considered. Austin therefore decided to supply the winch as part of the sail and a unit was

One of the many photos taken of the test rig for genoas

designed that formed part of the tack. From the drawing office paper to pattern making, castings, machining and into the sail took just a fortnight and was completed totally in the town of Ipswich. Impressive as this was, it was still twice as long as it would have taken during the war. The winch was designed using the lessons of some of Tom Thornycroft's ideas, and was a bronze casting with lugs for attaching it into the sail, which took a standard winch handle.

However, instead of having the normal ratchet teeth, it had a skewer that located through two holes in the main casing and went through various holes in the winch drum. To operate it, you simply wound up the required tension and pushed the pin through all the holes to lock the drum in that position. The unit worked perfectly and it was possible to control the sail shape exactly. The Ratsey Genoas were simply seized onto a luff wire and set as that with no means of adjustment.

IN BRIGHTLINGSEA IN the late 1950s the firm of 'Sailcraft' was set up by Reg White to build racing and cruising boats and in particular catamarans to the designs of Rod Macalpine-Downie. Austin was to do a great deal of work with Rod over the years, much of it frustrating at times. Rod was a self taught designer who, whilst having a fantastic eye for style, sometimes missed smaller details. In the early 60s, Sailcraft were offering the Hellcat, Shark, Thai IV and the *Yachting World* Cat, all Macalpine-Downie designs and also cruisers. These were very successful with different designs of varying length. One of the early successes was the 30 ft Iroquois which went through several marks before the company finally closed down in the late 1970s.

Reg first contacted Austin when the design for the Iroquois arrived and asked him over to supper to go through the details of the boat and rig. A few adjustments were needed in the scantlings to ensure the boat remained strong enough, although Rod was always concerned that Reg would build boats too heavy. They never were, but they were strong enough. It can be a fine dividing line. Rod seemed to regard a sailplan as a flat drawing and not as of a three-dimensional rig and sails. The sail plan drawings initially lacked detail and the rig drawings were checked to solve one or two problems which had not been foreseen, such as the jib being needed to be sheeted several feet behind the boat.

Eventually measurements were decided and Austin made the first suits of sails. However, the mainsails came out too long on the luff to fit the masts and it was only when Austin insisted on measuring the masts himself that he found someone could not measure correctly or, as he always suspected, someone had used a tape with the end missing. Once these early problems were sorted out the production became easy and many suits of sails were made for the class. The production of sails increased with the other Sailcraft designs including the Iroquois II, Apache, and the Commanche.

Nearly all these rigs were fully battened and very advanced aerodynamically for the time and this skill was applied to other boats as well. The two handed 'Round Britain and Ireland' races had started and a local Ipswich man entered with a catamaran called 'MIRROR CAT'. The boat was designed by Rod Macalpine-Downie and he crewed with the owner.

It was built by a freelance boat builder employed by the owner strictly to Rod's design and scantlings, with Rod pleased at last that this had been achieved. The design was basically a stretched Iroquois Mk I converted to forty feet, a lovely shaped boat, with the accommodation

Seahorse Sails on a Comanche

in the hulls and a centre trampoline. This was very advanced for the time. Austin became involved with the rig and at its first outing the sails set well and the boat slipped along nicely. Unfortunately, on her return up river, she was hit by a squall and took off, to be quickly followed by disaster as at least one centreboard folded up through the hull requiring rapid action to prevent the boat sinking. She was hauled out at Woolverstone and heavily rebuilt there with Rod wringing his hands about the weight being added. The work was successful and the boat completed the race, though by the time they finished it was good that there was accommodation in each hull as this saved talking to each other.

AN 'IROQUOIS' II was successful on corrected time in the Round Britain and Ireland Race, raced by Gerry Boxhall and with rig adjustments by Austin. Added to her wardrobe was a masthead genoa set down the lee hull. It was tacked onto the stem and sheeted at the stern, which gave a closer sheeting angle than if it had been tacked at the centreline and had been led all round the rigging. It set well with the mainsail and she pointed well and footed fast. This was a successful sail but much larger than her normal genoa and was not used for the production boats. Gerry Boxhall went on to crew with Sir Robin Knox-Johnston on the first really big cat 'British Oxygen', with Gerry the brains behind the project. This boat was built by Sailcraft at Brightlingsea to a Rod Macalpine-Downie design but, on an early outing, the main beam collapsed as

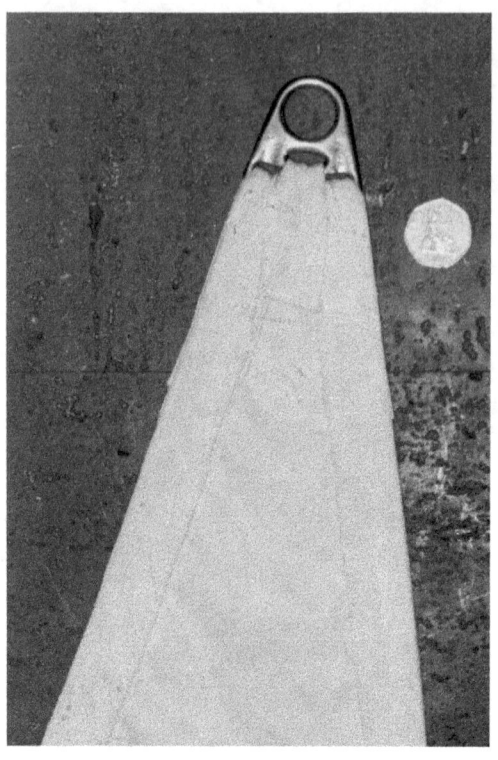

A head fitting as designed by Austin

a result of pushing technology and under estimating the loadings. This will happen when pushing race boat design. They sought structural advice from British Aerospace and the modifications were successful. A short while later Austin met Gerry Boxhall and Austin asked him how things were going. Gerry explained and said he was pleased with the results.

Austin said, 'I suppose they told you, you had 120 tons on the heel of the mast?' Gerry exclaimed, 'How did you know?' Austin said, 'It's my business to know this sort of thing. Why didn't you ask before?' Austin has always had a distinct advantage in that, with training as a designer and experience as a boatbuilder and sailmaker, he often sees the whole problem rather than one specialist area and had worked out the problem when the beam first collapsed. The boat then went to the south coast and Austin received a call from Gerry Boxhall saying that the boat wouldn't point and they had been tacking back and forwards across the Solent gaining about a foot on each tack.

Austin was invited down to sail as she was in the process of moving to Plymouth in readiness for the Round Britain and Ireland Race. Austin was to join for the passage there, which took the form of a race out of the eastern Solent and round the south side of the island. Next morning they were into West Bay and Austin remarked that if they wanted to solve the problems they would have to put the boat on the wind regardless of the race and stop running and reaching. This was done first on one tack with a compass bearing and then on the other, only to find the bearings were nearly 180° apart. There were several things wrong, one being the sheeting base was enormously wide because the crosstrees went out almost to the inside of the hulls. The genoa, working jib and staysail were all designed to be lead outside everything. This meant that the working jib went off the forestay at an angle of about 40 degrees and the staysail off the inner stay at about sixty degrees. This was obviously no use at all and the storm jib was substituted for the staysail which improved things a little as it did at least sheet through the shrouds.

Nothing could be done then about the working jib nor the massive luff sag on the forestay. Ratsey's had made the sails to Rod Macalpine-Downie's plan and were not helpful in re-cutting to solve the problems. They insisted that the stay must be tightened, but this was impossible. Although it might not seem a lot, there was still three feet of sag in the forestay and this could not be improved as with any more load the boat just bent. The working jib and staysail were discarded completely and Austin re-cut the genoa taking some five feet out to flatten the sail and to allow for the forestay sag, which although still too full, was now usable.

To complete the wardrobe Austin made a new yankee jib with a high clew and sheeting through the rigging. It had a full length luff of around sixty feet but, with the allowance for three feet of sag, was only fifteen feet wide. With this and the storm staysail she would now make quite good progress to windward. However, the mainsail was much too full and was reefed for most of the race to flatten the foot. Whilst the boat perhaps never totally fulfilled her potential, she did now show some pace.

The big cat British Oxygen

As so often with sailing campaigns, things are last minute and Austin delivered the yankee the evening before the race. Reg White, having built the boat, was also in Plymouth to do a few last minute jobs and one evening they took the boat for a sail around the Eddystone rock and back. Much to the consternation of some of the crew, Reg, with his brilliant sailing, skills flew a hull all the way back to Plymouth.

Rod became very ill towards the end of his life and his last major project was 'British Airways', which finally closed Austin's sailmaking in Ipswich, along with the boat building side of the firm. Rod's illness meant that often drawings were late, specifications changed and the entire work schedule became a disaster and contracts were cancelled.

THE OTHER GREAT multihull family in England at the time, and the only ones still in business today, was the Prout family. Roland Prout's small successful racing eighteen foot cat 'ENDEAVOUR' was developed into the very popular sixteen foot six inch 'SHEARWATER Mk

British Oxygen in Plymouth

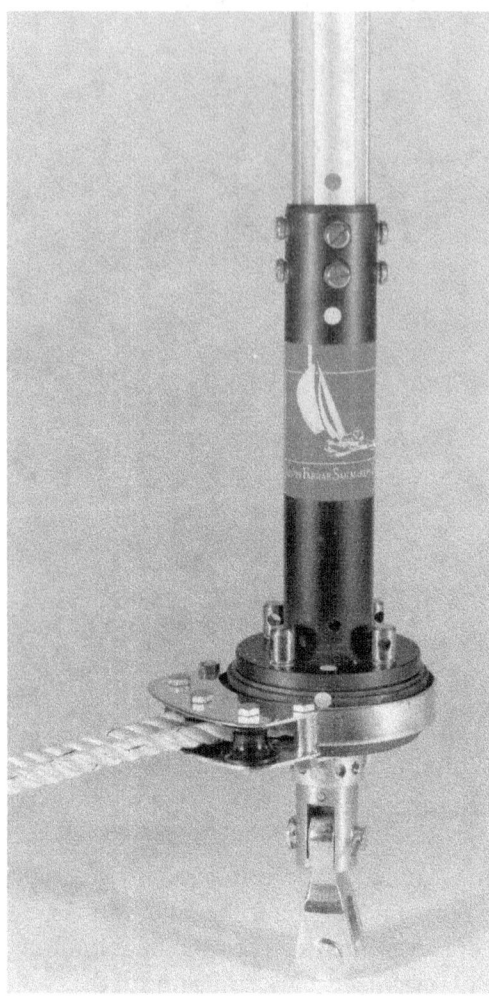

Austin's headsail furling showing the continuous line

An early roller reefing mainsail

III' design, and Austin also helped to develop their rigs, making sails for many of the class. At one Boat show at London's Olympia, Austin fitted the Shearwater with a set of very early taped transparent Mylar Sails. They caused so much interest that at one point they had to be taken down to give the boat itself a chance. He also made some sails for the various Prout 'C' Class Catamarans, used for the Little Americas Cup, of which more later. As an acknowledged expert in high performance rigs, Austin worked with many boats and designers, and various speed trials in England and was at the forefront of catamaran development in this country, including one of the early micro multihulls, the Typhoon Trimaran, built by Reg White, which used Tornado hulls as the sponsons.

Today, furling headsails are so common place on yachts as to be worth no mention. However, they are still a relatively new invention as we know them now. The Wykeham Martin furler had been invented back at the beginning of the century and is still in regular use but furls away the sail completely. What was now needed, particularly with the masthead rig and large headsails being fitted to cruising boats, was a system of reefing the headsail without having to go on deck to do it.

Several companies have developed systems over the years, and Austin produced his own system which used a continuous line. After Austin Farrar Sailmakers closed, the production was taken over by Sailspar in Brightlingsea, who still produce it today. One of the problems experienced was the sail becoming a very poor shape as it was furled. This was solved by careful cutting, and often the inclusion of a soft foam core to the leading portion which would absorb the spare material as the sail was rolled up. The furling system always formed an important display on the boat show stand, which they had every year at London. The loft also became involved in making sails for the first windsurfers to be sold in this country – the 'WINGLIDER' and 'SEA PANTHER' – by Gordon and Ken Way. Although Austin put time into developing their sails, it soon became clear that this was going to need a specialist loft as the demand was all or nothing, and he slowly moved out of this market. This subsequently became the case with lofts such as Tushingham and Gaastra, specialising in windsurfer sails only.

Austin and Charles Currey at the POW 1953 Lowestoft

Austin had continued to race dinghies other than the International Fourteens, although he attended every P.O.W. from 1946 to 1969, except 1959 when Charles Currey was not going to go and changed his mind at the last minute, by which time Austin had already committed himself to an offshore race. Most of these were with Charles, although a couple were sailed with other people including Sam Waters in 'WARRIGAL' in 1952 when Charles was sailing the Finn in the Olympics. Austin also crewed for other people in Fourteen regattas including the infamous 'Capsizing' Jack Blundell, with whom he sailed at Hunstanton in 1953, and could still not stop him capsizing – nor could Tony Rutherford the following year at Weymouth when they capsized every day and Tony eventually accepted a lift back in the rescue boat, while Jack sailed the swamped boat back, hanging onto the transom and steering from there.

Austin had raced a 'NATIONAL SWORDFISH' at the Royal Harwich Yacht Club with his cousin, a solicitor in Ipswich in the late 1950s. His cousin owned the Fairey built boat and there were a fleet of seven of eight racing regularly. If his cousin could not make it then a young sea scout would be taken as crew. This was the normal way of learning to race as a youngster, crewing in anything with anyone. The modern squad and school systems did not start until the

Austin sailing a Swordfish

505 sail development

late seventies. The Swordfish was a nice boat to sail but far too heavy on the launching ramp and Austin reckons it contributed to his bad back in a major way. Austin also had the use of other boats and would again take youngsters to give them the opportunity to learn to race. These boats included Charles Currey's Firefly for the 1949 National Championships at Harwich Town Sailing Club in the harbour approaches where he finished sixth. With his regular Swordfish crew, Austin had the chance to campaign a 505 one summer and was one of the first to sail at many of the local clubs in the middle fifties.

Ralph Wadham, the original chairman of Yachting Press who numbered 'Exchange & Mart' and 'Yachts & Yachting' among its publications, had ordered a new 505 from Fairey Marine and contracted Austin to collect it for him and deliver it to the Medway. On arriving in Kent, Austin found that Ralph was going to be abroad for several weeks, and he offered the boat to Austin to take back to Suffolk and race in the East Coast regattas to try and gain publicity for the new class. This was too good an opportunity to miss, and Austin sailed 'YANDY' (a name 'cleverly' derived from the initials of the magazine – Y & Y) in the different regattas up and down the East Coast, often having to choose between two venues for all of August. The boat gave the local handicappers a hard time and Austin often noticed that 'to handicap' seemed to mean 'to prevent winning' and not 'have an equal chance'.

The same year, Austin again sailed in 'YANDY', this time as crew with Charles Currey in a team racing regatta against the French in Ouistreham. The French were major supporters of the class, and large numbers were built with Hervé of La Rochelle being one of the leading builders. The French national authority – the FFV – put up a splendid trophy. Tiny Mitchell sponsored a team of three boats from the Cowes Corinthian YC. Team captain was Richard Creagh-Osbourne, crewed by Derek Pitt-Pitts sailing a Fairey demonstration boat. Max Johnson and John Westall were in Max's boat 'CORONA', which arrived in the cockpit of his motor boat, and Austin and Charles sailed 'YANDY', this and the other Fairey boat being taken on a double stacking trailer behind Creagh-Osborne's car. All the team had been made honorary members of the Cowes Corinthian YC.

Like most of the north coast of France, it is very tidal and sailing is restricted to a few hours either side of high water. The slipway was long and very steep except at high water and the boats were usually craned into the canal that leads to Caen, and then lowered in the lock to sail out to race. They were often towed back whilst there was water over the sands, except that one day they were kept out so long they missed the lock and had a very hard job pulling the boats up the slipway. Neither team had sailed as a team before, but the British seemed to master team tactics a little sooner than the French and went on to win the trophy.

Hospitality was generous and each team member was presented with large bottles of 'Benedictine', the local liqueur, with specially printed labels showing that they were prizes and not subject to duty. There was also an enormous bottle (possible a Magnum) for Tiny Mitchell.

Looking at the 505 spinnaker

On returning through customs, the smaller bottles were shown with no problem, but they left the larger one hidden in sail bags in the bottom of one of the boats, as they dare not risk showing that to the customs who would only believe so much.

Several weeks later the British team were invited by Tiny to a celebratory lunch at the Dorchester, at which the cup and giant bottle of Benedictine were centrepieces on the table. Austin rolled up in his by now very tatty Bentley, 'Bumble' and, much to his surprise, was ushered by the doorkeeper in a top hat into the prime parking place in front of the hotel. It was not until much later that he discovered that the then owner of the Dorchester was a keen member of the Bentley Driver's Club and staff were briefed to give reverence to Bentleys of any age.

As the sixties went on, Austin did less dinghy sailing and more offshore, although he does remember one other trip in a 505 with Harry Jonas, when he agreed to sail the boat to Lowestoft. He had already been to Roughs Tower and back, and Austin said no to sailing the boat to Ostend. In the event it was a very pleasant sail. They left Woolverstone early with a National Twelve rig for strong winds which blew up as the morning wore on. They put up the smaller rig and hiking the boat, not trapezing, they groyne hopped up the coast past Felixstowe, Aldeburgh and Southwold against the tide. After Benacre Ness, the wind and tide eased and they re-hoisted the 505 sails and trapezed, reaching fast across to Lowestoft Pier, where some people were

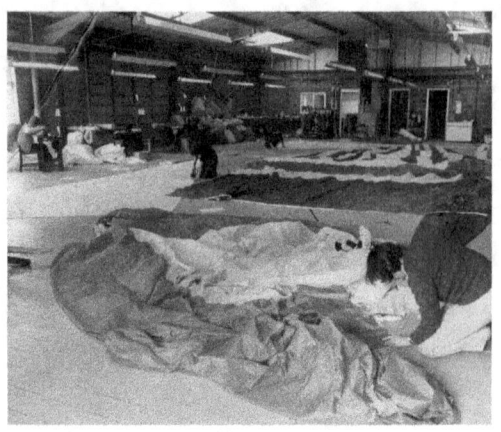

The sail loft at Martlesham

at first amazed to think that he had trapezed from Woolverstone. Harry's wife, Jeannie, was waiting with the trailer for the return trip. After this, they both did the Channel Dinghy Race which blew up hard and provided a tough beat for the last 5 miles into Bolougne. With the subsequent gale, all the dinghies were brought back on the ferry, where Austin elected to stay on deck so as not to be ill.

The loft continued with offshore sails, and Austin experienced racing with either Chris or Harry Jonas, who Austin had known from their first days in 505s, and had now bought an Ocean Racer each. Chris started with a Frans Maas 'BREON' built in Breskins, and Harry had a Nicholson 36, an early GRP boat. Later Harry had a North Sea 24 designed by Kim Holman on which Austin raced when not racing with Chris, including a Fastnet Race. Chris moved up to a Van de Stadt 'REBEL' moulded by Tyler's and fitted out by Southern Ocean Shipyards at Poole with an internal layout to his own design which was subsequently used in the production models. The brothers were successful land agents and travelled the country, but the boats were kept on moorings at Woolverstone and Austin was mate to Chris on many races in the North Sea and down Channel.

OCEAN RACING HAS changed greatly over the years, probably with the demands made on time in the modern world. These days there are still ocean races such as the Round the World Race, the Sydney-Hobart or the Fastnet, but particularly in the first case they need a full time commitment. The offshore races are less, partly because today's races are less comfortable offshore and partly because it is not easy to continually take Fridays off for the start. It is interesting to compare a race from 1964 with the races of today when the crew spend their entire time sitting on the windward rail eating only snacks.

Austin Farrar's sailmakers stand at the Southampton Boat Show

"In these days of shorter and shorter offshore races, with the sailors blaming the designers for producing yachts which require most of the crew sitting on the weather rail most of the time, and the designers blaming the rule makers for forcing them to design unstable boats, it may interest younger readers who have not experienced anything else, and bring back memories to the oldies who have, to look back over 30 years to the time when off-duty watch went to their bunks, and the ocean racers were perfectly capable of sailing across the Atlantic in the same trim in which they raced.

I think it is fair to say that, in the smaller yachts anyway, we used to go ocean racing as much for the adventure and challenge as for the chance of winning a prize. My first long race is the one I remember most clearly, and certainly had its share of adventure. This was the 1964 Yarmouth I.O.W. to Santander, 500 miles, coupled with the Santander to La Trinité which bought us half way home.

Our yacht was 'ZEELUST', a Breon class, designed and built by Frans Maas in Breskens. She was 36ft long by 10ft 6in beam, drawing only 4ft 9in. Owner/skipper was Chris Jonas, with his wife Eve who came as a member of the racing crew, and not as cook (which so often happens). Indeed we had a cook, Wilfred Underwood. Wilf did not pretend to be much good as a racing crew, although he would stand his watch. His hobby was cooking at sea, at which he was a real expert, with menus for each meal worked out in advance. He was only floored once, of which more later. There was Eric Willis from Lymington, Roy Webb, a doctor from Ipswich, Bill Gamblin, a Canadian gunner officer, who like many gunners was good at navigation, and myself.

With 42 entries, by starting first with the rest of class 3, we managed to keep out of trouble at the start off Yarmouth, but in the channel between Hurst Point and the Island, with wind against tide, there was a short steep sea which, with our short length, had us bucking like a bronco. Then an alarm call came from below: 'There's water over the cabin sole and more coming in.' When 'ZEELUST' was quite new, in 1963, there had been some trouble with the planking (she was strip planked on steel frames and edge nailed) and she had to go back to Breskens to have it put right, so the immediate thought was planking trouble returning. The water was gaining so quickly against our pumping that we were looking for a suitable spot in Alum bay to beach her. Then, when pulling up the floorboards showed that the leak was not along the garboards, it was found that the water was cascading down from under the cockpit. By hanging his head down in the aft locker behind the engine, Chris found that the hoses that connected the cockpit drains to the skin fittings were adrift, forced off by the slamming. There were no seacocks – a bad fault – but in the smooth water close inshore now, he managed to get the hoses back onto their fittings and tighten the jubilee clips securely. By the time we had pumped enough water out to get sailing again, the rest of the fleet were out of sight.

Losing about three hours while we saved the ship from sinking was bad enough, but by the time we had sailed diagonally across the Channel to Ushant it had cost us the tide around the corner. Ushant was a mark of the course – we could not take the short cut between the island and the mainland, so with the wind dying and the tide sluicing round the Ile d'Ouessant, we had to kedge and wait for the tide to turn. Not so easy as it sounds as the water was quite deep. We had a kedge anchor with a short length of chain, and then a drum full of line, but that did not reach the bottom. We added the spare halyards, and could feel the anchor bouncing along the rocky bottom as we were swept backwards. We then added the spinnaker sheets. We had to use every piece of string we could find, before the kedge found a patch of sand and got a grip.

The tide was going past us at about two knots – a good trolling speed – so since we were going to be there for some hours we got the mackerel line out. As there were seven of us on board, Chris had prepared the line with seven hooks and little metal lures and had hardly lowered it over the side before there were tugs on the line. He pulled it in again with seven fish on it. Fish unhooked, down again and another seven mackerel. After the third haul we called a halt. There were more than enough for supper, and mackerel do not keep. Wilfred began preparing batter for cooking them, and sharpening his knife for filleting. 'No, no – you don't cook mackerel in batter, you just gut them and grill them whole.' There are not many mackerel in the North Sea, and Wilf had not encountered them in the wild before, but had to admit that they tasted delicious grilled.

When the tide eventually turned, there was still no wind, but we pulled the kedge up and drifted, not round the corner, but south westerly towards the Atlantic – and back again with the following tide, dragging the kedge again until we must have been over the same sandy patch where we had stopped before. Eventually the wind filled in and we set off in a southerly direction into the Bay of Biscay, past the Armen buoy, which was another mark of the course, and into really deep water. This was idyllic sailing, but was not going to let us catch out competitors – we must have been last by a very long way.

There was one night watch when Roy Webb and I were treated to a pyrotechnic display in a sky already full of stars, when hundreds of shooting stars sped across the sky from the north-east. We were ignorant of it at the time, but discovered later that in the first week of August every year the Earth goes through the tail of a comet, when millions of small asteroids burn up in our atmosphere. In the murky English sky, few are seen, but these were ideal conditions for astronomy.

As we approached Santander we ran into the heaviest rainstorm I can remember, which went on for several hours. We had to locate a headland close to the harbour, and Chris, who had been in the RAF Transport Command, knew his way around by aerial beacons rather than the marine ones and announced that there was such a beacon on the headland. We proceeded to home in on it and then to circle it using just the hand held direction finder in a visibility of less than 100 yards. Suddenly there was the headland, and we just sailed round it and into Santander harbour. The rain continued, so after anchoring among the other yachts in front of the yacht club, all hands had a shower with soap on deck and felt a lot cleaner.

Although we finished last, we had caught up some time and finished only half an hour after 'Janessa,' and beat three yachts on corrected time.

Having lost so much time on the way, there was not much opportunity for sightseeing before the start of the return race, but we bought a few souvenirs and laid in a stock of wine and brandy. Apart from a few ready-to-use bottles of sherry and brandy, we loaded, from what looked like a petrol pump on the quay, six glass carboys of 16 litres each, filled with two kinds of sherry, red and white wine, all to be bottled and shared round the crew when we reached home. Two of these were stowed in the forecastle, and the rest under the quarter berths packed round with spare clothes and sails.

The start of the race to La Trinité was enlivened by a number of French yachts, some of them late entries, which had had their own feeder race from La Rochelle to La Lequito. It was a spinnaker run at the start, but the wind died away to drifting conditions before filling in with a pleasant breeze from the west. It seemed fine at the time, but looking at photographs today, one can see mares' tails in the sky which were omens of wind to come.

The westerly wind did increase gradually, with a long Atlantic swell to match, until we were sailing up one side of the rollers and down the other side, and when we were in the troughs the next roller seemed to be above our crosstrees. Somebody remarked that it looked as if the waves were 30ft high. Bill Gamblin explained that we were approaching the Atlantic Shelf where, with an underwater cliff face, the bottom shoaled from 1000 fathoms to only 30, and that waves will break in a depth of water six times their own height, so that if they started to break when we got into 30 fathoms, it would mean that they were 30ft high. They did, so they were. The wind was getting up to gale force, and we had to slow down because, instead of sailing down the back of a wave, we were falling off it and smashing into the next one at the bottom. So, with a reef and the small jib, we were more manageable but the helmsman needed a steady hand to keep her straight as she met the waves.

While this was going on, Wilfred cooked a meal of roast lamb and two veg, and we got through it while we could keep it on the plate – it took more than a gale of wind to put Wilf off his cooking, or the crew off their appetite.

We closed on the land during the night, by this time close reefed with the storm jib. The bigger yachts had entered Quiberon Bay and finished in the corner at La Trinité in the dark while the leading lights showed the way. Being one of the smallest and slowest in the fleet, we arrived at the entrance after dawn, with the lights extinguished, and with blown spume reducing the visibility to about 100 yards. There was no way we could find the rocks of the Cardinals off the south-east corner of Belle Ile which we had to leave to port, or the Le Four shoal off Le Croisic point on the mainland which guarded the entrance. The direction finder was no help, as it so happened that we were on a line between two radio beacons with no third beacon to fix our position along the line. We held a council of war, decided that discretion was the better part of valour, and that the legendary 'PRUDENT MARINER' would not risk the entrance. We turned round and went out to sea again until the weather moderated. It was not pleasant. We only saw one other vessel – a large trawler appeared over a wave a short distance away and vanished in the next trough, and we expected to see her again as she went about her business, but we never did. Our main concern was to keep sailing as slowly as possible to windward – we did not fancy heaving-to with a lee shore not very far away. We learned later that some of the small French yachts had given up and made for their home ports around the bay, and had failed to find their harbour entrances and piled up outside. One yacht was lost and one badly damaged, and five Frenchmen drowned.

A report by the RORC recounts: 'MARIE-GALANTE' gave up the race and ran for shelter towards the River Gironde, north-north-west of Cordouan where there are shallow banks. One big wave flooded her, another broke her mast, and a third sunk her.

Five of the crew, one at least badly injured, launched a partially inflated rubber dinghy. Two of them who were wearing submarine suits were still alive when washed up on the beach next morning.' And adds: 'Opinion at the time was that it had been a grave error of judgement to run into the Gironde where even big ships do not attempt to enter or leave in bad weather.'

We kept watches with one on the helm and another sheltering in the hatch ready for action. On one occasion I had just come off watch, having handed over to Eric Willis, shed my oilskins, visited the loo, and was part way across the cabin to my bunk when Eric accidentally let 'ZEELUST' gather way. She sailed off the top of a wave and fell into the trough. Watchers said that I flew across the cabin – I maintain that I was stationary in space and my bunk came across and hit me. Anyway, we met with such force that the Mahogany bunk board was broken, and I cracked two ribs. I rolled into the bunk and passed out.

A major incident was when Eve was on the helm and Chris was sheltering in the hatchway. He saw the bow go straight into a wave and two feet of green water surging towards him over the coachroof. He slammed the hatch shut and the wave swept over and hit Eve, who hung onto the steering wheel and turned her head away from the water. The wave hit her with such force that she broke two of the spokes of the wheel and was swept back to the limit of her lifeline. It also carried away her glasses, and she was on her knees fumbling for them in the lee scuppers when she dislodged a lifebuoy which went over the side and drifted away. The lifebuoy, with the yacht's name on it, drifted ashore in a couple of hours, somewhere in the La Baule area, and since we should have finished days before, and had not been sighted, we were reported missing. The Press were informed, and the Daily Telegraph reported our loss – to the distress of various friends and relatives – including locally, Bill Gamblin's wife Teddy, who had come out to La Trinité to join us.

Aboard' ZEELUST', of course, we knew nothing of all this. We were uncomfortable but cheerful. Unless on watch we kept to our bunks, and I could hardly get out of mine anyway. I woke up once to a delicious baking smell – Wilfred was baking scones, buttering them and handing them round.

The gale blew itself out in the end, and we headed back towards Quiberon Bay. We saw a French aircraft, which flew round us at low altitude and went off again. Apparently they were supposed to be searching for us, but although our sail number was in full view above our reefs, they never reported us, and when we reached the finish we were treated as if we had returned from the dead.

We certainly packed a lot of incidents into quite a short race, and in retrospect it felt as if we had been battling the elements for several days. However, looking at the results kindly provided from the RORC records, I see that the leaders, having started on Sunday afternoon, finished in the early hours of Tuesday. Most of the small class were in by breakfast time before the visibility got too bad. We eventually finished 36 hours later – but it seemed much more – and we still weren't placed last.

There was some drying out to be done on board, and stores to be replenished. Roy bought a large roll of sticking plaster from the chemists and strapped my rib cage until I resembled an Egyptian mummy. I had to keep it on for three weeks, and it was a major job eventually getting it off again.

We cleared all the sails out of the forecastle onto the deck so that Bill and Teddy could have it as 'married quarters'. Teddy went to the fish market for a selection of goodies, and gave Wilfred a rest while she prepared a marvellous seafood chowder.

After all we had been through we were determined to get some relaxation while we were in Brittany. We purchased a Brittany courtesy flag to fly from the spreaders while we went to explore the Gulf of Morbihan. This is an inland sea like a miniature Baltic – it is only about 20 kilometres across but is reputed to contain 365 islands (or so the Romans said when they discovered it), some big enough to have a village and a ferry to the mainland, while many just have a farm, and some support only a pine tree.

The entrance from Quiberon Bay is narrow and rockbound, and with a 30 foot rise and fall, the tide goes through at about nine knots. We could feel 'Zeelust' going downhill while we motored at full throttle to keep steerage way as we were carried through the entrance. Once inside it was quite peaceful, with children's sailing clubs, and a few traditional craft carrying their Brittany ensigns.

The Bretons consider themselves separate from France, so when we closed on one we dipped our blue ensign and toasted them with 'Vive la Bretagne'. They responded with a dip, a raised bottle of wine and 'Vive la Grande Bretagne'.

Back in the Bay we landed on Ile Hoedic, one of the small islands. There we found a Napoleonic fortress, and a more recent and very rusty German gun – put there against the English.

Eventually Teddy left us to make her way back to England, and we set off round the coast. It's a waste of time trying to buck the French tide around a headland if there is not much wind, so we put into Audierne and anchored until the tide turned. Further on we entered the Rade de Brest and went ashore at Camaret to fill up with diesel; we also bought a 25 litre plastic jerrycan full, and were glad of it later. We were saddened to see several large wooden fishing boats rotting on the beach, but it is only a repeat of the scene at Lowestoft, where Lake Lothing used to be full of abandoned sailing trawlers.

We left at dusk to take the night tide through the inshore channel, rather than the Chenal du Four which is the main shipping channel between Ushant and the mainland. Although a relatively minor passage, with rocks everywhere, it is very well lit and visibility was good with clear starlight. We then emerged into the English Channel in dense fog. Being a very busy corner, there were ships hooting all around us. We felt very naked with no radar reflector, so we set to and made one – basically a cardboard tray which had held Carlsberg larger, cut into four corners turned so that all the points came together to give the effect of the three planes crossed at right angles, securely stitched with a sail needle. Then we covered it with kitchen foil and it looked like a professional reflector. We hoisted it to the spreaders and the next invisible steamer was hooting at a greater distance.

We motored the length of the Channel, still in fog with no wind and without seeing land. Once we thought we had sighted Dungeness nuclear power station – a square white affair dimly seen, but while trying to take a running fix on it we discovered it was in fact the superstructure of a large tanker, miles from land.

Eventually, with the fog thinning somewhat, we found Dover and we set off up the North Sea. We were met with a stiff breeze across the Thames Estuary, arriving in Harwich harbour at about four in the morning. In those far off days, the place to clear customs was Felixstowe dock, so we tied up alongside the 'dummy' used by the ferry, and managed to get a message to the Customs Office to report our arrival. In due course Mr Brown appeared, which was a great relief as he was senior officer and very helpful. Chris greeted him with: 'I hope you've got your testing equipment, because we are importing some wine.' He had not brought his testing gear and did not want to go all the way back, so said he would inspect what we had got before deciding if he needed to measure its gravity. We pulled up the mattresses in the quarter berths and revealed our carboys of wine, which had survived unscathed (but we had drunk all the bottles and the brandy). 'I see,' he said, and wrote down on his inspection form, 'Six bottles of wine.'

The sailmakers logo

TODAY THE BOATS would probably not survive a trip such as that and certainly the crew would not have been able to rest and feed as well with the limited facilities on modern race boats. Also, I suspect the Customs may not have been so generous.

Early on, Austin had joined the Association of British Sailmakers, having already been a member of the Ship and Boatbuilders Federation to which the ABS was affiliated. He did his term as President when the time came (it was not a choice) and in 1993 the ABS honoured him with a presentation in 'Recognition of his contribution and years of service to sailmaking and the marine industry'. This was presented at their annual dinner but, as Austin says, having to speak as guest of honour rather spoils the meal with nervous anticipation of the speech to come.

CHAPTER 7
POST WAR DINGHY SAILING, THE OLYMPICS, THE IYRU AND THE LITTLE AMERICA'S CUP

A USTIN'S REPUTATION AS a good crew prompted Tom Thornycroft to ask him to crew for him in the 1946 Prince of Wales Cup in Torbay, the trophy he had won in 1930, and this subsequently led Austin to be involved with Tom Thornycroft's Olympic sailing in 1947 and 1948. Tom Thornycroft had sailed Fourteens since the very early days in the 1920s, always designing his own boats, although they were built for him by Uffa Fox until 1934 when, short of time, he took a stock boat from Uffa Fox, No 325 'GYRINUS'. He was still sailing this boat in 1946 and eventually gave it to Austin, who subsequently left the boat to the National Maritime Museum at Greenwich as part of the National Small Boat Collection. This collection is now part of the National Maritime Museum Cornwall.

AUSTIN WROTE OF sailing 'GYRINUS' in an article in 1991:

"The fourteen Foot Internationals turned out with 59 boats – their best ever – for the first post war Prince of Wales week (POW) at Brixham. Peter Scott and John Winter were sailing 'THUNDER & LIGHTNING' again, and they won the cup again, while Charles Currey had been lent 'THUNDER' and was crewed by Phil Gick. I went as spare crew and transporter, as Charles's Morris Eight had blown up and was in bits, so we hitched 'THUNDER' behind 'Bumble', my ancient Bentley, and trailed her down to Brixham. We had booked in to stay at a crowded bungalow but it turned out to be rather squalid and Peter Scott insisted that we move up to the Lupton Hotel – formerly the home of Lord Churston and very grand, with a statue of him in the hall.

Mrs Richardson (14. K421 'HAPPY RETURN' and known in the class as Aunt Phyllis) had booked most of the hotel for her friends and she said, 'You can come and stay at my hotel, and you, but not you – you're too noisy!' We had a long table down the middle of the dining room and the residents were rather pushed into a corner.

Also at Brixham was Tom Thornycroft with 14. K325 'GYRINUS'. He was living aboard his big motor boat 'KING DUCK' but without a crew, so I crewed with Tom, which was a wonderful experience. Tom had bought back the 77 foot 'KING DUCK' from the Army after the war (she had of course been requisitioned.) She was still in her wartime camouflage and had been re-engined. Instead of her original pair of 75HP diesels, which gave her 12½ knots (though her model had been tank tested to 30 knots), she now sported a pair of Hall Scott petrol engines of 300HP each which gave her 23 knots. Unfortunately, only one of the engines would work, but this gave her about 15 knots and the tanks were full with 800 gallons of aviation spirit which lasted her for the season, after which she was given diesels again.

'GYRINUS' was designed and built by Uffa Fox in 1934. Tom Thornycroft had designed four earlier Fourteens for himself, the earliest being 'GARGANY' in 1927. He had nearly won the POW in 1929 with 'PINTAIL', but was piped by Uffa in 'DARING' when he was half filled with water at the last gybe. He did win, though, in 1930 with 'GOLDEN EYE'. In 1934 Tom was too busy with other things to design himself a new boat so he had one of Uffa's standard ones – not unlike Stewart Morris's 'R.I.P.' – which was very flat in the floor and a splendid planing boat.

In 1946 'GYRINUS' had hardly been in the water in the last 12 years and Tom was 65. He felt he could not hold up the whole rig so had cut two feet off the masthead, and we sailed with a permanent reef in the mainsail. But 'GYRINUS' had been re-measured with a six foot spinnaker pole to get some of the rating back with a penalty J-measurement, and it fairly helped the spinnaker on a reach. (This could have been a look into the future – modern asymmetric spinnakers!) We spent the early part of the week getting used to each other and wishing we had the full rig in the light winds. In the POW race on Thursday, Tom made a perfect start, as shown by the press photo from the committee boat, but we could not hold our place and finished about fourteenth.

That evening there was a dinner party at the hotel perched on the cliffs above Brixham. After dinner, from the terrace outside, we looked across the bay and above Torquay we saw a fantastic display of the Aurora Borealis – said to be the best this century, which astronomers are still talking about.

On the Friday there was a race off Babbacombe, round the corner to the North of Torbay, where I had memories of racing 12-Metres in a gale. We went round from Brixham in convoy, 'KING DUCK' carrying two boats and towing several more, while Ralph Farrant with his spritsail barge, 'JAMES PIPER', towed a lot more of the fleet.

Babbacombe has a tiny bay under a 400 foot cliff, and the wind tends to come down in vertical squalls. 'THUNDER & LIGHTNING' found one of these squalls and capsized before the start but was righted again in time. Starting inshore, the course was a triangle out into the open sea, where the wind was steadier and quite strong. 'GYRINUS' revelled in it. She was so stable that, while planing with the spinnaker set on the broad reach, I was able to walk up forward to fetch the bailer. We won the race and a splendid cup.

POW winners 1946 with the Mayor of Hunstanton and Austin, back row, second from left

The finish was accompanied by a

thunder storm with torrential rain, but it was lit up by the sun shining under the storm cloud with a golden glow, turning the huge drops of rain splashing into the water around us into little golden waterspouts. As we sat in our boats, waiting for the rain and the rest of the fleet to finish, I called out to Peter Scott in 'THUNDER & LIGHTNING', 'What a scene, Peter – it ought to make a splendid picture.'

He replied, 'It's no use making a painting of it. No-one would believe it.'

K396 is TAIYARA with K407 DEVELIN owned by Stuart Morris

From the Fourteen it was a natural step to crew for Tom in the 'SWALLOW', the new two man Keelboat designed by Tom Thornycroft for the Olympics. In 1946 the Yacht Racing Association announced that a small keel boat was to be introduced, and the IYRU decided at their November meeting to adopt it as an international class for the 1948 Olympic Games. The initial idea was to replace the 'DRAGON', but a storm of protest allowed their reprieve and continuance in the games until 1972. Fourteen designers were invited to submit designs, the only requirements being for a two man boat with 200 sq ft of measured sail area, capable of being sailed single handed with a permanent backstay and no runners, and also economical to build. In the event, only four designs were submitted from Morgan Giles, Tom Thornycroft, Uffa Fox and Robert Clark – all having built boats at their own expense for the trials off Cowes in early December.

Two days of light weather and one of heavy, with the boats sailing against the stop watch so as not to take each others wind, provided the committee with the information to make a choice. The trials should have continued but an onshore gale halted the proceedings and two boats were damaged on their moorings by other yachts going adrift. Tom Thornycroft's 'TOUCAN TOO' was voted the fastest all-round performer and the most responsive to sail. By this time the class rules had been formulated and the design published so that the 'Swallow' class, as it would be called, could be built in other countries. 'TOUCAN TOO' (built by Uffa Fox) was found not to measure. Tom had decided to take part in the Olympic selection trials and therefore needed a new boat. He ordered a batch of three from Morgan Giles – 'ADVICE' for himself, 'SCAUP' for his two sons to share and 'SYMPHONY' for a friend. Tom was already an Olympic Gold Medallist – but this went back to

Pinching a 14 around the Weir Buoy on Chichester Harbour

Tom Thorneycroft

1908 when the Olympics were previously held in England and when motor boat racing had been an Olympic sport. He had designed and built his own boat, designed and built his own engine, and then raced it into first place. The boat, of which he had a photograph in the saloon of his big motor boat 'KING DUCK', was called 'GYRINUS', which is appropriately the name of a small beetle 'which when aroused proceeds in small circles emitting a noxious odour'.

During the early part of 1948, Austin and Tom would visit Morgan Giles's yard at Teignmouth in 'KING DUCK' to see how the Swallows were getting on. Two weekends were spent this way, with an early departure from the moorings in Hamble on Saturday and arriving in Teignmouth at teatime, spending the night on board and returning Sunday afternoon. 'King Duck's' compass had not been re-swung after the new diesels had been installed and she had a southerly bias on an easterly course, although correct when heading west. On the first return trip they nearly missed the Isle of Wight. The second time, they gave her 10 degrees of northing, aiming the see Portland Bill ahead. The wind was rising to a south-westerly gale and there was quite a nasty following sea. After running the distance, there was no sign of the Bill when suddenly they spotted it through the murk about half a mile on the port beam – they were heading straight into the race. Tom spun the wheel and they made off towards the Bill, skirting the race, and with the throttles set for 13 knots, she surfed down waves at over 17 knots. The boat was fantastic, never trying to broach and they dashed past the Bill to shelter in Weymouth for the night, carrying on the next morning when the winds and seas had moderated.

The Olympic selection trials for the Swallow class were to be held in Torbay on the same course as would be used for the games. After a trial sail, the boat was collected from Teignmouth and towed on 'KING DUCK'S' stern wave, at 13 knots, to Brixham.

KING DUCK and the Star Class

The Swallow course was closer to Brixham than Torquay and Tom decided to base himself there to avoid the turmoil on the other side of the bay.

The selection trials were quite hard work with the Swallow as a two man boat – they are sailed today with a crew of three. The spinnaker is large and can be difficult to hoist and recover.

Austin and Tom had adopted the dinghy practice of setting from a bag to leeward and taking it down in the lee of the mainsail. However, if it was to be reset on a different gybe, it would mean sending the halyard round the forestay with the sheets to be the right side for hoisting again. For setting, Austin would start the hoist and then hand the halyard back to Tom, who would steer standing with the tiller between his legs to have both hands free. Austin would fix the pole, cleat the guy and trim the sheet while Tom cleated the halyard at his end.

David Bond transferring a spare sail from Swift

TORBAY HAS A reputation for fluky conditions and Austin's pre-war experience in 12-Metres and dinghies was most valuable. Most of the 'flukes' are in fact predictable and obey natural laws – such as the way the wind tends to come off the land at right angles to the shore – so if the windward mark has been laid off a headland, two winds will tend to converge at the mark. Not everyone understands these things, even today, and previous experience is very valuable. Whatever the experience, the bay can throw up some very unpredictable occurrences. Austin remembered returning towards Brixham after one race with the spinnaker set, only to see two Dragons sailing towards them, both with spinnakers set and about a hundred yards apart. Austin and Tom actually sailed between the two Dragons and none of the spinnakers collapsed.

Their principal opponent was Stewart Morris in 'SWIFT', and he was selected by a narrow margin. The margin would have been even narrower had Austin and Tom not tried a different mast in the middle of the trials. It did not help and cost them several points. For the games themselves, Austin was nominated reserve crew, in the case of Stewart's regular crew, David Bond, falling ill. 'ADVICE' was loaned to the Canadian team and Austin and Tom promoted to Judges with 'King Duck' on the Star/Swallow course. Judging involved also helping with the measurement of the other classes before the racing started and so they were kept busy. The Canadian Swallow crew were a pair of teenage dinghy sailors who had never been in a keelboat or set a spinnaker in their lives – but were keen to learn. Tom and Austin took turns as instructors and the lads worked very hard, eventually managing two seconds and finishing seventh in a

Spinnaker measurement at Torquay

Fireflies launching at Woolverstone

fleet of fourteen.

They were also able to help Stewart Morris who, whilst doing his own tuning, needed support with spare sails which were kept aboard 'King Duck'. He looked the most promising for a gold medal, with the Portuguese – sailing another of Tom Thornycroft's boats – the main threat with three first places. Stewart had two firsts, but never fell below fourth except for a DNF (Did Not Finish) which he could discard. The Portuguese had more total points and had to discard a fifth place, allowing Stewart to beat him by just a few points. The last race was very tight with Portugal leading and Stewart in fifth place needing to finish fourth or better to beat them on points overall. His chance came on the last reach when, with the others all going along at maximum displacement speed, Stewart picked up a local squall, lifting 'Swift' onto the plane and hurtled past Brazil in fourth place at seemingly twice her speed just before the leeward mark. He then covered Brazil up the last beat to the finish, and took the gold medal.

They saw a little of the Firefly course – the single handed class – where the youthful Paul Elvstrøm from Denmark was winning his first gold, and some of the racing of the Six Metres and Dragons who were out in the mouth of the bay where they had the full benefit of the wind when it blew and the flukes when it did not. Light, fluky winds can be very frustrating, but the wind can be seen as cats' paws on the surface, particularly from a height. One of the Six Metres always seemed to know where to find the wind - until a man with a walkie talkie was discovered 400ft up on Daddyhole Plain from where he could see most of the bay. Although behaviour was probably more gentlemanly than today, there are always some people who will try to take advantage.

For the 1952 Olympics, Charles Currey was representing Britain in the Finn Class in Helsinki and therefore Austin crewed for Sam Waters in 'Warrigal' for the POW - finishing second. Austin was still sailing for pleasure during the late 1940s and early 1950s - despite the demands on time made from the shipyard - at the Royal Harwich Y.C. racing the 'Swordfish' to try and support this new class - this was the boat shared with his solicitor, a distant cousin. It was the perfect arrangement; he owned it and Austin mostly sailed it. Whenever possible Austin also used to slip off to Itchenor to do the club racing in Fourteens, driving through the night across the centre of London in the Bentley. His usual helm was Charles Currey.

In the early 1950s it became apparent that a replacement for the ageing 12 sq metre Sharpie was needed for the two man Olympic boat, and trials would have to be set up. These trials would establish a new two man centreboard class for International status. The new class would almost certainly be used for the Olympics in 1960, the 1956 classes having already been set and keeping the '12 sq metre Sharpie' as the two man centreboard boat. The need for a new design had been recognised and initially the IYRU had asked Uffa Fox to design a new two man boat. Uffa was not keen to design a hard chine boat, being more used to round bilge designs. However, he was persuaded to draw a new design, and came up with a light plywood sharpie as requested. Unfortunately, it was not at all successful and a very poor boat. The design was called the 'TYPHOON' and very few were built.

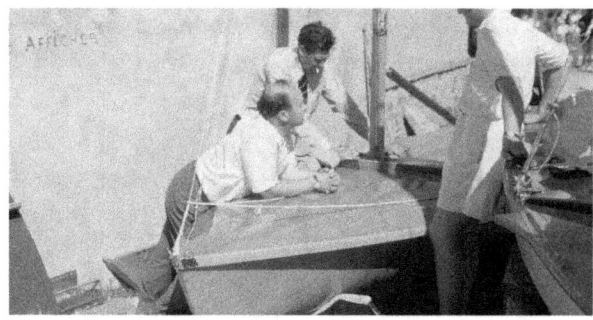

Peter Scott discussing Coronet at La Baule

The first gathering of boats took place at Loosdrecht Lake and the Ijsselmeer in Holland in 1952. Sixteen boats of different designs, from seven countries, attended and the 'FLYING DUTCHMAN' from Holland, the 'HORNET' (designed by Jack Holt) and the 'OSPREY' (designed by Ian Proctor), both from the UK, were among those boats that showed promise. The Hornet had a sliding seat but all the other boats were hiked normally. The FD seemed best in the lake conditions whilst the Osprey had an edge on open water. This questioned the FD's all round performance and further unofficial trials were scheduled for the autumn in Chichester Harbour. Austin was asked to meet the Hook of Holland ferry at Parkstone Quay near Harwich and tow the boat down overnight to Itchenor, having grabbed a quick meal in Colchester. The boat docked around 7 p.m. and so, with Austin towing and two Dutchmen with him in a Mini, they all eventually arrived at Charles Currey's house at about 2 a.m. The trip had meant Austin organising a 50mm tow ball as things were not at that time standardised and across London the route required a diversion down the Mall as they wanted to see Buckingham Palace.

Trapezes were now starting to be used and the boats were developed at every outing. Apart from the FD, most of the boats were from the UK so it was not a totally fair comparison, but similar results to the first trial were obtained. Because of this, another set of official IYRU trials were arranged for August 1953 at La Baule in France. These were organised by the French sailing federation, the FFV, and the trialists were put up in great luxury at the huge Hermitage Hotel or in private houses. Several interesting new designs now appeared including John Westall's 18ft 'Coronet',

Cornette's spray deflectors in action

Lifting in Stars at Torquay Olympics

Uffa Fox's 18ft 'Jolly Boat' and Claude Nethercot's 17ft 'Marianne', round bilged and with a sliding seat. There were other boats there including Jack Blundell with 'Thunderbolt' – Austin's design. It has to be said, however, that some competitors were there more for a splendid sailing holiday than with any hope of being selected as a new Olympic Class. As usual, politics were just below the surface.

The Dutch, who were and still are strong 12 sq metre Sharpie sailors, had been working on a new design for some time under the leadership of Conrad Gulcher. The 'Flying Dutchman' probably started life as a keel-less Flying Fifteen with International Fourteen influences drawn on a tablecloth by a group of sailors at the 1950 Olympic Classes championship in Holland. This group included Shorty Trimingham from Bermuda and Charles Currey, both great Fourteen sailors. The tablecloth reputedly found its way, with Conrad Gulcher, to the designer U. Van Essen who flattened it a bit more, pulled the heel of the stem forward to give less overhang and a hollow waterline ending, and the design had a character of its own which became the beautiful boat it is today. Meanwhile, the French were looking for a replacement for their 'Caneton' class. The IYRU still supposedly wanted a sharpie although none were at the trials.

Austin crewed for Charles Currey in a souped up International Fourteen called 'Fleetwing'. Fairey Marine had produced a standard hull, but decked and with a self draining cockpit – one trapeze and a larger genoa. Determined to uphold the honour of the Fourteen class, they quite often led at the windward mark, but downwind the longer boats would pass them. The course was basically an Olympic triangle, but after the first day, by popular request, a beam reach was included. This was a reach across the course and back at the gybe mark between the two broad reaches – here the Flying Dutchman and the Coronet could really perform. Strangely, enough local knowledge helped even though they had never sailed there before.

Austin and Charles were used to racing in Torbay and on arriving in La Baule they discovered that the bay there was the same shape and orientation as Torbay with the harbour and beach in a corner equivalent to Brixham. With a tidal range of 30 feet the whole bay dries out to hard sand and sailing was only possible for about three hours either side of high water. They applied Torbay techniques and found that they worked well. They named the various parts of La Baule Bay the same as those of Torbay to ensure that they knew which way to go. Comments would follow along the lines of, 'Let's take a tack in towards Paignton.' It would have made an interesting recording in the middle of France. Sailing in La Baule was a pleasure, with the water so clear that crabs could be seen on the sandy bottom. After the standard open Fourteens, sailing a decked self draining version with a trapeze was a joy and one which the class itself would not allow for many years. They had one strange encounter when, on a screaming reach in relatively deep water, they were suddenly brought up all standing with Austin very nearly flying round the forestay on the trapeze. Thinking that they must have snared a fishing net, they were rather surprised to find that they had ploughed into a giant jellyfish with the centreboard.

John Westall had designed the 'CORONET' which was similar to a modern 505 but some 18ft 6ins long and with more angular flared topsides. The French liked this boat very much and asked John Westall if he would do a slightly smaller version for their Caneton replacement. Austin's Fourteen design 'THUNDERBOLT' was there, although with Jack Blundall steering she spent much of her time capsized. Shortly afterwards Austin received a call from John Westall asking that now Austin could not use his flared topsides on his Fourteens, could he use them on his new design. Austin was more than happy for them to 'have a good home' and the new design was born to become the highly successful 'INTERNATIONAL 505'. It shows John Westall's talent that the 505 is as modern looking today as it has ever been.

John Westall was not a full time naval architect and designed very few boats over the years. He worked as a journalist and was on the staff of Yachts and Yachting. Austin had first met John sailing with his crew around the coast in an ancient Fourteen to get to a POW in North Norfolk. They had started from Devon and were camping on beaches at night. They put into Woolverstone on the way up with time running short. Austin realised that they would never make the regatta and put their boat on his trailer and took them there himself.

IN TOTAL THERE were at La Baule eight UK boats, seven French, two Dutch and one Italian. All the main contenders had sliding seats or trapezes and the two Flying Dutchmans had new lightweight hulls and much bigger genoas than previously. The races were supposed to be pure trials, with no inter-boat tactics, but that was a very naive requirement. The two FD's sailed as a team (why else would there be two of them?). But the two French 'CANETON's' seemed to be precisely the opposite of a team and the bitter rivalry of the season came to a head at La Baule. At the weather mark, after an untranslatable shouting match, the crew of one boat leapt into the other and physically punched home his points.

The FD's, Coronet and Osprey each won races at La Baule and a contemporary report said – 'Taken all round, there was little to choose in performance between the Flying Dutchman, Coronet and Osprey, though the two larger boats had the slight edge over Osprey to windward. The FD's planing in a strong wind was impressive, but the Coronet appeared easier in a seaway and Osprey was fastest on the runs.' Various people tried each others' boats and the FD eventually succeeded though, like the Osprey, which was subsequently modified to encourage home building, the FD needed strengthening before production as after the trials some 50% of her very light side deck beams had broken.

Austin's involvement with the YRA and IYRU during the 1948 Olympics led to him becoming a measurer for several classes including the Dragon. Austin measured all the Dragons built by Ernie Nunn at Waldringfield in Suffolk and they were very good boats. The first one, however, was nearly a disaster. Ernie Nunn had built the boat during the autumn and winter, taken the moulds out and started the fitting out of the other boats in the yard for the new season. He did not get back to the Dragon until all the other boats were afloat. By this time it had changed shape by inches and although the deck was sprung into place, when Austin came to measure the boat it would never be a legal Dragon.

Ernie Nunn was nearly in tears and Austin desperately tried to work out what they could do to salvage the situation. Eventually the deck was taken off and all the timbers removed. The moulds were then forced back into place and the hull re-timbered. With the hull well braced the deck was refitted and Austin was able to re-measure the boat. It measured – just. A measurer should always try to help and make the boat measure if he legally can. Too many measurers are less than helpful. The last Dragon that Ernie Nunn built was to be a real beauty. Most of the boats had been built with fairly heavy mahogany but this one was to be built with Honduras Mahogany. Austin checked the boat before she left the shed and it was spot on.

All that remained was to weigh her. They used to borrow some hydraulic scales from Ransome & Rapier – the Crane builders in Ipswich – which were all certified. When Austin arrived, the boat was hanging from the scales in the yard. 'Spot on she is,' called Ernie Nunn but, when Austin went to check the reading, the boat was two pounds under weight. This was a little puzzling and Austin went into the shed to check something. When he came out a little while later the boat was now four pounds underweight. Another two hours and she was six pounds underweight. A bright spring morning and a warm breeze was slowly drying the boat out as she hung on the scales, having been there since first thing.

A boat must be weighed dry so Austin worked back to the time the boat left the building shed when the weight had to be recorded and calculated that she was just over the minimum weight with maximum corrector weights allowed and therefore fully legal. The rules for the Dragon class were being progressively tightened and every boat that Austin measured required more figures or a new template. Towards the end of the season Austin received a call from the owner asking if he would check the boat over and re-weigh her as it was assumed that she must have taken up a little water and some of the corrector weights could be removed. The corrector weights in a Dragon were to be placed in little wooden boxes just inside the cabin on either side.

Austin duly arrived, having collected the scales on the way, and on examining the boat found that these boxes contained a pair of binoculars one side and some other bits the other. He eventually found the corrector weights down in the heel of the bilge. Not at all legal, but she had taken up enough weight to remove all the corrector weights, although Austin never found out what the owner was thinking.

The measuring continued with being appointed official IYRU measurer for the combined Flying Dutchman World Championships and FD Week at Whitstable in 1959. The World Championship was decided on one boat per country, but the Week was an open event. This would be a very interesting championship, being the Pre-Olympic year. The club at Whitstable had worked hard to make the event a success, organising accommodation and entertainment for the many overseas competitors. Austin got to know several of these and it offered an insight into how various nationalities travel and their expectations. There were fifteen entries in the World championships from as far afield as Sweden and South Africa and twenty eight entered in the Week including several from Britain.

Austin's duties began with the check measurement of sails, the validity of measurement certificates, and the measurement of new sails not already entered on the certificate. Competitors arrived during this pre-race session, and Austin remembers a call in English asking for help in unloading boats. It turned out to be the interpreter for the Russian team – a sixteen year old schoolboy who spoke perfect colloquial English without a trace of an accent, although he had never been out of Russia before. The team of five had driven from Moscow in a Volkswagen van, sleeping in the van with one boat on a trailer and the other on the van roof.

The team manager arrived by air and turned out to be a friend of Austin's, Ordzonikidze, a Dragon sailor and grandson of the admiral after whom the notorious cruiser was named. He had been the Russian delegate at the IYRU conference for several years. The main difference, however, was that while at the conference he communicated through a lady interpreter who was evidently the political commissar. In Whitstable he communicated with everyone, speaking very passable English. Austin spent some time with both of them, asking the young interpreter how he had become involved, since he was a footballer and not a sailor. It turned out that an advert had appeared on the school notice board asking for someone to go to England as interpreter. He put his name down, although he came in for some ribbing with claims that the English would not talk to him and would be very horrid. He was pleased to find that this was not the case. The one thing that no one could convince the Russians was that Whitstable had not been spruced up and the shops filled with desirable goods especially to impress them. They spent some of their allowance on sweaters and jeans.

The racing was very good with fine weather most days and only one blow. Because of the tidal nature of the venue, the start times had to move an hour each day, but it could still be a long walk, with the boat on a trolley, to the water's edge. The world Championships were won by Mario Capio from Italy, with 'Adrian Jardine' crewed by Angus Fryer in second place for Great Britain. Third place went to Rolf Mulka, who also subsequently took the bronze at Naples the following year. 'Slotty' Dawes of Whitstable was selected to represent Great Britain in Naples, where he was to have problems with Mario Capio.

After hard racing, entertainment ashore is important at any major event, and at Whitstable included a Grand International Football Match which seemed to be Europe versus the rest, with four balls on the field at the same time. Finally the crews' race, where the crew steered, was sailed in Cadet dinghies designed for youngsters up to the age of seventeen. This would have been amusing enough, but for the added excitement of a Le Mans start and a falling tide, which required pushing or carrying the boats around certain marks. A good time was had by all.

Having been a measurer and judge at the 1948 Olympics, in early 1960 Austin was honoured to be asked by the IYRU to be part of the measurement Committee for the 1960 Olympics in Naples – for which he was given a tie and a beautiful badge. This committee did not have to do the actual measuring, only oversee the whole procedure, and consisted of the chairman Artù Chiggiatu, a naval architect from Venice, James McGruer, a naval architect from the Clyde and Austin as IYRU technical delegate. The committee was in frequent touch with the International Jury via their secretary general, Bruno Bianchi, and sometimes joined their meetings for technical support.

There were about thirty Italian measurers working under them to do the actual measurement, and they were allotted to the five classes in the three different yacht club harbours which were the sailing bases. The measurement Committee moved around from one to the other each morning, paying a routine visit to see if there were any problems. They usually travelled on foot or in Artù's car, having politely declined the use of the Vespa scooters allocated to them, after seeing the way Neapolitan traffic was conducted. There was often something to sort out in the various classes in conjunction with the International Jury. Artù's yacht club in Venice had reciprocal arrangements with the YC Canotteri Savoia in the Santa Lucia yacht harbour where the Dragons were kept, so the committee usually lunched at the club, guided through the menu by the chairman. He also guided them through the menu at the Hotel Vesuvio where they were staying, and where they dined by candlelight in the roof restaurant overlooking the lights of the bay of Naples. During the month they were there, never once were they served spaghetti.

The 5.5 Metre class had a query with one boat where, whatever they did, the numbers would not add up. The rule is a formula of length, displacement and sail area, all being interactive – a longer, heavier boat has to have less sail area and visa versa. The boat was placed in the floatation tank and really did not look right. It was long but light on displacement and adding more ballast just made it longer still. Austin dryly remarked to his colleagues, 'There seems to be something wrong with the displacement. Do you think we ought to get Archimedes on the job? He used to live around here.' Bruno Bianchi replied, 'What a good idea. I wonder what his number is on the Elysian Fields.' (Elysian was the abode of the blessed after death in Greek myths). They then discovered that the Elysian Field was actually a telephone district on the outskirts of Naples. Unfortunately, this did not help the boat, which required major correction before it could be allowed to race.

The Dragon Class also had its problems with the Australian Dragon failing its measurement completely and causing a lot of problems. It apparently had a valid measurement certificate but, when checked, some of the measurements did not agree with the drawings. Austin worked his way thorough the scantlings, which had been adjusted for Australian timbers of unknown weights, and found that the gunwale construction bore no resemblance to the specification. The most blatant error was at the stern, and the committee could only conclude that the original measurer was either half blind or was measuring in a shed so small that he could not get round the back of the boat. The rules required the transom to be flat and basically more or less rectangular. This one was semi-circular, making it look more like that of a 5.5 Metre. The committee and Jury met and decided – The Australian Dragon 'Ghost III' is not a Dragon and never has been. She is therefore ineligible to compete in the Olympic Regatta. The Substitution of 'Gabbiano' was approved'. The covering letter to the Australian team manager included: 'The Jury reached this decision with reluctance, bearing in mind the great distance you have brought the boat, but they have ruled that she is not and never has been a Dragon.

They were therefore left with no alternative. They have, however, accepted the substitution for 'Ghost III' of the Dragon 'Gabbiano', kindly lent by a local owner, and have granted you permission to race with this boat......'. This substitution caused a bizarre problem in the first race. The Australian crew took the new boat with their own sails for the first race, only to find they had been disqualified on their return for leaving out a turning mark. The crew protested that they had rounded all the marks and finished eighth. It then transpired that the support crew had taken out 'Ghost' to watch the racing, and – incredible as it may sound – had sailed in among the competing boats on the course to get a good view. The course marshals would not expect two boats with the same sail number and did not see both at once. When they saw one apparently leaving out a turning mark they reported it. Disqualification was automatic and the real one was not timed in at the finish. The protest hearing that evening was very dramatic, but eventually the truth came out. With a severe reprimand to the Australian team, their boat was reinstated in eighth place.

Another clever Dragon builder had tried to fair the back end of the keel into the rudder with a little bit of extra casting grown on. The Committee gave him a hacksaw and a couple of blades and told him to saw it off. It took him all day.

Whilst most of the measurement problems were caused by carelessness or ignorance of the rules, some sailors will still try to gain advantage by various methods – and get away with it. One class with potential problems was the Finn class single handed dinghies. The Committee had an inspection of all the sails from the Finn class after practice and before racing to check that no one had tampered with them. All the equipment for the Finn class was supplied by the organisers and the committee went over each sail with a magnifying glass to check the sails had not been re-cut. Everyone was there to see Paul Elvstrøm's sail checked as, with three Gold medals – the first in 1948, aged eighteen – he was notorious by this time. His sail was fine but he was complaining bitterly about his mast which he claimed was far too bendy and floppy like macaroni. He was asked what he expected in Italy although the joke was not appreciated.

The Belgian was then complaining that his mast was too stiff, just like a telegraph pole. He couldn't sail with it. The Committee considered swapping the two masts over, but first took both masts into the shed – without the sailors – and hung weights on them to compare the two along with at least half a dozen others. The masts were identical. They told the two sailors this but Elvstrøm still claimed his would break.

They were both told that they were the masts and that was the end of it. Shortly afterwards Elvstrøm set off for a practice sail and to try to break his mast. He sailed around the coast out of sight but did not realise that the motor yacht a little way off contained three members of the International Jury quietly keeping an eye on him through binoculars. They observed Elvstrøm trying desperately to break his mast by pulling on the mainsheet, jumping up and down and kicking it. He did not break the mast but did break the boom. He was allowed another one with a stern warning. It all seems slightly pointless as the mast still allowed him to win his fourth Gold Medal, a feat that stood unbeaten in sailing until 2012, when Ben Ainslie won his fourth Gold Medal, also in the Finn, and fifth in total. Whilst in Naples, Austin wrote and narrated the script for a film of the event. Unfortunately, although several copies were sold around the world shortly after the event, the finished master was lost when the company went bankrupt and no copies are at present known. Austin was unable to get the master returned from the receivers so there is a possibility that it still exists somewhere, locked away with no knowledge of what it is.

THE SELECTION OF sailors for the British team has not been our strong point. In 1948, for the single-handed class, the position went to Commodore MacDonald who, whilst a competent National Twelve sailor, was not very good single-handed in the Firefly. He was too old to be competitive in the Olympics, particularly against the likes of the eighteen year old Elvstrøm. Charles Currey was the team manager and in the last race it was blowing like hell. With a reefed sail it was not possible to use the kicking strap, so Charles stabbed through three or four rolls of sail with his knife and fixed in the kicking strap lug. He was sent out with the instructions that now you're reefed so stay reefed. On the way out to the start he decided that the wind had eased and so shook out the reefs. On arriving at the race area he decided that perhaps the wind had not eased and put them back in again, only afloat he could not locate the kicking strap lug and therefore could not use the kicking strap. Without it the sail was next to useless.

Some years later we again chose someone who was too old to be competitive and to take the pressure of top Olympic competition. 'Slotty' Dawes had been selected for the 1960 Olympics in Naples and, although a good Flying Dutchman sailor, he was not as proficient as the Jardine brothers. It was pressure that finally finished 'Slotty' in Naples. After the first race he protested the Italian boat for missing out a mark. This protest he duly won but from then on the Italian had it in for him. Every race after that the Italian protested 'Slotty', ensuring late nights in the protest room. The Italian was not worried about the result of the hearing and expected to lose all the protests.

THAI, SWIFT and JUMPAHEAD **catamarans at Thorpe Bay**

He was therefore relaxed and slept in the waiting room. 'Slotty' could not relax and spent each evening late into the night under great pressure and tension in the waiting room. The Jardines would have coped much better under this pressure.

Austin was again involved with trials in the early 1970s, for an Olympic multihull, this time being part of a design. There were entries from several countries including the USA, Australia and Great Britain. They were held at the Catamaran Yacht Club on the Isle of Sheppey. Britain had several designs including the 'THAI IV', the 'SHEARWATER III' and two 'TORNADOS', one with a sloop rig and one with a Una rig. The 'TORNADO' was designed by Rodney Marsh as commission for Reg White and followed on from the prestige of 'LADY HELMSMAN' and had a Una wing rig scaled down from 'LADY H'. ('LADY HELMSMAN' was a very successful boat in the 'Little America's Cup' and will be dealt with later).

One evening Austin received a phone call from Reg asking his opinion of the rig for the 'Tornado', bearing in mind it was to be used for one-design fleet racing, not match racing as in the 'Little America's Cup'. Austin said that he thought it was unsuitable for that use in that the crew would generally have nothing to do and it was supposed to be a two man boat. A fully up-dated sloop rig offered far more potential. Reg asked Austin to design a sloop rig and he would build two boats. Austin duly developed the rig, drawing on his experience from the earlier 'C' Class catamaran, 'Emma Hamilton'. At the trials, the una rig took the lead, but after having missed stays a couple of times the rig fell down from a fitting failure and the sloop rig went on to win the trials, becoming the Olympic class in which Reg won the first Gold Medal in the class in 1976 in Kingston, Canada. Austin never found out whether Rodney Marsh was happy about an alternative rig, but the royalties from the thousands of boats actually built must have softened any objection.

Committee work with the IYRU started around 1950 when Austin was asked to attend the Annual Conference to explain the concepts of cold moulding to be used on the new two man centreboard boat for the Olympics. Austin's expertise was obviously needed and he found himself on the small boat committees as an advisor for some forty years. The committee to which Austin had been summoned was chaired by The Crown Prince Olav of Norway, who took an active interest in the class and had been a helper at the 1948 Olympics. He was a stickler for correctness in meetings and Austin remembers an incident where the Dutch delegate was talking in Dutch to his technical advisor over his shoulder. Olav rapped the table to draw attention, but they did not stop. Olav then addressed them in perfect Dutch and gave them a roasting. He then said, 'Gentlemen, the language of this meeting is English. Shall we continue?' No further trouble. Austin advised the centreboard and multihull committees regularly, and was available for the keelboat and measurement committees. At that time Francis Usborne was at the head of both the IYRU and the YRA and they were run from the same office. At times it was difficult to tell which hat he had on. The Union was fairly small at that time but has grown larger and larger with more and more committees and all the associated politics and paper work that they generate. Austin remained a technical advisor in his own right for many years, with input into many projects

Testing a spinnaker on the 'C' Class wind tunnel model

including the IYRU Measurement Manual. Being independent and not elected by a National Authority meant that he could express his views gained from real life with sailors and not have to express the views of the Authority that elected him. The Union continued to expand and as these changes took place Austin decided that he no longer wished to be involved and the expectation that he would have to pay his own expenses as the meetings moved around the world finalised his decision to resign. Strangely, being involved with the IYRU meant that he had very little connection with the actual committees of the RYA, although he worked as a measurer and had input in various projects.

One of the major developments in small racing craft rigs was the wingsail and, if for nothing else, Austin should be remembered as a world leader and for setting the standards which took others a great deal of time to equal.

The International Catamaran Challenge Trophy, which became better known as the Little America's Cup, was held by Britain for seven years after the first Challenge and Austin played a crucial role in its defence with the development of the sails and rigs.

SINCE LOSING THE cup to Denmark in 1969 we have only made one very unsuccessful challenge and people have forgotten about this trophy.

The trophy grew out of the 'One of a Kind' regattas that were held on both sides of the Atlantic after the war. In the States in 1959 Bob Harris from New York won the series sponsored by the magazine '*Yachting*' with 'TIGERCAT'. The design was widely acclaimed as the finest available. In Britain John Fisk and Rod Macalpine-Downie had won the 'One of a Kind' series sponsored by the RYA with Rod's design Thai Mk IV. Obviously John and Rod felt that theirs was the superior craft and they were confident that the British were more advanced in the catamaran field than any other nation. To settle this point, John Fisk wrote to Bob Harris suggesting that a series of races be instituted between catamarans and intimating that they would be prepared to meet the Americans on their own water for the first match. The idea was met with great enthusiasm and the task of detail was put under way.

The Eastern Multihull Sailing Association of America had accepted the challenge and invited the Sea Cliff Yacht Club to organise the match. It was agreed that the boats were to be limited to 25ft length overall. 14ft beam and 300 square feet sail area. These basic rules, with a few others to ensure sense, were agreed and, apart from one or two minor modifications, control the International 'C' Class Catamarans to this day.

Rod was busy designing the beautiful and advanced design 'Hellcat' and much of 1961 was spent tuning and practising. She was felt to be too lightly built to stand an Atlantic crossing (on board a ship.), so 'HELLCAT II' was built identically but in fibreglass for added strength and shipped to The Sea Cliff Yacht Club on Long Island Sound for the September competition. The Yacht Club's response to everything was magnificent and they donated the highly original International Catamaran Challenge Trophy itself.

The American defender was 'WILDCAT' from San Francisco, designed and built by Sanderson and Hickok, and sailed by John Beery. She was smaller and considerably lighter than 'HELLCAT II' and had been dominant in the American trials. However, 'HELLCAT II's superior windward ability proved too much for 'Wildcat's' downwind speed and the British won four races to one.

EMMA HAMILTON at speed

The Americans were obviously shaken by this setback to their international catamaran fortunes, and immediately made a challenge for a match in Great Britain for September 1962. Chapman Sands Sailing Club accepted the challenge and invited Thorpe Bay Yacht Club to host the event. The Americans were obviously determined, and several new boats were built, with the final choice being 'BEVERLY', a Bob Harris design sailed by Bill Saltonstall and her owner Van Allen Clark Jnr. At first, defenders were a little thin on the ground, particularly as Rod Macalpine-Downie had made a decision not to be represented again by his now comparatively old design 'HELLCAT II' – we believe she was left in the USA – and the fact that he felt he could not design a new boat within the time available. However, A.R. Holloway bought the old 'HELLCAT I', had her refitted and, with Ian Norris and Nick Pope sailing her, Britain again won with four races to one.

'HELLCAT I' again proved superior to windward but had difficulty in holding 'BEVERLY' downwind. The racing was spectacular, silencing any critics, and downwind the boats would reach 30 knots with 'Hellcat I's fine hulls diving in up to the main beam and stopping before surfacing and leaping off again. Fine forward hulls

Emma Hamilton crosses the line to win the 1964 Little America's Cup

could prove difficult to sail, and 'Beverly' had extra buoyancy added forward after she pitch poled on an earlier occasion.

Interest in catamarans was growing worldwide and for 1963 a challenge was received from the Australian Catamaran Association with the Sandringham Yacht Club taking up the challenge. Again, the challengers mounted a concerted effort, selecting their team from five 'C' class catamarans which had been built in Australia. Two boats, 'Quest' and 'Matilda' were eventually shipped to England to finish tuning and selection on the race waters off Thorpe Bay. To defend, Bertie Holloway had commissioned Rod Macalpine-Downie to design 'Hellcat III', to be built by Sailcraft and, though many plans were made, no other boats were built until a late attempt by John Fisk with 'Boadicea'. This boat was developed quickly and won some late racing in England including the trial race week when 'Hellcat IIIS' suffered damage.

'Hellcat I' had unfortunately been badly damaged in an accident (she was later re-built) and Bertie Holloway had commissioned 'Hellcat IIIS' with all the latest ideas. This boat had proved to be the fastest, particularly in a straight line and John Fisk withdrew 'Boadicea' in favour of 'Hellcat IIIS' knowing that this was their best boat to defend. After an eventful series against 'Quest', designed by the Cunningham Brothers and with one of the brothers on board, 'Hellcat IIIS' won the series four races to nil.

In 1964, The Americans were back with 'Sea Lion', designed and built by two amateurs, the Hubbard Brothers – British born and originally from Colchester in Essex. At last several British boats had been built to challenge for the defender position and they included the latest Hellcat design called 'Emma Hamilton'. She was owned by Bertie Holloway and again had Reg White onboard. She fought hard to claim the defender title and in the match against the Americans eventually won four races to one. This was by no means the easy victory it might seem as 'Sea Lion', with her Una-rig, certainly had the advantage in light winds and, as is often the case, the weather and luck played a part in the outcome. During one race when the Jib halyard broke, Reg climbed the mast to repair it before continuing with the race.

The Australians were back in 1965, with another well developed boat from the Cunninghams, 'QUEST II', again raced against several other contenders in Australia. Bertie Holloway had commissioned Reg White to design and build a new boat called 'Ocelot' and, although potentially the fastest boat, there was not enough time to tune her to perfection so 'EMMA HAMILTON' was again in contention.

A hard fought series showed several boats with potential speed including 'Thunder II' and 'Miss Senior Service', but in the end 'Emma Hamilton' proved consistently out in front. This was the closest series yet with a final score line in favour of 'EMMA HAMILTON' of four races to three. 'EMMA HAMILTON' had a new high aspect ratio rig, but was up against 'QUEST'S' wing mast. 'QUEST' was certainly the better boat, but Reg White was a much better tactician. As always, the British boat showed better pace to windward and the Australian boat better speed downwind. As the series went on the teams tweaked and tuned, and by the last race, with the scores level, the Australian boat now showed an edge to windward and the British boat speed downwind. With 'QUEST' fractionally in front, a vicious squall ripped across the race course and she capsized, allowing 'EMMA HAMILTON' to take overall victory.

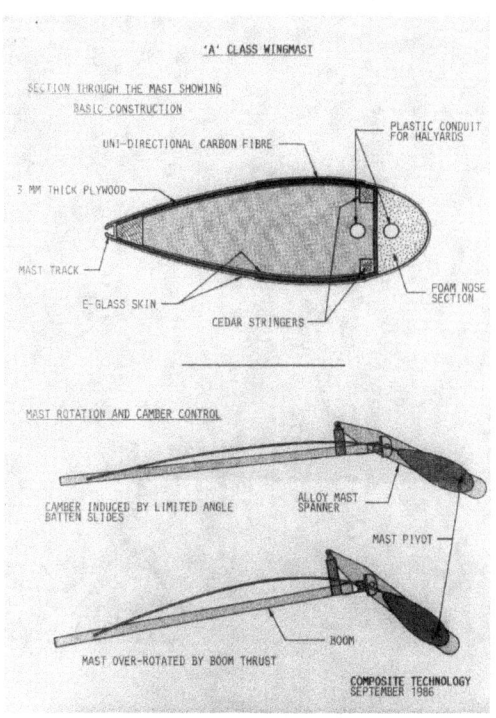

How a wing rig works

The result was too close for comfort and in 1966, when the Americans challenged with 'GAMECOCK' and her 40ft high wing mast, work would be needed by the defenders. An impressive line up of cats, each with wing rigs, competed for the defender's title and included 'THUNDER II', 'MANTA C', 'WILLS VENTURER II & III', 'MISS SENIOR SERVICE' and 'LADY HELMSMAN'. The latter was a development of the 'Hellcat IIIS' with a knuckle forward rather than the spray rails. This gave added buoyancy as the hull buried. As the trials developed it was a close race between 'THUNDER II' and 'LADY HELMSMAN' with the latter eventually proving the best across all conditions. Whilst there was obviously disappointment in the other camp, this extra competition helped Reg White and John Osborne to tune 'LADY HELMSMAN' to perfection. The matches were close and 'LADY HELMSMAN' eventually won the series four races to two, but not before both boats had suffered breakage and bad luck.

The Australian determination was undiminished when they returned in 1967 with 'QUEST III', again designed by the Cunninghams. Although Una rigged the sail

Lady Helmsman

sleeved over a standard mast and was not a wing mast, as was now becoming the norm, she proved herself in the Australian trials. 'Lady Helmsman' had a crew change with Peter Schneidau steering and Bob Fisher crewing, and there was competition from 'Wills Venturer III', 'Miss Senior Service II' and 'Ocelot', Reg White's design from 1965 and sailed by father and son, Bob and John Osborne. Although 'Lady Helmsman's' crew suffered from lack of practice, the boat still proved she could master the situation, and went on to win the Cup series against 'Quest III' four races to one. 'Lady Helmsman' was much the faster boat and her only loss was due to retirement after breaking a centreboard and driving it into the hull.

For 1968, America returned with 'Yankee Flyer', sailed by Greer Ellis and Bill Hooten, with a complex wing mast. It must not be forgotten that, as ever, fine racing machines are expensive to build and maintain, and many of the boats were subsidised with sponsorship, 'Lady Helmsman' being owned by Sanderson Paints. In the defender trials she had very little competition against boats that had many minor problems, and she was herself having teething problems with her new wing rig that had been tested in the Southampton Wind Tunnel. The drive for development meant that more and more time was spent testing ideas and theories. The actual cup was well fought with both boats suffering breakages, but an eventual win by 'Lady Helmsman' with four wins to one.

The end of an era was drawing to a close when Denmark entered the arena for 1969 with a boat called 'Opus III', with Gert Frederiksen and Leif Wagner Smitt.

Lady Helmsman **with wing rig**

The defenders were weak, with only one new boat having been built and several sponsors withdrawing. 'Lady Helmsman' had been retired and Reg White was sailing a modified Ocelot with his brother-in-law, John Osborne. Although she had been that year's European and National 'C' Class Champion, she borrowed 'Lady Helmsman's' rig for the cup races to increase her potential. Unfortunately, the rig was too heavy for the boat and it was not to be, and Britain lost the cup four races to nil. Since then we have only made one challenge in 1987, with the same losing score line.

For the rest of its time the cup has alternated between Australia, who eventually won it in 1970, and the USA, who claimed it for the first time in 1976. It must be remembered that the boats mentioned were not the only 'C' class built, although the class itself has now died. There were several boats built to the HELLCAT III design and there was even a HELLCAT IV with straight stems, although this was not a successful shape.

Austin became involved with the cup after being asked to make the sails for the first defence. Seahorse was already involved with Sailcraft, the boat builders run by Reg White, who were building Rod Macalpine-Downie designs. Austin was making the rigs for the very successful 'IROQUOIS' cruiser/racer catamarans and therefore was a leading exponent of fully battened catamaran rigs. He made the sails from the first defence back in England and became more and more involved over the years, not only with making the sails but also the design of the actual rigs.

General Parhams curved spar rig on BELINA ANN

AS TIME PROGRESSED, and the Australians turned up with a wing rig, the pressure was on, and Austin spent some time developing our own wing sail. Whilst Austin had already built the wingsail for the International Canoe in 1949, a much more successful sail would now be needed. Living close to Austin in retirement at Hintlesham was General Parham. One of the old school of innovators, General Parham had been involved with army flying during the First World War and was a member of the Royal Aeronautical Society. He had always experimented, including converting his aeroplane into a glider when the original engine fell off.

After his death in the 1960s, his daughter came across the manuscript of a book written by him during the last war in the Far East called 'Flying for Fun'. This was eventually published and was subsequently televised by the BBC with one of his granddaughters playing her own grandmother. He constructed many experimental craft, often crudely, including a wooden bicycle which he used around the village. Austin had a standing invitation to call in for tea and a yarn on his way home from Hadleigh, and many interesting discussions were held. The General had developed two wing rigs, of which neither was wholly successful, but it was Austin's combining

The wing rig with virtually no twist

of the two that led to the new rig for 'LADY HELMSMAN', to the delight of the General. He had been responsible for doing early experiments with Austin and determining the amount of twist required in a sail as it went up the mast. Certainly, as photos at the time showed, there was no twist in a small craft rig. These experiments were done in a Swordfish dinghy towed behind the yard launch at an appropriate angle for beating. They deduced that even if all possible twist was removed there was probably still too much. He took his experiments very seriously and even had his own small wind tunnel. This he had found after the war in Germany and it was eventually given to the Royal Aeronautical Society. The General and Austin borrowed it back when they made their short film called 'Simple Aerodynamics'. Unfortunately, this film has been lost.

The General's first rig had a bendy mast to match the sagging leech but was difficult to tack, requiring the mainsheet to be slacked off, the mast swung through 120° and the mainsheet hardened in again. This was too slow and was hardly suitable for the race course. The bendy mast bowed to leeward to match the sagging leech of the mainsail and so removed the twist. It had possibilities if it could be made to tack more easily. Reg White saw this possibility and made a very tall and very flexible mast which was tried on one of the HELLCATS.

Trying the wing rig on a Tornado

Known in Brightlingsea as the Lunar Rig, it could turn on a ball mounting, and had conventional shrouds and forestay to about ⅔ height, but also two lower shrouds each side which were kept slack but adjustable to control the bow to leeward. It gave a good shape to the sail, but needed to be physically turned by a 'spanner' to the new leeward side every time the boat tacked, otherwise it would be left bowed to windward on the new tack. This happened once too often; Reg at the helm gave a tug on the mainsheet, hoping to make the mast click across, but instead it collapsed in a shower of splinters.

The other rig had a rigid symmetrical section which would tack but was inefficient because it had only a solid symmetrical section. Having established that there is no measurable twist in the wind for a small craft's rig and that the bendy mast made a sagging luff to match the sagging leech, the 36ft mast for 'Lady Helmsman' was symmetrical.

It had a straight leading edge and a curved trailing edge in an arc of a circle, making it nearly 4ft wide at half height narrowing to 4 inches at the head and 2ft at the foot. It was more than ⅓ of the total sail area of 300 square feet. The luff of the sail had a slightly greater curve than the mast so that it fitted when the mast was turned to one side or the other, and would 'click' across when tacking.

The Tornado catamaran showing the rig adapted from Emma Hamilton

The curved trailing edge, when swung to leeward with the sail, matched the leech of the sail when seen from astern so that there was no twist in the sail, and the junction between the mast and the sail was always fair. The large radius leading edge fairing into the sail at the trailing edge combined to make an aerofoil which resembled the low speed glider wing sections developed at Göttingen in Germany before the war. Blending the two produced the 'Lady Helmsman's' rig and it was tested in the wind tunnel at Southampton University.

All the earlier 'C' class wing masts from America and Australia had been straight with a constant section and could be turned so that, in theory, the lee side of the mast lined up with the sail. However, in spite of enormous leech tension there was always a knuckle line where the sail met the mast, either in the upper or lower part, because of the twist in the sail.

After Lady H's successful rig, Austin developed an improved model with a fatter forward section which had been shown in the wind tunnel to be more effective downwind. However, this was built by someone who did not fully understand the requirements and the rig would not work. Austin also designed an all plastic version

Icarus with her Tornado rig and hydrofoils

built by Derek Nunn, who built his own boat called 'Early Bird' for the 1968 trials. This was a foam structure skinned in silver Melinex and looked magnificent. Unfortunately, whilst the rig was good, there were problems during the defender trials, with teething problems and gear failure, and the boat was unsuccessful, never completing a race. Much work was done in the Southampton wind tunnel on different sections with a scaled down rig which was designed for a fifty foot Trimaran in the USA. Because the rig would be expensive to build, the client was more than happy to subsidise the testing in the tunnel and they had a model Trimaran to go on the turntable. With the middle hull removed it worked very well as a 'C' class test rig. Like so many other projects the Trimaran was never finished, through a fire in the USA. Austin was, however, paid.

The logical route for further development was a variable camber sail. 'Lady Helmsman's' rig was a fixed camber, which could not be changed other than letting off the kicking strap to allow the head to twist off when overpowered. There were only two ropes, both with eight part purchases. The aft purchase worked as the kicking strap on a full semi-circular track and was controlled by the crew with the line led forward. The helm controlled the middling line which set the rig angle. In going to windward it would take both crew to sweat the sail in hard to eliminate the twist. Austin began to work on new designs and an early variant was wind tunnel tested. However, with the loss of the Cup in 1969, further work was stopped and the development left to other people. During the life of sailmaking Austin designed several wing rigs, but few were built.

Icarus with her Tornado rig and hydrofoils

Perhaps the most successful development from the Little America's Cup was from 'Emma Hamilton's' tall rig which, slightly scaled down, became the 'International Tornado' rig. The Tornado design had been commissioned from

Rodney March by Reg White for the IYRU selection trials and it came with virtually a Lady H wing rig. Reg phoned Austin one evening, saying that he did not think that this is what the selectors would be looking for, for a one design class. He wisely reckoned that a two man one design would need something for both crew. Austin scaled down 'EMMA HAMILTON's' rig and Reg built two boats, one with the EH rig and one with Rodney March's wing rig. The trials were held off Sheppey, with designs from all over the world. In the first race the wing rig sped into the lead but got into irons on the first tack and then the mast fell down. From this the sloop rig dominated and won the trials convincingly.

CROSSBOW **at speed**

Austin was already on the Catamaran Committee of the IYRU and found himself co-opted into the Speed Sailing Organisation. He had only attended the first trials as a spectator, but his knowledge was invaluable and he soon found himself roped in, initially to do some measurement. Honorary life president of the Amateur Yacht Research Society (AYRS) followed, although Austin never actually belonged. He believed strongly that the Society was for amateurs, and he was a professional. This was not to put down their work, but the organisation was not set up to deal with both sides. The Weymouth Speed Weeks were certainly the main speed events in Europe, and Austin attended them until their first demise in the early 1990s, following growing costs and the need for big prize money. They have subsequently been revived by AYRS on an amateur basis. The original weeks had a growing reputation and were supported by the Royal Yachting Association. An army of time keepers and marshals would descend on Weymouth for the Autumn Equinox and varied craft from all over the

Crossbow II on a run in Portland Harbour

world would try to break the speed record. This was held for many years by Crossbow until Windsurfers took over the sport in the 1980s. Austin spent much of his time measuring sail areas, as this divides the classes for speed sailing. He did not get directly involved with any one team but did make sails for several of the various craft. The types of craft would fill every form of imagination and while some were reasonably successful, most were not.

Austin did have the opportunity to sail on board 'BRITISH OXYGEN' at that event, helmed by Reg White. The course used was a clock face with a centre point and a ring of marks. A press boat asked Reg how close they would go to the centre point, as he wanted to get a really good shot. Reg, with his normal mischief, said he would come fairly close and proceeded to thunder this seventy foot catamaran right past the press boat with inches to spare and dowsing the occupants. Reg was such a skilled driver that he could control a boat to the last degree. During his 'LADY HELMSMAN' campaign, a local photographer had asked to get some photos and requested Reg come as close as possible. Always happy to oblige, Reg sailed the boat straight at the photographer, lifting the hull high above the boat, putting it down the other side.

One piece of design that was directly for a speed campaign was an 'A' class wing rig for 'ICARUS', the foil borne Tornado sailed by James Grogono in 1986. Based on the 'LADY HELMSMAN', rig it was built by Nick Barlow to withstand 60 knots, but that year the wind failed to blow and the rig was unproven. It was used again in 1987. The rig was used and tuned on a standard Hurricane 5.9 by Reg White, then on 'Icarus' at Portland, where she took the 'A' class record, but 'ICARUS' and the rig suffered by being left up overnight on the night of the Great Storm. The last rigs were three identical wing masts built by Euan Seel for Reg White to use on his Hurricane 6.5. This large 6.5 metre catamaran was devastatingly fast, with the crew using ladders and racks to project themselves outboard. The three boats successfully completed some of the big open cat events but proved too expensive for a production market. These rigs were nomex and carbon built with epoxy, the latest technology.

For the British, Tim Coleman's 'CROSSBOW' and 'Crossbow II' built the unlimited sail area world record up from 26.3 knots in 1972 to 36 knots in 1980 using sails designed by Austin. This record stood for six years until broken by the Frenchman, Pascal Maka, on a sailboard at 38.86 knots. The sailboard had arrived. During one year with 'CROSSBOW II', Austin had his motorboat in Weymouth and had a cameraman onboard. Despite the high speed of the motorboat, they could not keep up with 'CROSSBOW'. Weymouth was not really large enough for this craft and she was still accelerating at the end of her run.

CHAPTER 8
RETIREMENT? & OTHER PROJECTS

Having left the sailmaking business at a time of life when many would have thought of retiring, Austin was able to become involved in many various projects and interests, working from home.

On the dinghy front, in the mid 1990s, Austin was approached by two of the Olympic classes to help up-date their rigs. Firstly, the Flying Dutchman class and their chief measurer, Cle Jeltes, asked for ideas on a new rig. Austin designed a more modern and powerful rig utilising two trapezes, a fully battened mainsail and a much larger spinnaker with longer pole. The Dutchman still had the very short 'J' measurement pole, dating back many years. The class liked the general concept but felt that the mainsail and extra trapeze was a little too far at present, but that the spinnaker would be good. More detailed work was done and the spinnaker halyard moved up the mast a little. Rule changes were made and passed, and today the boat sails with an approximately 20% larger spinnaker and longer spinnaker pole.

Austin and Charles Currey had been invited to a Finn Class supper at Bosham Sailing Club at about the same time and, as so often at these functions, various things were discussed which led to their chief technical officer, Richard Hart, to again ask Austin to re-design the rig to make it more suitable for lighter sailors – such as those from the Far East – in the Olympics. Charles Currey, although he had not sailed the boat a great deal after his silver medal in Helsinki, was still involved with the class and helped with the trials. Austin again developed a fully battened rig which, on an un-stayed mast was fairly revolutionary, and the sail was made by Eddie Hyde. Tried out for the first time at Bosham, where there is a Finn fleet, it proved very satisfactory and, although not necessarily greatly

Flying D model test rig

The cold moulded motor boat

more powerful, according to the sailors it was definitely more controllable. This rig was trialled for a time but plans for introduction into the class were shelved. As a current Olympic Class, it always takes a great deal of time for any changes to work through.

Austin's one foray into powerboats came in the late 1950s when Austin read that Ray Hunt, designer of the famous Fairey powerboats, had been inspired to design the 'BOSTON WHALEr' range by the Hickman 'SEA SLED'. Austin felt that the thinking was not necessarily correct. Austin knew about the Hickman 'SEA SLEDS' because Philip & Son had the English rights to build them and there were several lying around the yard in Dartmouth during his apprenticeship, though there were none built when Austin was there. Quite by coincidence Austin had built a model of a 'Sea Sled' whilst he was at school. The 'SEA SLED' had two hulls, but had a tendency to land heavily off waves and split. This had happened to a sixty foot version built for a Swedish industrialist who had ordered a boat to commute to his hunting lodge up the coast. It was fitted with two aero engines and, although fine and achieving the specified sixty knots on the first outing, the second in rougher water resulted in a splitting hull that limped home in a sinking condition. The engines were put into another craft and the wrecked hull was in a shed when Austin was at the yard. Ray Hunt added the third central hull which certainly improved the sea keeping, but faired away the two wing hulls, leaving one hull with a deep-vee at the stern.

Austin felt that this was wrong in that the centre hull should flatten out to a shallow tunnel at the stern giving a cushion of air to ride on. The original 'SEA SLED' achieved this effect, but the 'BOSTON WHALER' could not. Austin, with another boat builder, built two wooden cold moulded prototypes in the barn at Stutton, for their own use, Austin using his as a tender to the 'C' Class catamaran racing at Thorpe Bay. The boat was painted white outside and, arriving one day with the boat on a trailer, an American approached him remarking that it was a very nice GRP moulding. It was only as he got close enough to look inside that he exclaimed, 'Good God, it's wood!'

The motor boat showing a clean ride

Reg White took a mould off this boat and a number were built by Sailcraft before the mould was sold on – without Austin's knowledge. It passed through two or three hands until Austin found the boat being exhibited at the London Boat Show. The builder said who he had bought the mould from but that he did not know the designer. Austin told him the facts and asked for royalties. Although there were obviously legal fees, Austin did at least receive some before the boat went out of production for the last time. How many were actually built is not known, but if you know what to look for, they can often be seen in various

The FIRORE **sailing on the River Orwell**

harbours around the country. In the mid 1990s Euan Seel, of Demon Yachts, made a new mould with a little more beam, and one prototype was built. The boat is superb and handles with great accuracy and safety as the author can vouch for, having spent one evening putting it through its paces. The other feature is that the same performance can be achieved with less horsepower compared to other dory type craft. As yet it has not been possible to put it back into production, although it is a very special opportunity in waiting.

International Youth sailing is well supported by the various National Authorities around the world, culminating in a World Youth Sailing Championships once a year with one representative from each country in each discipline (single handed, two handed, girl or boy, etc). To train these young sailors various schemes are used and different boats chosen for the different age groups. Most of these classes have become successful through natural selection. In the early 1990s the RYA decided that a new intermediate trainer was needed for thirteen to fifteen year olds before they went into the 'INTERNATIONAL 420' class at around sixteen. It was hoped that this new design would become a well supported international class. People were invited to build – at their own expense – prototypes and to attend the trials.

Austin decided that he would enter with a form of tortured ply construction, which would allow home completion and build on the success of the 'International Mirror', with its 'stitch and glue' method. Although the boats were very different, Austin believed that the ability to build a competitive boat at home or in schools would allow more youngsters into the sport, rather than restrict it to the parents that could afford to buy and maintain relatively expensive dinghies such as the '420'. The 'Furore', as the design came to be called, was an excellent little single trapeze dinghy of some twelve feet in length and was built by Euan Seel of 'Demon Yachts'. It was well behaved and, managed by two lightweight youths as required, its performance sparkled. At the first trials in Dover harbour the boat performed very well but the conditions were light. At subsequent trials in more wind, the boat again performed very well but was still unsuccessful, there being amongst some of the judges an

The cold moulded wooden car

obsession with boats from one manufacturer only, despite the financial limitations this places on many parents. As Peter Johnson points out in his book '*Yacht Rating*', 'Rules, and indeed yacht racing classes in general, originated by institutions, have a bad record. Amazingly, as late as 1993, the RYA took it upon itself to choose a youth dinghy, the '405' – it flopped.' This is unfortunately true and the '405' has never gained many numbers and is certainly not successful as a class, despite the company Hobie Cat agreeing to build thirty on spec in France. This was hardly supporting British boat builders, particularly considering the expense that so many people had been put to.

Using the same method of construction, Austin also entered a design competition for a small yacht tender in the American magazine 'Wooden Boat', the details of which had been passed onto him by his friend John Leather. Eventually Austin heard from the magazine that he had been unsuccessful and, when hearing of the results, which were all hard chine flatties, he realised that it is very difficult to change the perceptions of a nation. The sharpie type of shape has always been enormously popular in the States for all types of boat and our designs look as strange to them as theirs often do to us, despite the fact that both designs do the job equally well.

It is quite common for many designs to be completed to some stage or another from basic sketch to full worked up drawings, and for the project then never to happen. Whilst at the London Boat show around 1991, Austin found himself talking to the manager of the Suffolk Canoe Company, who was new to the business and boat

The wooden car

shows. As so often at shows, the requests and inquiries are many and varied from sensible sales to the completely eccentric. However, one enquiry that seemed quite serious was for a thirty foot electric canoe, as seen sometimes on sunny afternoons on the Thames. During conversation Austin agreed to do the basic design so that at least a sensible discussion could be held with the client. It would be done on the basis of commission, if and when the boat was built, and working plans were drawn. Sometimes, the more serious the enquiry the less that comes of it, and nothing was ever heard after the first initial contact. So there is a design for an electric canoe waiting to be used.

Austin remained in contact for several years, and obviously the Suffolk Canoe Company hoped that one day another customer would walk in wanting a beautiful and elegant craft such as this, and the design could actually be built.

OVER THE YEARS, Austin was involved with several special cars and the further use of Aerolite glues and cold moulding was demonstrated in the late 1950s with the building of a wooden car body. Slightly thinner veneer was used to cope with the tight curves and a very elegant car was produced. It had initially been the brainchild of a local character, Bill Bunbery, now Sir Charles Bunbery, who had taken up sports car racing and decided to have a special built. Coe's garage in Ipswich did a lot of specialist engineering as well as normal cars and Lawrence Coe, the son, was to build the chassis and tune the engine – a souped up Standard Ten – while Austin completed the body. The first open top car went very well and was successful, winning several meetings. Building on this success they decided to go in for a sports saloon with a different moulding. The first was on a welded cruciform chassis and the second was to have a tubular aluminium one, both with the tuned Standard Ten engines. Unfortunately, Bill Bunbery's father must have decided not to support him any more and the funds dried up. Coe's were left with the chassis and Austin with the body, not quite but nearly complete. It sat around for a long time until eventually it was given to Martin Kendall of Custom Boatbuilders in Shotley, who has spent many years finishing it – the chassis was never completed. The sizes were right for it to be worked on to a Triumph Spitfire chassis, which is what has happened. What happened to the open top car is not known, although it may still be in the Bunbery family's ownership. Only the two bodies were produced. Austin did try to sell the idea to Colin Chapman of Lotus but, whilst a very good product, it was a little too late and was superseded by glass fibre.

Also, during the time at Woolverstone, Austin constructed a diesel Rolls Royce. The yard needed a new general purpose hack and Austin's brother, Norman, who worked for Paxman's Diesels in Colchester, informed him that the company were disposing of some fifty horsepower diesel engines that had been prototypes for a war project and were no longer required. One had been given to a farmer friend who successfully put it into a Fordson tractor, and another could be Austin's if he could find a suitable chassis.

Austin knew of an old Rolls Royce Silver Ghost chassis with a wartime ambulance body on it in a field at Hayling Island which, when measured, would just take the engine. Its own engine had been shattered by ice and there were bits of cast iron over the bonnet. After an exchange of about £20.0s.0d., the Rolls Royce was towed back to Woolverstone behind Austin's Bentley – which was a very, very long tow. The diesel was fitted – although it was an awful job – and a new, more useful body built but the vehicle was not actually a success. The engine was not powerful enough. It would go about fifty-five m.p.h. flat out and was not very economical. It would tow well, but was awkward and very unpleasant to drive, and parking was murder. It sat around for some time, but was eventually sold and lost until 1997 when Austin found out that, having passed through a couple of hands a new owner had it, still with the diesel and wooden body. His intention, it is believed, is to restore it to a full Rolls Royce.

Today we cherish the old cars, and it is difficult to realise that only fifty years ago or less they were thrown away as scrap. It was from a breaker's yard in Southampton that Austin

The steam car discovered

acquired a very special car, a White Steam car. Austin had gone there when in Southampton to set up the net making facilities, in company with an RNVR colleague who was in charge of the net making. The RNVR chap was a keen car enthusiast, and he and Austin would tour the breakers' yards on bicycles in the evenings, looking for anything of interest. He always regretted that he had nowhere to store many of the objects to be found which would not be believed today, and of course would now be worth a fortune.

White steam car

One yard even had a nearby field to park cars as an overflow and included vehicles such as a 1910 Napier and an Eight Litre Bentley. Under a pile of junk, Austin noticed a wheel standing up with the word 'White' stamped on it. Going right back to before his apprenticeship Austin loved steam in all forms and this rang a bell in the memory about steam cars. Austin dug down a bit and, sure enough, there was the chassis of a White steam car. This was too good to miss, and potentially valuable, and he made some arrangements to get it away, when the breaker's yard man said there was a body for it somewhere, last seen slung up in the roof of a timber yard some five miles away. They travelled over to look and, sure enough, there it was, still slung up in the roof. Covered in dust it was complete and paying £5.0s.0d for the lot, they bolted the body on the chassis and moved it back to Suffolk by rail. It was towed to the house in Stutton from the goods yard at Bentley station on its own wheels and put into the corner of the barn for many years, waiting for Austin to have time to restore it.

Of course this never happened and, when a man from Lavenham took an interest, after much persuasion Austin sold it for £400.0s.0d after storing it for over twenty years. Although he reckoned to be able to restore it, Austin never heard anything from him until one day, out of the blue in the early 1990s, he received a telephone call from Bob Dyke in Penzance, asking if Austin had once owned a White steam car, because he now had it and it was running. It had obviously been sold on from Lavenham and was now owned by Bob Dyke. He had

The White steam car and Bumble

Bumble

spent many months restoring the car and making new parts for the engine, some of which were machining masterpieces. There was to be a rally in Norfolk where he met Austin, who at last had the promised ride in his steam car.

Austin already had his own Bentley by this time, known to most people by the nickname 'Bumble'. It was a 1924 three litre Red Label. He had acquired it whilst still working at Shoreham, again from a breaker's yard at Lancing. 'Bumble' was full of junk and old bottles and, when cleaned out, the upholstery was rotten. However, the engine would turn over by hand, but the aluminium water jacket was corroded away and what was left was half full of oatmeal, once used to cure leaking radiators.

It was towed away behind Austin's Morris Eight to the garage which Austin shared with the man across the road from his digs. The garage was large and stored Austin's Morris Eight and the Austin Seven. It was Austin giving a lift to this person to the breaker's yard to replace the rear main bearing on the Austin Seven that led to the Bentley in the first place. Rather than just a bearing, they selected the most likely complete Austin Seven and towed that away instead, uncovering 'Bumble' in the process – along with a couple of Daimlers, a Sizaire Berwick, which had belonged to the manager of the Grand Hotel in Brighton, and many others from really good to old wrecks. The coming of petrol rationing had meant that many cars had just been dumped as they could not be run.

The following Saturday, for the princely sum of £20.0s.0d., they returned for the Bentley. Temporarily in the main garage, it was then moved to another garage next to the boatyard. With half a pint of petrol it proved to be a runner, and Austin spent some time replacing the worn engine parts. It was taxed, although probably not insured, and Austin started to drive it occasionally. When he went to the Admiralty, the car stayed in Shoreham until Austin was able to have the car put in a railway truck from Shoreham and moved right into the 105 shed in Southampton Docks where he was able to continue working on it. The Morris Eight was chartered to Charles Currey's engineer for the duration, as he needed to drive around Portsmouth. It was sold after the war. Austin's need to travel during the war allowed him access to petrol and enabled him to use the Bentley. 'Bumble' had a tow bar, which must have been unusual for a Bentley, and worked hard until about 1964, by which time the car was very decrepit, especially the brake drums which had been skimmed so many times they distorted when the brakes were applied and the oversize linings barely touched the drums. This was hardly safe and the car was retired to a spare corner to be replaced by a Triumph Herald which, as a closed car, was far more useful when sailmaking.

In about 1988, Austin began to restore 'Bumble' with the engine stripped down to the last nut and bolt, and completely rebuilt using a Bentley specialist in Swindon when necessary. The chassis was overhauled and reassembled, and the body refitted. The woodwork had been restored and strengthened by Euan Seel, and it was re-panelled by Smith's the coachbuilders in Gt Bentley.

Bumble fully loaded

New wings were bought to replace the old ones which had corroded away. In 1998, the car gained a new MOT and is again running on the road. The car has had some modifications over the years, including the replacement of the carburettors with SUs, the upgrading of the starter motor and the exchanging of a dynamo to an alternator. Having said this, the essential Bentley parts have matching serial numbers.

Of the many bodies that Austin has been associated with, the Royal Institute of Naval Architects is particularly prestigious. He joined the Institute during the war, and was a founder member of that body's Small Craft Committee over forty years ago, and was at one time joint chairman. The committee was formed to look after the interests of designers of small craft, although they were very careful not to draw any dividing lines other than perhaps that small craft were not large ships. It included yachts, tugs, dredgers, fishing boats, work boats and small coasters up to roughly two hundred feet. They decided to be different to the main body of the institute, which gives awards for learned papers, and decided to award medals for actually doing something, be it designed, built or something done with an outstanding craft, not just a learned paper. An example would be the award of the Small Craft Group medal to Ben Lexen, who designed the 12-Metre with the wing keel that broke the American stranglehold on the America's Cup. Austin was honoured with the medal in 1988 for 'Outstanding contributions over many years for the design of rigs, sails and high performance racing craft.'

Austin wrote and reviewed regularly for the Small Craft Group magazine, '*Ship and Boat*', and followed various projects, such as visits to boatbuilding industries including trips to Sweden – the first to Scania marine engines and the second, which whilst interesting was very hard work, to twenty-five firms in six days. He had also presented papers on 'Sail Balance', 'Sail Cloth Development', 'Sail Design' and 'Hull Design' for 'Computer Aided Design Conferences'. Another position, linked with RINA, was his assistance with the Engineering Council. This is a collection of all the learned societies associated with engineering. The Engineering Council is a collective voice and one of its ideas was encouraging engineering in schools. Engineers were encouraged to join with their local schools and Austin helped at the local Holbrook High School. Various projects are approved including lectures – Why a boat sails –

Austin on SNR business

and challenges. Recent projects have included building model bridges to support a minimum weight, wind turbines judged on highest voltage and model boats to transport a 'dangerous' cargo the length of the swimming pool in the shortest time. These projects bring together all the skills learnt in science and technology, and the winning team receive certificates and good prizes.

Over many years, Austin had a deep interest in the history of maritime subjects, and had been involved with 'The Society of Nautical Research' since his time in Dartmouth. He became friendly with a family who came every year for their summer cruise – the father was then secretary – and a founding member of the SNR. At that time he took very little interest in the son, but he remembers the daughter as being rather nice. In the early 1960s, Austin was approached by George the son, who was himself now secretary, and was invited to sit on the SNR Council, to which Austin agreed. Shortly after, he attended a conference on the 'Preservation of Timber in Ancient Craft' presented by Olin Peterson, the head of the Viking Boat museum at Roskilde in Denmark. On the way downstairs to lunch, he was tapped on the shoulder by a lady who said that George, the secretary, said she should get in touch. She was looking for a boatbuilder who was also a Naval Architect. This was Austin, and the lady was Honour Frost, a leading Marine Archaeologist.

She had been working on the excavation of the 'Punic ship' found off Marsala in Sicily, and needed someone to help decide what shape it originally was. On the seabed the pieces were scattered but they had mapped each piece and its relationship to others around it. So far, a French computer expert reckoned he could do it, and a model maker from Liverpool had made scale models of all the planks, with the intention of reconstructing at a smaller scale. Knowing where the ship was built and the width of the slipways, a maximum beam was known and Austin worked this knowledge in with the shape of the recovered floor timbers. From this and the other information available, a full lines plan was worked up. When the three drawings were overlaid, it was remarkable how similar they actually were.

Austin visited the site in Sicily at the time the last timbers came out of the preservation tanks in about 1965. There he was able to help build up the parts which were in an old wine factory, which Austin described as like being in a cathedral with the strong arches. It was long enough for the whole boat – some 110 feet – and on the new concrete floor cast keel blocks were laid to accept the keel. Austin was responsible for lofting things out, which makes him the only man to loft a Punic ship in about the last two thousand years. It was not ideal circumstances lofting on polythene sheeting but the local carpenters, who were splendid fishing boat builders, welded up strip sections from the lofting and set them up with 'Acro' jacks to hold them and the planks – still showing their original mortice and tenon construction – and timbers were fitted. It worked superbly with even the nail holes lining up.

Austin remembers this as a very satisfying experience. One unusual feature found before reassembly was a belt of planks where the water line would have been some four or five planks deep, which were five sided and not like the other planks in the carvel construction. Why? This caused a great deal of discussion and speculation, because it was obviously a design feature and carefully placed. The academics, with little understanding of practical design and construction, formulated theories about making it easier to plank the boat – which hardly seems right when only used there, and not on other every day ships of the period where standard carvel construction was used throughout, as it was for the rest of the Punic ship. However, Austin, with his greater practical experience, saw it in a different light and realised that they were

Model showing tab and peg method used on the Punic ship

almost certainly spraybreakers. It must be remembered that these ships were rowed into battle and the oars would be naturally close to the waterline for most efficiency. Therefore, anything which would deflect the spray and water away from the oar ports could only be an advantage. Austin prepared many notes and slides on this subject, and the cause is today championed by Honor Frost whenever possible. The tragedy of the whole project is that, having got the ship re-established, there was to be a museum constructed with the ship as the central feature. However, with internal local political wrangling, the funds were never forthcoming and everything fell into disrepair, and today there is nothing left. Everything has been lost, except the knowledge, which hopefully rests in a filing cabinet somewhere.

Austin was on the SNR council for about twenty years until made an Honorary Vice president and helped with the day to day running of the SNR. Probably the principal project of the SNR is its involvement in HMS 'VICTORY'. The SNR was involved from its earliest days in the preservation and restoration of Nelson's flagship and today works just as tirelessly to maintain the standards, and raise funds for restoration work. One of 'VICTORY's' former Captains, Peter Whitlock, had remarked during one of his many lectures that her complement of boats was not complete and she should have a pair of cutters on her quarter davits. After his death it was decided that a fitting memorial would be to complete 'Victory's' complement of boats and build two cutters.

Austin found himself with the job of producing the lines plans for the two boats, both Clincher built. One would be an exact replica to be a display boat, and the other would be built in epoxied plywood to be used as a sailing exhibit which could be taken to various maritime festivals. One member, an academic from the National Maritime Museum, managed to produce a sheer draft of a cutter of 1805. Unfortunately, his latter inputs have been less helpful. Austin took the sheer draft and produced the full lines and Jack Chippendale in Norfolk produced the plywood cutter with no problems, and it has been a great success at festivals all over Europe. The other replica was built at the Chatham Dockyard and ran into no end of troubles. The first boat built was terrible, with unfair plank runs and

A model of the keel scarf on the Punic ship

Half model of the Victory cutter

other problems. After much discussion, it was rebuilt and most of the problems have now been ironed out for it to be on display in Portsmouth. The builders in Chatham were not helped in their task by changes in specification. Austin had taken great care and constructed models to check that twelve planks per side would work and this was proved by the boat built by Jack Chippendale. Without reference, the academics changed the specification to ten planks per side – which Austin already knew would not work – and then specified no scarfs. Unfortunately, a complete lack of practical knowledge led to insurmountable problems. It perhaps brings home the problem, when in a book an author can claim that for a cutter of 18ft length it would have oars of 24ft in length. The Navy may have strange traditions, but they are reasonably practical and this shows that even in academic text books the 'facts' must be treated with care.

WHILE ON THE council, Austin was a prime mover in the re-establishment of the SNR Small Craft Committee. Austin had been given a copy of the out of print Science Museum's ship collection, which lists work done by the SNR Council Committee in the mid 1930s. Then they had accurately recorded the detail of some hundred local boats around Britain. Austin produced this booklet at a Council meeting and said that, with the original work over sixty years ago, it was time to do new studies, hence the formation of the new committee. It will again seek to research and record the many types of native craft in the various areas of Britain. To help with this work, Austin developed a method of taking lines off a boat by photography. It involves marking sections on the boat, placing marked vertical ranging poles at each station and taking photographs from several positions. When developed the photographs are processed with basic trigonometry and turned into a lines

The seahorse on Bumble

plan. Great interest had been shown in the method as it will allow recording of lines between tides and should prove a very useful tool.

The skills of sculpture and medal making have been honed over the years, beginning with the Seahorse sculpture used as a mascot on 'Bumble' and subsequently the logo for the sail loft. It was made during the war in the evenings when Austin was fire watching at the WPL workshops. Quite often there would be little to do and there was scrap timber and tools available. Austin had a little dried seahorse which he had bought in St Malo at the end of a race on 'ORTAC'. Using this as a model, he scaled it up two to one and carved it in Obeche. At first it was copied faithfully, including the dried dorsal fin which had lost its shape but looked like a little cleat. Blakes of Gosport cast it in gunmetal and at first it took pride of place on the Morris Eight. The wooden original sat on the mantelpiece in Austin's office at the Admiralty.

One day a man came into the office, saw the model and said, 'Ah, a seahorse. You've got the fin wrong.' Austin asked him what he knew of seahorses and found out that he was a marine artist who had done the murals for the liner 'Queen Mary'. He re-drew the fin for Austin on the back of an envelope, but it was ages before Austin discovered it was nearly twice the size it should be. However, he had already altered the wooden pattern and thought it looked really nice so it was left. The old casting was melted down and re-cast. This new moulding sat on 'Bumble' for many years until it was retired and Austin made a new mould for a new casting. In Austin's last car, a Saab, there was an actual size casting taken from a real seahorse.

IN THE 1980s Austin completed a Lion Rampant for the Royal Harwich YC to become the Jubilee Trophy for the Royal Harwich One-Designs on their fiftieth anniversary in 1987. This trophy was carved from a solid block of carving wax and the final trophy was cast in bronze by Cire Perdu of Brightlingsea. Austin had first used this

The MARY ROSE gun model

Detail of the Mary Rose gun

firm some years ago when he was making wax patterns and moulds for sail fittings which would be cast in gunmetal and stainless steel using the lost wax technique that he had first heard about from his friends at Aero Research. They also cast a scale cannon for him which he subsequently bored, had proofed and fired. The interest in casting grew and led to more knowledge of the sorts of waxes and techniques used for casting and medal making. Although Austin had always had an interest in old guns, having had one at school at a time when you could buy gunpowder across the counter.

This proper little cannon would fire a lead ball, but when it broke a window in the sports pavilion about half a mile away things had to be toned down. Austin could not remember what happened to this gun, but the interest in miniature cannons probably started again when, killing time near Liverpool Street Station in London, he came across a toy and model shop in which a dilapidated Basset Lowke kit had been marked down going cheap. It made an interesting model of a Waterloo Cannon and Austin, having completed it, spent time looking at other examples in museums.

The model cast in Brightlingsea is a copy of one of the guns from the 'Mary Rose', recovered when some artefacts were lifted in the late 1700s and is now in the Tower of London. He gained permission from the Tower of London to crawl all over the original, taking measurements and recording detail. He then went to Woolwich to see the other recovered guns – these are now all in the 'Mary Rose' museum at Portsmouth – until he had completed his research. As can be imagined it took many years and in fact from beginning research to completing the gun took ten years.

It involved meticulous attention to detail to ensure the decoration and inscriptions

The wind turbine

were correct, and it required various waxes and plasticene to achieve the necessary moulds. Having finished the 'MARY ROSE' cannon, Austin then went on to produce a replica of a gun from HMS 'WARRIOR' which, without all the ornamentation, was 'comparatively' easy. These models were correct in all their details and were exquisite working models.

To fire them, a firearms certificate is needed, and Austin had one for many years, after being taken shooting by Tony Breirly at the Viking Pistol Club, where he subsequently joined and bought a 22 single shot pistol for target shooting. He used to do some competition shooting, but admitted to never becoming that accurate. However, belonging to the club meant that he was allowed to hold a firearms certificate and use the cannons occasionally, at the range and as specified on the licence at the RHYC for ceremonial purposes. Sadly, with the new government regulations, Austin had to give up his firearm certificate and these beautiful guns had to be decommissioned. However, they are still in existence and were left to the Royal Harwich Yacht Club for their display cabinet after Austin's death.

The first medal that Austin designed was for the RINA Small Craft Group which features a Viking ship and is awarded for outstanding achievement or contribution, and from that medal grew the SNR 'Victory' medal which shows HMS 'VICTORY' under sail and is awarded to the Dockyard chippies who have worked on the ship. Following this, Austin did another medal for the SNR as part of the prize – money and the medal - for an essay competition. This medal shows the SNR ship which, when seen, will leave the reader in no doubt as to the complexity of making the pattern and mould. The essay competition is aimed at students with an interest in maritime history and the winning article would be published in the SNR quarterly periodical, 'The Mariners Mirror'. All these medals are awarded today at the appropriate intervals.

AUSTIN NEVER STOPPED designing nor innovating and spent the last few years working on a new design of wind turbine to drive either pumps or generators. The idea came from the wing mast designed for James Grogono to put on his hydrofoil 'Icarus', to

Wind turbine on test rig

attempt a world speed sailing record. As previously mentioned, the mast was built in Southampton and used at a Weymouth Speed week. The company building the mast also built wind turbine blades for average size windmills. The more Austin looked at the windmills the more he felt a vertical axis with aerofoils like wing masts would be better. He started with two, found three was better, as were four, and carried on until he had completed a full circle. He realised then that if they all closed to form a drum it would be a safety device with minimal resistance as the wind built to dangerous strengths. This is one of the main selling points against the horizontal axis type which need huge brakes and suffer very large loads. Austin's design should continue to work in far higher wind strengths than the other, which makes it far more efficient and economical. A full size was envisaged at about forty feet in diameter and blades of about sixty to eighty feet high, although overall it would probably be considerably lower than the windmills used today.

Obviously, scale versions have been constructed and tested in wind tunnels and on a test rig on top of the car. A prototype with a pump and with a generator have been made and patented and both versions have proved highly successful. The costings are better than the horizontal type, not needing a gearbox and development will hopefully continue. After Austin's death, all his research work and models were passed on to a group who were to continue the experiments.

A letter in a magazine had started an earlier experiment with propellers, when it was claimed that it would be impossible to sail directly into the wind by any method. The letter was passed to Austin, who constructed a small model with an airscrew on one end of a sloping shaft and a water propeller on the other, which indeed would sail directly into the wind and this was photographed and filmed. There was much correspondence with two people being for and against the theory. This ran for some time until the magazine discovered that these two were one and the same person arguing both sides.

Over many years, Austin travelled round the various sailing clubs and yacht clubs giving illustrated lectures. Quite how or why it started he was not sure, except that he had taken many colour slides and had given a few shows locally. It was well received and so he placed an advertisement in *Yachts & Yachting*, announcing a lecture tour of a particular area and inviting club secretaries to arrange a date. For several years it became quite successful with autumn and spring tours planned. The tour could often be a dozen lectures in a fortnight, starting in Oxford, up as far as Newcastle and back down the East Coast. He took all his own equipment with projectors, screen and slides and a home built auto-changer for the slides of some three different lectures. This was long before the modern carousel type projector and Austin used a pre-war 'Zeiss', boosted with a bigger lamp and a fan. The lectures started in the late 1940s and continued until he commenced sailmaking when there was then no time to spare. Then, however, it helped with money, which was in very short supply. It was very informative on venue acoustics from very poor in the hold of a tank landing ship at Chatham Dockyard through mediocre at the Royal Corinthian at Burnham to the best at the Foreign Office in Whitehall for the Civil Service Sailing Association. The lectures would be on a variety of subjects including the film of the Naples Olympics and slide shows of the Racing Rules, Racing Tactics and a general show called 'Colour Afloat' which had a variety of images. These lectures were very popular and reports of them can be found in magazines such as *Yachting World*. In April 1955 they reported:

"IN HIS TALK on tactics, organised by the Central Council for Physical Recreation on March 23rd, Austin Farrar used a new idea to illustrate it. He began his lecture by showing, on the screen, colour photographs of the start of an Itchenor Burgee race for Fireflies. The leading boats sorted themselves out and the next slide showed a model of the position of the first six boats soon after the start. Further similar diagrams followed. Just when one was beginning to think he had got the models into an impossible position, he would show a 'live' picture to prove that it actually happened. Farrar used models from a protest set fitted with sails marked with the correct sail numbers moving on 'water' of crinkled glass. Under the glass, near the crêpe paper 'shore', sand coloured paper indicated shallows, while blue paper showed deep water. The first pictures were taken from fairly high up, and some were photographed from 'water level' with a Chichester Harbour backdrop, which gave a realistic effect. Thus the audience was able to follow the race move by move. So successful was the lecture that it is to be repeated at the end of May."

This second lecture subsequently took place on June 15th 7.30 p.m. at the London

Austin giving one of his many lectures

Austin with Rita on Bumble

School of Hygiene and Tropical Medicine in the University of London. *Yachting World* continued to report the lectures and advertised them also: 'LECTURE TOUR: Austin Farrar, M.I.N.A. is planning a tour of the Midlands in mid-October. Lectures are well illustrated and subjects include dinghy racing and tactics. Club secretaries should write to Mr Farrar at ....' This was from an issue in August 1958.

Austin's vast and varied experience over the years meant that he was often consulted on many subjects, and would usually have succinct and accurate advice to offer, whether it was accepted or not. This approach led to a certain amount of surveying over the years, often for the insurance company, 'Navigators & General'.

The garden at his house proved very productive over the years with both fruit and vegetables and allowed Austin to indulge in another interest, that of home made wine. Many types had been tried and they were successful in judging at the local horticultural shows and I can vouch for the taste and quality.

Austin continued to work on many projects with undimmed enthusiasm and was never afraid to try new ideas and to offer help and advice where he could. At a little over eighteen months before his death, he sketched out a new design for an International Fourteen showing all of the new developments and that he was still in touch with the modern high performance racing craft. He always maintained his contact with this class and was made an Honorary Life Member of the Association for all his input to the class over many years.

It was only in the last year of his life that he became frail and stopped working. He relished the visits from friends and long telephone conversations until the last few months and it was only then that he left his beloved house and garden for a nursing home close by where he passed away peacefully on the 6th July 2004 at the age of 91. Those who met him found him a kind and generous person who was always willing to encourage, help and to pass on knowledge. It was a privilege to know Austin and when reading this book it is hoped that others will be inspired to also see the potential for innovation in the years to come.

One of the many Christmas cards that Austin made

APPENDIX 1

INTERNATIONAL 14 DINGHIES TO AUSTIN FARRAR DESIGN

Sail No	Year	Name	Builder	First Owner
583	1950	Windsprite	Woolverstone Shipyard	B.B.Banks

P.O.W. Winner, 1950, 1951, 1953, 1955.
This was the only one to this design built in the U.K.

Sail No	Year	Name	Builder	First Owner
NZ593	1952	Quicksilver		G.C. Smith

Built to the Windsprite 583 design.
Austin sent out the plans at the end of 1951.

Sail No	Year	Name	Builder	First Owner
596	1952	Warrigal	Woolverstone Shipyard	S.H.G. Waters

New design. Although not a P.O.W. winner still very successful.
1952-2nd. 1953-6th. 1954-5th. 1955-6th. 1956-6th.
Ordered after the successful work by Austin on the Fairey K555 'Barilea'. 'Warrigal' was to replace Sam Waters earlier Fairey K557.

Sail No	Year	Name	Builder	First Owner
NZ606	1953	Christine	L.D. Brookbanks, N.Z.	L.D. Brookbanks

Built to the Windsprite 583 design, from 1951 plans.

Sail No	Year	Name	Builder	First Owner
NZ609	1952	Zephyrathes	C. Wild, N.Z.	J. Smale. N.Z.

Built to the Windsprite 583 design, from 1951 plans.

Sail No	Year	Name	Builder	First Owner
NZ610	1952	Atua Hau	C. Wild, N.Z.	N.Z.

Built to the Windsprite 583 design, from 1951 plans.
P.O.W. Winner 1958.

Sail No	Year	Name	Builder	First Owner
KB26	1953	Ilys I, became Dream	Woolverstone Shipyard	R. Spurling, Bermuda

Built for Rowe Spurling, and then sold to Hartly-Watlington who renamed her 'Dream'. Development of Warrigal, finished 5th in 1953 P.O.W. Hartly-Watlington had previously owned K463, a 1946 Fairey.

Sail No	Year	Name	Builder	First Owner
634/ KB28	1953	Ilys II.	Woolverstone Shipyard	R. Spurling

Built to the Warrigal 596 design. Finished after 635 Thunderbolt with modified rolled down gunwales to meet new class rules. This boat was shipped straight to Bermuda.

N.B. All KB boats painted, not varnished, to protect from sun. Either RS or HW importer of an American brand of paint which was sent over to be used. Boats painted bright yellow.

Sail No	Year	Name	Builder	First Owner
635	1953	Thunderbolt	Woolverstone Shipyard	J. Blundell

Built to the Warrigal 596 design. This boat had flared gunwales extending the beam to 6' 6" giving 40% more leverage. This was promptly banned and the beam fixed at a maximum of 5' 6".

667	1956	Bolero	Woolverstone Shipyard	S.H. Morris

New design. Drawings and plans dated 1954.
P.O.W. Winner 1957, 1960.

669?	1955	Reveille	Woolverstone Shipyard	J. Hartley Watlington

Shell ordered off the mould 1955. Probably this number, although not attributed in International 14 class records. The shell sat on the new mould for a year before being taken off and finished as this boat.

Austin sells Woolverstone Shipyard between 1954/56 and has no further direct contact with building boats.

668	1956	Catalina	W.H, D.W. & C.A. Scott	D.W. & C.A. Scott

Built to the Bolero 667 design. Finished shell.

672	1956	Stormcloud	W. Holeman	I. A. Williams

Built to the Bolero 667 design. Shell sent down to Exmouth for final finishing.

676	1957	Calypso	W.H, D.A. & C.A. Scott	W.H. Scott

Built to the Bolero 667 design. Finished shell.

677	1956	Ballerina	H.S. Southerland, N.Norfolk	T. Atkins, Bermuda.

Built to the Bolero 667 design. Finished shell.

683	1957	Shearwater	Woolverstone Shipyard	Dr. C.J. O'R. Morris

Built to the Bolero 667 design.

Sail No	Year	Name	Builder	First Owner
685	1957	Machs	B.R.R. Mc Donald	B.R.R. McDonald

At the request of *'Yachting World'* Austin allowed them to publish the lines of one of his Fourteens. However, they were not the exact design of any yet built but a slightly modified 'Warrigal'. This boat was built from the lines in *'Yachting World'*.

692	1958	Caduceus	Woolverstone Shipyard	F.C. Durbin

Built to the Bolero 667 design. Shell only, finished by owner.

693	1958	High Fidelity	Woolverstone Shipyard	Dr. G.G. Wells

Built to the Bolero 667 design.

728	1960	Polyester	Woolverstone Shipyard	J.J. Allen

Built to the Bolero 667 design. P.O.W. Winner 1963.

730	1960	Velocia	H.S. Southerland	M.J. Ellison

Built to the Bolero 667 design. Shell only.

744	1961	If-Anjatim	Lawrence & Plater	G. Derrer

Built to the Bolero 667 design. Shell only.

770	1961	Mystere	Woolverstone Shipyard	R.C. White

New Design. (3 skin diagonal outer.)

778	1962	Woolverine	Woolverstone Shipyard	A. Farrar

Built to the Mystere 770 design. This boat was a prototype built in GRP, though not accepted at the time. Built on Mystere plug which was then cut up. GRP failed on not having a constant thickness of hull at overlaps. Boat never granted a certificate. Boat now lost?

779	1962	Matelot	Woolverstone Shipyard, Shell.	R.J. Ogle

Built to the Mystere 770 design. Finished by Eric Willis at Esher, Surrey. AF had run in with R. Ogle who after the boat came from E. Willis found traces of GRP on the hull and accused AF of taking a mould off the boat. AF categorically denied this but suspects that E. Willis might have done it. AF mentioned that he would have to investigate infringement of copyright and R. Ogle went quiet as the boat was in his charge and he would be responsible.

Sail No	Year	Name	Builder	First Owner
N.B.			J. Fisk built his own tooling.	
828	1963	Le Mirage	J. Fisk	Sir G. & S. Bull

Built to the Mystere 770 design. Built with 2 layers of 2 ply. John Fisk modified this design slightly.

Sail No	Year	Name	Builder	First Owner
840	1964	White Cloud	J. Fisk	I.A. Williams

Built to the Mystere 770 design. Built with 2 layers of 2 ply.

845	1964	Restless	J. Fisk	R.C. Edbrooke

Built to the Mystere 770 design. Built with 2 layers of 2 ply.

846	1965	Sargon	J. Fisk.	L.R. Llewellyn

Built to the Mystere 770 design. Built with 2 layers of 2 ply.

851	1964	Geronimo-Ole Miss	J. Fisk/Plycraft	G. Douthwaite

Built to the Mystere 770 design. Built with 2 layers of 2 ply.

948	1970	Maxtoo	B.R.R. McDonald	B.R.R. McDonald

Built to the same plans as his earlier boat K685, Machs.

US 666	1964	Salute.	------------------	Dr Stuart Walker

Built to the Bolero 667. P.O.W. Winner 1964. Complete hull sent out to U.S.A.

P.O.W. Cup Winners

583		Windsprite	1950 Hunstanton	Bruce Banks
			1951 Plymouth	Bruce Banks
			1953 Lowestoft	Bruce Banks
			1955 Seaview	Bruce Banks
667		Bolero	1957 Hunstanton	Stewart Morris
			1960 Falmouth	Stewart Morris
610K.Z.		Atau Hau	1958 Ryde	Geoffrey Smale
728		Polyester	1963 Torquay	Mike Peacock
U.S. 666		Salute	1964 Lowestoft	Dr Stuart Walker

APPENDIX 2
OTHER ASSOCIATED ARTICLES

Most of the articles in this appendix were written by Austin for *Yachting World* in the 1930s and the money paid was used to buy the various volumes of books by Uffa Fox. These articles, whilst not in the main text, are equally important.

First published in Yachting World, October 11th 1935

The Wishbone Rig
Results of a Practical Trial

Having read so much in the Yachting Press, both English and American, of what the 'Wishbone' should do for a mainsail and little or nothing of what it actually will do, except for topsails, I decided to give it a trail myself in my Dart One-Design dinghy. These boats are clincher built, mahogany, 12ft 6in O.A., 4ft 6in beam, carry 100 sq.ft. of sail in a Gunter-Lug, and with a 90lb cast-iron centre-board give very good sport in river and open sea. As the Wishbone rig was to be only experimental, and to be ineligible for class races, and could only be used for unofficial races when Bermuda rig and vertical cloth sails made an appearance, it was necessary to leave the boat structurally unaltered, so that the standard rig could be put back at short notice. In the interests of economy the ordinary sail was used, on its yard without the boom.

Outside Everything

I had never seen a wishbone in the flesh, except 'Carrina's with the sail stowed, but in all the pictured ones the spar comes to the mast with a gooseneck. The outhaul, led along one of the arms, needs constant adjustment. Far worse, the shrouds have to be scrapped if the sail is to be eased off more than about 45 degrees – Uffa Fox says his mast bent like a piece of rubber hose – it must have been remarkably tough to stand at all. I decided to overcome these objections by taking the spar right outside the shrouds. The two arms, meeting 2ft. foreside of the mast, were strained back by uphaul and downhaul tackles to push out the clew of the sail, which was held directly to the spar by a pin through the clew earring. As the spar now projected over the bow the forestay was in the way; but, on giving the matter some thought, I realised that the only purpose of a forestay, when not required for sail setting, is to counteract the downwards pull of the mainsheet trying to flatten the twist out of the sail.

As the wishbone now did the 'pushing down', and the mainsheet merely pulled it amidships, the forestay was quite out of a job and better out of the way. (I have since used a single part mainsheet in winds of force 5, the only objection being that it fouled the tiller when gybing.) Being warned that the usual tendency of the extreme head of the gunter yard to bend aft when close hauled would be a good deal worse, I put a stop to that by making the standing part of the uphaul do duty as a sort of topmast forestay – this works admirably. The uphaul and downhaul were led through blocks stropped to the sailing thwart, and belayed on cleats on a board clamped to the middle thwart, proving handy to the crew, or helmsman, if single handed.

Constructional Details

The Wishbone spar was steamed up in two parts of Silver Spruce, 1¼in x 2¼in rounded rectangular section, laid flat wise so the larger dimension resists the bending strain due to compression. At the after end they were mitred together and through-fastened with copper boat-nails riveted on roves. At the fore end they were squared off and bound together by a brass strip inside and out and through-riveted. The outer strip carried the lugs for the uphaul and downhaul blocks. I think the spar is unduly heavy (it weighs 15lb.), but having no idea how much strain there would be, I decided to make it strong enough so that it could be lightened later if necessary.

So much for constructional details, which may be of use to anyone who wants to build a Wishbone for his own use; I believe the I.Y.R.U. 14ft Class rules allow it.

Does it work?

Yes, it certainly does work. In light airs it does not seem to make much difference, but my boat is so notoriously sluggish in light airs, anyway, that it would take nothing short of a motor to make her go. In a good breeze, however, enough to have one sitting on the gunn'le or outside it, it makes a marked difference; the boat will point a lot higher, apparently about 3½ points off the wind. Sailed on the same course as boats normally rigged and close-hauled, she takes the sheet eased and sails

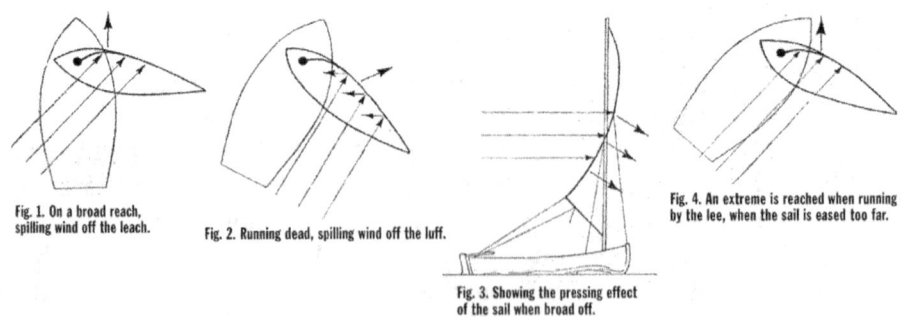

Fig. 1. On a broad reach, spilling wind off the leach.

Fig. 2. Running dead, spilling wind off the luff.

Fig. 3. Showing the pressing effect of the sail when broad off.

Fig. 4. An extreme is reached when running by the lee, when the sail is eased too far.

proportionately faster. Presumably this is due to there being no twist in the sail, so that when properly set and adjusted, the angle of incidence is the same all up the luff. When the sheet is eased too much this begins to shake everywhere, instead of just at the top, while the bottom is still close hauled.

In Actual Practice
On a dead run there is obviously no difference in speed, but when reaching the downhaul can be eased, which gives more belly and more lift. Like this she has left the other boats fifty yards behind after reaching for a quarter of a mile. Coming on the wind the downhaul has to be hauled out again till the sail just does not touch the spar. The uphaul normally stays put, and is only for adjusting the height of the spar.

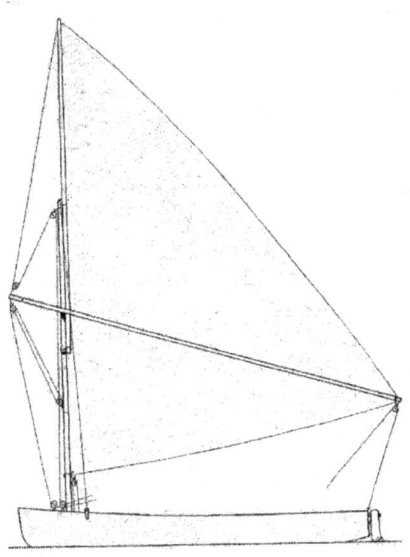

The ingenious method of rigging without a forestay.

Sailing the boat under the new rig was very strange at first; in fact, the first time out, with the sail evidently adjusted to give too much lift, I was struck by a strong squall when broad-reaching and did a spectacular capsize to windward!

My experiments are only in the nature of a 'lash-up', but with a hollow spar and wire and winches to control it, and a mitre cut sail, I expect results would have been even more remarkable.

First Published in Yachting World: January 3rd 1936

Warning to Would-be Wishboners – Theories on Capsizing to Windward
HAVING NOW ACHIEVED the feat of capsizing to windward under 'bones', I feel qualified to write a sequel to my last article and theorise on the reasons. The first time it happened we had only been under way for three minutes after fitting the rig for the first time, and things were happening too quickly to take an academic interest; but I do remember that just before 'it' happened I eased the sheet to try to minimise the effect of a specially strong squall; the next instant we were grabbing at the lee gunn'le as it soared above our heads. I think it shows great presence of mind that I kept my wristwatch above water till rescue came. When we started salving, my crew and I had great fun deciding which of the many strings we should cast off to get the sail clear – we needed the rigging blue print! There were various theories among the waterside cognoscenti –'Er wooldn't never goo over ter wind'ard. Er must ha' jarbed sudden like.'

Out for Fun
On Sunday, October 20th, my crew, thinking perhaps that discretion was the better

part of a wet shirt, did not turn up; so, there being some wind, I pulled down a reef and had a very pleasant beat up-river by myself, singing at the top of my voice.

Returning, with the wind blowing straight down river, I was 'tacking to leeward,' as, owing to the great speed when broad-reaching with a wishbone-rigged boat, I think this is the fastest means of progression down wind. I should estimate my speed in the stronger puffs as about seven knots, planing. I had to bear up, however, and run dead before on port gybe so as to pass in front of the steam ferry which was ploughing its lonely furrow across the river. I was just passing her, sitting well back on the weather gunn'le and going like a train, when I noticed I had not eased the sheet from broad-reaching trim to 'square-off'; I eased it gently, and an invisible hand picked the boat up by the lee gunn'le and threw me in the ditch. Having unwittingly caused all the trouble, the ferry very decently launched a boat to my aid, and two yacht skippers put off from Philip's yard and helped me salve the dinghy, but the water was so cold I laid her up rather than risk another swim.

In the first condition (Fig.1), when broad-reaching, the sail takes its proper aerofoil section between the wishbone spars, and the wind striking the sail as shown by the light arrows, and setting up a suction on the foreside, produces a resultant pull along the heavy arrow. This is elementary, Manfred Curry, and is proved by there being no leeway with the plate up, practically no weather helm, and only a small heeling force. Now, without altering the trim of the sheet, we bear up dead before the wind (Fig.2). It will now be deflected from the clew to the luff of the sail, and the resultant will be sufficiently to leeward to merit one's weight on the weather gunn'le. With a normal boom it is impossible to ease the sheet past the point when the boom touches the shrouds, when the wind, striking the upward twist of the sail, gives a downward resultant (Fig.3), which gives very much the same effect.

Disastrous Results
But the wishbone encircles the shrouds, and there is nothing to prevent the sail taking up condition (Fig.4) (the shroud makes a flat across one corner of the sail), when the angle of incidence is the same as in Fig.1, but this time the resultant is to windward, with disastrous results. The small amount of movement of the sheet from position 2 to 4 (exaggerated in the drawings) would, I think, account for the suddenness of immersion. I suppose it should be possible to find a happy medium for which there is no tendency to heel one way or the other, but it would be a rather unstable equilibrium. These are only my own pet theories as to the capsizes, and I should like to hear what the expert aerofoil theorists think about them.

An answer was not long in being published and on the 17th January, 1936 the following letter appeared from L. T. Bundock of Hereford.

"IN HIS RECENT 'Warnings to Would-be Wishboners' Mr Austin Farrar has rather mis-stated the case, I think. One gathers from his article on the subject that when he capsized he was really running by the lee and, but for the fact that his wishbone is so arranged that it will let the sail considerably farther forward than will a normal sail, I believe he would have had a gybe before the capsize.

In effect, when the sheet is eased right off, the wishbone really acts as a weather yardarm, and the wind pressure is certain to tend to turn the boat over to true leeward even though that happens to be the side on which the sail is not. Sometimes the lee side of a ship is loosely defined as the side on which the boom is carried. Usually this is true of the fore-and-aft rig, but Mr Farrar does not seem to have realised that the wishbone rig as used on his boat may act as 'half of a square sail' and still draw when the sail is on the windward side of the ship."

Austin recalled these events again in an article in 1989

In 1935 the yachting papers were full of the Wishbone Rig, with pictures of ketches with wishbone topsails, the spar on a gooseneck, and the Florida Suicide Class with the spar encircling the mast and pulled towards it with a halyard. There was lots of theory but, apart from the topsails, very little practical information about how a wishbone rigged boat really sailed, so I decided to give it a try myself in my Dart One-Design dinghy.

Since the experimental wishbone rig would be ineligible for class racing, the boat had to remain structurally unaltered, so that the standard rig could be put back at short notice. The regular sail would be used, on its mast and gunter yard without the boom. It was evident that if the wishbone had a gooseneck on the mast it would foul the shrouds when off the wind, so I made it big enough to go round them when lashed in towards the mast. This meant doing away with the forestay but, as I argued that most of the forestay's work was resisting the down pull of the mainsheet, and that work would be done by the wishbone, it would be redundant anyway. Not knowing what the thrust angle would need to be I made the height adjustable, with uphaul and downhaul purchases pulling it back towards the mast, and the standing part of the uphaul led to the head of the yard to stop it bending backwards. The uphaul and downhaul were led through blocks stropped to the mast thwart and belayed on cleats on a board clamped to the middle thwart for easy adjustment. It really was a bit ahead of its time!

The new rig certainly worked; taking all the twist out of the sail made the boat closer winded, while off the wind the downhaul could be eased to make the sail fuller when she would pull away from other boats in an unofficial race. Sailing with it took some getting used to though. On the first time out I got things wrong on a broad reach and did a spectacular capsize to windward, so that my crew and I found ourselves grabbing at the lee gunwale as it soared above our heads.

I had a repeat of this performance, single handed this time as my crew, a young sea scout, was busy coxing the junior four for the rowing club. I was taking to leeward down the river with a fresh breeze, enough to have me sitting out on a broad reach, as this seemed safer than running dead. But I had to bear off onto a dead run to pass ahead of the steam ferry which was ploughing its lonely furrow across the river. I was just passing her when I noticed I had not eased the sheet from broad reaching trim to square off. When I eased it gently, an invisible hand picked the boat up by the lee gunwale and threw me in the ditch. Having unwittingly caused all the trouble, the ferry crew very decently launched a boat to my aid, and I qualified for a paragraph entitled Harbour Rescue, in the local paper.

Taking account of the small movement of the sheet and the suddenness of the immersion, I set about working out the theory and concluded that reaching with a normal twisted sail (the kicking strap had not yet been invented) there is quite a downward as well as a leeward force on the lee side. With the untwisted wishbone sail there is no downward force and a reduced leeward force – until the sheet is eased too much because the shrouds do not stop it – when it suddenly becomes a windward force, with disastrous results.

All this is well known today to anyone sailing with an unstayed Una rig such as a Finn or a Laser, and they probably have a knot in the mainsheet to prevent it going out to danger point, but at the time it was pioneering work which made headlines in the yachting press.

Austin continued to write with the following being published during his time with Robert Clark.

Yachting World August 26th 1938

Spring Delivery
A New Boat in Very Mixed Conditions

IT IS HARD for a peace-loving dinghy sailor to write about cruising, but it seems the custom for one member of the crew to write up a 'hard-case' cruise (whether to encourage others to emulate it or warn them from such foolishness I have never discovered), and I was the only one to do the whole trip, the rest of the crew changing about. Eight tons, 'Inverie' is a Robert Clark design built by Millers at St Monance, on the north side of the Firth of Forth.

The Start
We arrived at St Monance the day before handing over, and found 'Inverie' high and dry against the harbour wall watched by a crowd of fishermen and small boys and enveloped in the activity usual in any new boat just about to leave the yard for good. Besides building yachts beautifully in a big shed, the only industry in St Monance is herrings, and nobody talks of anything else. We heard that the drifters had been having bad markets lately, but were going out again that night, so I walked to the end of the harbour wall to photograph them. The entrance is very tricky, as it has a right-angled bend too narrow for the drifters to steam round, and they have to warp in and out assisted usually by a small boy on the wall who surges their warp round a huge cleat.

We slept on board 'Inverie' that night with the wind singing wild songs in our solid wire shrouds, which always exaggerate, but it was blowing quite strong in the morning when 'D', the third member of the crew arrived. Mr Miller said, 'Of course, you won't start?' but it eased down considerably by the time we floated at midday.

We bent on the trysail, cut from a Six-Metre's mainsail, and about equivalent to second reef, and a baby jib politely called the spitfire. Watched by the entire population of St Monance we motored out of the harbour (our 32ft 9in overall not being long enough to require warping out), and hoisted our sails while head to wind in the narrow entrance, then eased off with wind abeam (W. Force 4), stopped the engine, and headed for the Bass Rock across the Forth. Wind was against tide and there was a lump of a sea, especially about half-way over, where we afterwards found there was a shoal patch but, except for one dollop when a vertical wave crest toppled over on to the deck, we were remarkably dry. During the whole trip 'Inverie' never plunged her nose into it or took solid water on the deck at all but, as she bounces off one wave on to the next, a sheet of fine spray drives across from about the rigging. 'Inverie' took this reaching course with helm amidships, which surprised me, but not so much as her responsiveness for, although absolutely steady if the helm was not moved, when a big wave showed up a quick jerk spun her off to take it on the quarter. We had to knock her off more and ease the sheets a bit when we found the flood was setting us above the Bass Rock, and with the wind freshening we tore along. Then it backed to W.S.W. and blew harder, so that I was 'lifting' the mainsail, dinghy fashion, to ease her.

All or Nothing
Now, if one has to lift more than a third of a dinghy mainsail for most of the time it is time to reef, but there weren't any reefs in our trysail. Having been a roller-reefer, it was all or nothing, so when it got to the stage of flogging almost the whole sail we took it down with some difficulty. I would arms around it while 'D' passed the tyers. At this stage the sea was much less, as the tide had turned with the wind, which was now so strong that it blew the tops off everything in a white smoke, and our own spray blew right over the boat and did not reach the water again till twenty yards to leeward. Meanwhile we were making about four knots under jib alone, about six points off the wind. All this nonsense lasted about an hour, after which conditions moderated and, deciding we weren't going fast enough, we reset the trysail, our course now being along the coast, keeping about three miles offshore past Dunbar and on to St. Abb's Head with the wind about a point free. We were very wet, but for some reason quite warm and, therefore, happy, and it was no discomfort to roll into damp blankets and sleep under the drip of the skylight. This had no cover, and some of the sheets of spray found their way below.

We met a small motor drifter returning probably to Dunbar, and right under St. Abb's Head half a dozen steam drifters were lying kedged. 'D' said, 'Do you see anything funny about that lighthouse?' We both looked, and then noticed the ominous South Cone on the flagstaff. It was the first time I had seen one from the water, and in the gathering dusk was not too cheerful a sight. Our intention had been to get down to Bridlington if everything went well or else put into Blyth but with a new boat and untried gear, wind backed to S.W. and now blowing gale force, we did not fancy going outside the Farne Isles with the subsequent dead plug to windward, so we decided to make for Tweedmouth.

We put 'INVERIE' on the wind (not Solent stuff, but a good sea-going 4½ points) and kept along the coast. Tweedmouth was hard to recognise at night, as its rather feeble lighthouse got mixed up with the coal-mine lights, and we arrived before we expected. 'D', who was navigating, was not prepared for 5½ knots on the wind over a foul tide. After following the south side of the mole till it tailed away, we made our right angle turn to the south, hoping the instructions were right, as it was too dark to see. A man on the mole shouted, 'More to the left! More to the left!' So we did that and went slap on a shingle bank.

An Easy Entrance
It is possible the man said 'More to the West,' but anyway there we were for the duration: 9 o'clock and no possibility of floating again till midnight. Meanwhile, we ate our supper at an angle of fifty degrees, oilskins standing out from their hooks in the most ludicrous way. We awoke when it got light and followed the shore round to the entrance of the little dock. It was quite surprising how easy the harbour entrance looked in daylight – and the old dock-master, hospitality itself, came and moored us up to a pile pier to wait for high water when the dock would open. 'You needn't put out fenders,' he explained, 'The flood setting through the piles keeps you clear, and on the ebb there's an eddy does the same.' A most admirably arranged dock pier! After some tea we turned in again till 10 o'clock when we had a nameless but large meal and spent the rest of the day drying our gear with clothes, bedding and sails festooned all over the ship: there was plenty of 'Dryth.'

When we got into the dock we left 'INVERIE' tied up between bollards across a corner, which seems the ideal way to leave a boat when there are not many others in the dock. We had supper on shore and caught the night train back to London and the office full of determination to reach Bridlington next weekend: 'Brid or bust' was to be our watchword. We took the trysail with us to have a tear mended (a batten had flogged its way out of the wrong end of its pocket when handing the sail off the Bass Rock) and to get a six foot reef put in. The 45 miles we had achieved in 9 hours under way seemed a poor beginning for a trip to Burnham, but at least it knocked three hours off the journey by train, and 'INVERIE' had reached England.

The second weekend's crew consisted of Henry, who was skipper, navigator and cook, and Hal, both ocean racing toughs and myself. The clerk of the weather at the Air Ministry had promised us fresh to strong North Westerly winds with frost and possibly sleet. The cold part was in evidence when we got aboard as we slithered about on a deck covered with ice. Our night train brought us in at 6 a.m. and the deck hands bent on the trysail and jib while the cook produced breakfast. After this we cast off and motored out of the dock and round out of the harbour, hoisting sail as we went, and when well clear of the mole, squared away for the Farne Islands.

Rolling Wildly
There was a big swell from the North, not running true with the wind, which made us roll frantically. At the risk of being flung overboard we tried to hold the boom still while a foreguy was rigged, but the four involuntary gybes, the boom being flipped over by the rolling, were followed by an extra hard one which burst the trysail so that it split right across about half way up. The topping lift had the boom which we pulled inboard and secured by the main sheet while we got the sail down – a shake into the wind was necessary to get it clear of the crosstrees – and bundled it below. Then we ran on under jib alone, rolling drunkenly in the heavy swell. This kind of progress soon began to pall, being too slow and far too uncomfortable, and we cast about for something to set abaft the mast. The mainsail was on board but unstretched and verboten (and too large, anyway) but we plumped for the ship's working jib. Some of the Metre boats, I believe, carry a set of mainsail hanks with specially large eyes into which can be slipped ordinary piston type hanks for using a jib as an emergency trysail, and it is an idea any Bermuda-rigged cruiser might well copy.

Very 'Ljungström'
We did not have these and had perforce to unsieze all the hanks from the jib, replacing them with ones taken from the trysail. This took about two hours, while we reeled on feeling rather squeamish. Lowering away the topping lift we tried to secure the boom end on deck, but it got badly in the way so we lifted it right off the gooseneck slide and lashed it right on the side deck. Then, shackling the tack to the main tack purchase, and the main sheet boom block direct to the clew, we shot up into the wind and hoisted it, and were overjoyed to find that not only did it set very nicely but the sheet lead was just right. We had rounded the Outer Farne by now, hauling our wind slightly which brought the wind more on the quarter and the sea dead astern. With our 'Main & Jib' set and looking very 'Ljungström', we were fairly steady and much faster, much easier to steer too, though at regular intervals a succession of three waves larger than the rest would need to be carefully met dead on or they caused some excitement below.

The Northumberland coast is very beautiful seen from the sea, with grassy slopes down to a low cliff, and a succession of old castles looking most romantic, but in the afternoon the castles ceased abruptly in exchange for coal mines with their huge slag heaps, and the grime of the industrial North. We discussed putting into Blyth, but as we were going so well decided to hang on and make Bridlington on Sunday afternoon. We were very cheerful though bitterly cold, wearing three changes of raiment at once as there was no water coming aboard and they were not wanted as changes. In the evening Henry produced a wonderful Sea Curry with a bully beef basis which was a great success, and we settled down to a watch of one at the helm for three hours and then six below. The helmsman could easily do any minor sheet trimming and no sail changes were contemplated, as indeed we had nothing to which to change.

The wind went quite light at times during the night but by morning had made up to about force five again, and dawn found us tearing along about two miles off a coast of horribly steep cliffs. Whitby was passed about breakfast and Scarborough a little later. My breakfast was rather spoiled by a squall of about force seven, but the other two revelled in it and consumed all the bacon and seven eggs between them. After following the coast for some time past headland after headland, we were out of sight of land across the big bay to Flamborough Head, where we met the steamer lane with its coasters and curious Flat Iron colliers. We also saw several Yorkshire Cobles working their nets or pots which were marked by big dan buoys.

Into Bridlington
Rounding Flamborough at about one o'clock we were close hauled for the four mile stretch into Bridlington, and just congratulating each other on getting real yachting conditions when down came another force seven screecher which lasted until we were in harbour. We crossed Bridlington Bay like a scalded cat (this simile was confirmed by the onlookers ashore) with the helm hardly getting any attention at all but hanging loose most of the time while we crouched down to shelter from the icy spray which was driving over us. Topham and Rooke, the builders, were expecting us and turned out in force for a welcome. They moored us up alongside a Dutchman, promised to do all the clearing up and get the trysail mended, and whisked us off to hot baths and an enormous tea of Yorkshire ham and eggs. Then we went off for our train, determined to make Burnham next weekend if it took all Monday as well.

Yachting World, September 2nd, 1938

On to Burnham
Continuing 'Spring Delivery' from the North

WHEN WE REJOINED at Bridlington on the Friday evening there was a forecast of 'Moderate north-westerly winds, warmer,' so we slept on board 'INVERIE' aground in the harbour, all prepared for a crack of dawn start on Saturday. The trysail had been mended and the hanks we had taken from it seized on again by the rigger, 'who,' Topham remarked, 'ought to have made a good job of it. He's been at sea for forty years.' 'Man and boy?' asked Clark politely. We roused at 4 a.m. and got away after a quick breakfast. It was still too dark to see if it were a nice day, but it looked very grey and the wind was all of 'Moderate.' Trysail and working jib we set, and tore out of the harbour into the grey North Sea, setting a course, when we made our departure, for the Outer Dowsing.

Reducing Sail
It soon became evident that there was too much wind for the working jib, and I had a jolly time on the spray-swept foredeck changing to the spitfire. This eased matters for a time, but an hour or so later we realised that if the wind went on hardening as it was

then we should need a further reduction, so decided to reef the trysail. We pulled the jib up to windward, which I have read is the time honoured method of heaving-to, but 'INVERIE' went on sailing almost as fast. We put the helm down, which also seems to be part of the ritual, and she showed that she would come about against the jib. We got the trysail down without much difficulty, and the boom in the crutch and found that was the way 'INVERIE' liked to be hove-to: no mainsail, jib to windward and helm a-lee, and even the experienced Hal remarked on how quietly she lay, hardly moving through the water sideways or forwards so that the log line hung all slack. We tied down our reef in comparative comfort, hoisted the trysail again and bounced on.

A conference held at about this time decided us that with a falling glass, a rising gale, visibility down to about two miles and two compasses which did not agree, we should do better to make for the Humber than to go hunting lightships in the North Sea. There is, I believe, a way into the Humber estuary from the north by following close along the shore, but the chart showed overfalls and it was probably quite as rough as further out, with the added difficulty of picking a way through sandbanks. So we shaped a course for the Humber Light which is at the official entrance to the estuary, but about 15 miles out to sea by my standards. This bought us about 5½ points off the wind and going very fast with spray driving so hard that it was very painful to look to windward through screwed-up eyes. We passed a small motor drifter having a very rough time, her mizzen not steadying her much, as the helmsman couldn't spare a hand from the wheel to respond to our wave of greeting. The Humber lightship was sighted fine on the weather bow and we trimmed sheets for it. A small tramp came out of her course to have a look at us and steamed across our stern to read our name, but I bet she couldn't see it. We rounded the lightship and close-hauled 'INVERIE' for the long beat up to Grimsby, hoping to get in before the tide turned against us.

Degrees of Misery

I have not mentioned the passage of time and, indeed, I had no idea of it, but it was now mid-afternoon and our tide lasted till 7.30. We were wet, cold and miserable, with varying degrees of sea-sickness. Hal and I decided that a farm in the country was about our mark, with perhaps some ducks. We had to make tacks of only about a mile each way because of the sands either side of the channel, and it brought home to us the severity of the gale (officially force 10 at Spurn Head) when we saw steam drifters, which one usually sees with the mast hinged back in its tabernacle and a mizzen set – even in dry dock – now with the mainmasts up and trysails set, beating to windward under sails and steam, and we were delighted when we overtook one and passed it to windward. A crash and a coil of wire on deck announced a port lower shroud gone, or rather the shackle which attached it to the mastband. As the remains of the shackle could be seen aloft, we promised ourselves an inquest.

With One Shroud

There are two shrouds a side, and although we had promptly thrown about onto starboard tack we could not go on like that for ever and had to risk port tack again with one shroud. Not for very long, however, as the continual flogging of the trysail had chaffed the lashings to the hanks and, one by one, starting with the top, they all came off. You can't set a trysail flying so, of course, we had to take it in and carry on with the jib only. Like this, 'INVERIE' sailed almost upright and was a lot more comfortable, but would only do about six points from the wind and, not unnaturally, refused to come about and had to be worn round every time. As ship's engineer I started the engine, a 6 h.p. Watermota, which helped a lot, but she kicked her propeller out of every decent wave and, in an extra big one, must have got the water inlet out, as the engine got very hot indeed quite quickly and stopped. After a few minutes to cool off, it started again without difficulty but seized again. I unshipped the valves on the water-pump and evidently destroyed the air-lock, as water gushed through but, unfortunately, the engine got drowned by a wave during the operation and refused to start again.

As long as the flood tide was running we continued to go up stream – we were inside 'the land' now – but when the ebb started we began to lose ground, and on our next tack shorewards we anchored off Cleethorpes, about two miles below Grimsby Docks – our goal. Then began a night of trouble beside which the day was a joy ride. I consider 'INVERIE's' 15 lb. C.Q.R. anchor was a size too small, and she now has a 24 lb. one but, all the same, a shingle bottom is not ideal holding ground with a spring ebb and a sou'wester blowing, and we dragged – with a horrible rumbling which travelled up the chain and reverberated through the ship. The chart showed a sandbank to leeward and we sheered across for it, but sheering increased our drag and we got only the end of the bank for holding ground but the rest of it must have sheltered us a bit. Then the anchor shackle broke; anchor chain should have a long link in the end to take a shackle at least a size larger but with an ordinary link our 5/16-in. chain would only take a ¼-in. bow shackle and this broke. We had a spare anchor and, hauling up the chain, we tied this to the chain with a round turn, three half hitches and then seized the end back. During the excitement we had, of course, lost our friendly sandbank and the anchor went back again into shingle.

Beam On
There must have been less tide here, for 'Inverie' had lain head to wind and tide, but now with the windage of her mast she tried to lie beam on. We were roused from our bunks, where we were trying to keep warm, by sounds of trouble forward, and found that the chain had leapt the guides of its roller and was bearing hard against the forestay bottle screw. While I fought with the chain (it really was bar taut – I couldn't get even an inch of slack), it chewed through the ⅜ in. stem of the rigging screw and the mast lurched backwards. I succeeded in guiding the chain into a mooring fairlead as it passed and then lay on my back holding up the mast by the forestay until Hal brought a coil of line with which we made a lash-up from the remains of the rigging screw to the chain roller. Rum was issued and a conference called. We decided we were in a bad way. Even if we seized on the trysail hanks again we could not set it, lacking a strong forestay, and we were short of a mainshroud. We could, however, set

the jib which would help support the mast. As we could not make seamanlike repairs with the gear on board it would be foolhardy to go out to sea to ride it out hove-to. There is a bight inside Spurn on the north side to which we could blow across if we could find the entrance, but visibility was bad and the pilot damned its shelter with faint praise. More than likely we should have piled up at the entrance.

Less Heroic
If we stayed where we were, or rather went on dragging as we were, we should be a salvage case after about four miles and we had already covered two. The committee decided that as it was not our boat it would be better and more comfortable, if less heroic, to be saved before the last eventuality took place, and a motion was passed to burn a flare. We tore one of the owners blankets into strips, soaked one of them in a basin of petrol and tied it on the backstay but it refused to be lit with matches – if the match was struck far enough from the blanket not to be soaked in petrol, it blew out before getting there – but the galley mop dipped in petrol and lit in the cabin made a fine torch. The effect was a most satisfying flare which lit up the water in a wide circle, but after burning three strips of blanket and about a gallon of petrol without anyone taking the least interest on shore, we got bored, and I salved the last strip to wind round me as a very welcome 'tummyband.'

Although I have no idea of actual times, I think we must have all slept for a while, probably soothed by the rum, for the next thing we knew 'Inverie' was lying stern to wind though still dragging with it, so the tide had turned. By making a broad sheer across and then putting the helm down suddenly it was possible to get stern to tide and then steer towards the anchor while the other three manhandled the chain. When the anchor came up, burnished bright by the shingle, we were horrified to find that it was attached to the chain by a solitary half hitch! Then up went the jib and we set off to windward, still doing our six-points-off-the-wind-and-gybe-every-time business, but the strong flood pushed us up very fast so that we were soon opposite Grimsby docks. We nearly went into the trawler basin by mistake, but found the right entrance in time. The gates to the inner dock were open and men waving us on, but we couldn't point for the opening. Just as a matter of interest I tried the engine and, having dried off during the night, it started at once and in we went, and tied up alongside a tug in the far corner.

Shackles and a Moral
Feeling that the food we had on board would not do justice to our great hunger we went ashore for baths and breakfast, and Clark and Hal went straight off to London by train, while Bill and I stayed to clean up the ship.

A trip up the mast showed that the broken shackle had a flaw (Moral! Always get tested ones), but all the others were distorted so a new set a size larger were ordered. We got some seizing wire and made a seagoing lash-up of the forestay rigging screw and the anchor chain. The owner of a converted Morecombe Bay Prawner hospitably invited us to moor alongside him and drove us all round the docks in his car. We watched a fleet of trawlers coming in on the afternoon's tide – it was a hair-raising exhibition as they queued up and dashed through the narrow entrance. Bill and I slept aboard Sunday night. It was bitterly cold and we shared all the remaining blankets. After breakfast we dressed for the part and went to see the Fish Market in action. I have never seen so many fish. Then, after paying dock dues for a week and one penny dues to the Humber conservancy for keeping the sandbanks in order, we too went back to work in London.

When the crew assembled the following Friday evening at King's Cross station, we caused some attention by reason of our new C.Q.R. anchor which the porters could not understand at all.

On to Burnham

We got aboard in time to lock out to the outer dock at midnight for an early start but, as I had to fit a new set of shackles aloft, I voted for the smooth water of the inner dock to do it, so we slept in peace. It took most of the morning, slacking off one shroud at a time and we locked out at one o'clock and had lunch as we motored down the Humber, then set sail as the fishing fleet steamed past us. We were close hauled out to the Humber Lightship, and then eased away with wind on the quarter. There was a rolling swell as when we left Tweedmouth, but rather less wind.

'INVERIE' made good speed past Lincolnshire, and tore across the Wash at 7 knots, sighting the North Norfolk coast at about midnight. There were only three of us this time, Clark, Buster and myself, and we worked 3 hours on deck and 6 below through the night. When I looked out at 7 a.m. on Sunday we were right off Lowestoft, and almost becalmed with the end of a fair tide. We fanned along, snooping inside sandbanks to cheat the foul tide, and followed right down the Suffolk coast about half a mile offshore in glorious sunshine but the coldest, for daylight, we had experienced. We sailed through a maze of crab pots off Aldeburgh, and got one round the propeller, but cleared it without damage. After Orford Ness, the tide being our way, we went outside everything to the Gunfleet where, late in the afternoon, we turned on the engine to save our tide up the Crouch.

It seemed vandalism to run the engine on such a lovely evening with a gentle sailing breeze, but we were delivering a yacht and not strictly yachting at all. Also it was bitterly cold and the engine did help to warm the cabin. We ran it for four hours, and picked up a mooring in Burnham just as the ebb was starting.

One final article is of interest in that it recalls a specific yacht built during his days in Dartmouth and was published in 1993.

The 'NAGMATI' for the Maharao of Kutch

PHILIP & SON's yard at Dartmouth had quite a name for building motor yachts in both steel and wood. One of the larger wooden ones was 'NAGMATI', built in 1932 for his Highness the Maharao of Kutch. She was 100 ft long overall and 135 tons

Thames Measurement. Because the Indian Ocean is infested by the Teredo worm, which eats most timbers except teak and greenheart, she was built mostly of teak with a greenheart keel about 80 ft long which had probably been imported for dock piling. Incidentally, greenheart, which comes from South America, is so dense that it will not float! She had a pair of straight eight 160 horsepower Gleniffer diesels, with reduction gears to the propeller shafts, and these were estimated to be able to give her 13.5 knots. The engines were started by compressed air, and the reverse gears were operated by a wheel above the gear box which turned one way for ahead and the other for astern. It was not immediately obvious which way was which until Cecil Inder, in charge of installation, with the yacht lying alongside the pontoon and the engines ticking over, tried the control wheel of each engine first one way and then the other, and noted through the porthole when she moved ahead.

The engine had been run in and thoroughly checked on the test bed at the builders' works, and when we took 'Nagmati' out on trials we went out of Dartmouth harbour at half speed accompanied by the yard tug and round to Start Bay where there is a measured mile. All was peaceful, if not exactly quiet, in the engine room until the engines were brought up to full revs for the first run over the measured mile when the heat started to cook the asbestos lagging on the exhaust pipes which went dry up to the funnel, and the engine room was filled by something akin to tear gas. Cecil and I beat it for the deck coughing and with eyes streaming, and we finished the run with no one down below – then Cecil tied a wet towel round his head and ventured down to close the throttles. This was before the days of bridge control, and there was an engine room telegraph from the bridge to signal orders to the engineer. We lay head to wind for some minutes for the ventilators to clear the engine room of fumes and then opened up the throttles for a return run over the mile – again with an empty engine room, but the fumes were getting less as the dressing burnt out of the asbestos. However, when times were averaged and speed calculated, it appeared we were only getting 12.3 knots instead of the promised 13.5, so we did another pair of runs with the same results. This was rather serious as it appeared that the engines were short of power.

Angus MacMillan of Gleniffers arrived from Glasgow and discussed the situation with Philip's directors and the Maharao's project manager. We took the head off one of the banks and drew out a piston and con rod for examination: nothing apparently wrong. Then on a sudden thought Angus asked, 'Which way have you got the propellers turning – inwards or outwards?' 'Why, outwards,' said Cecil, 'starboard prop turning clockwise, the same way the engines are handed.' 'Ah – there's your problem – the engines are handed to turn outwards, but the reduction gears make the shafts run the other way. You've been running full speed astern so it's no wonder the gearboxes were getting a bit hot.'

Nobody at Philip's had noticed the small print about the engines which gave this vital piece of information! Fortunately it was not necessary to lift the engines and swap them over. We docked the yacht and swapped the propellers overnight so that the (now) starboard prop turned anti-clockwise for ahead, and went out for trials again the next day. Now 'Nagmati' would do 14 knots and everyone was satisfied, and the gearboxes were so robust that they had not suffered from being run flat out in reverse for several hours.

Shipping the yacht to India was done on the 'BELRAY', a specialist heavy-lift ship which already had eight barges stowed two deep on deck and sticking out over each side. She picked up 'NAGMATI' with her big derrick, heeling 20 degrees in the process, and swung her inboard to stow diagonally across the deck. It looked a most ungainly load, but was all in the day's work for the crew of the 'BELRAY' who lashed everything down securely, and duly arrived in India without incident.

INDEX

505	125, 130, 148, 149, 165	ARZILA	19
10 Sq. Metre Canoe	90, 122	Association of British Sailmakers	156
12 Metre	42, 47, 80, 139	ASTRA	43, 46
12 Sq Metre Sharpie	162	ATLANTA	10
15 Metre	16	Atlanta	69, 104
19 Metre	16	ATLANTIC	51
1948 Olympics	104, 118, 165, 171	Aumonier, John	95, 123
1952 Olympics	162	Austin Farrar Sailmakers	132, 133, 146
1960 Olympics	136, 168, 170	Australian Catamaran Association	174
1976 Olympics	171	Autoclave	104
23 Metre	44, 46	AVEYRON	9
5 Rater	10		
5.5 Metre	120, 137, 168	**B**	
6 Metre	16	Babbacombe	45, 158
		Banks, Bruce	108, 111, 116, 120, 131
A			134, 140, 206
A33 Monospar Cloud	62	BARILEA	112, 203
Abeking & Rasmussen	80	Barlow, Nick	182
Actaeon Net Defence	85	Bateman, Peter	131
Admiralty	79, 85, 96, 196	Bavier, Bob	137
ADVICE	159, 161	Beale, Joan	105
Aero Research	103, 126, 197	Beale, Martin	105, 108,
Aerolite	103, 187	Beery, John	173
Agba	106, 110, 117	Bees Wing	118, 119, 122
Aircraft dope	122,	Bell, Mrs	92
Aisher, Owen	137, 138	Bell-rope	77
ALARM	110	Bembridge	33,
Albacore	104	Bembridge Redwing	121
Albermarle Street	32	BENBOW	74
Aldeburgh	11, 120, 124, 149, 220	Benedictine	149
Aldeburgh Yacht Club	128	Bentley	149, 157, 162, 188, 190
Allen, Jon	136	Bermuda	112, 114, 116, 164, 203, 204
Amateur Yacht Research Society	181	BESSIE	9
America's Cup	44, 51, 80,	BEVERLY	173
ANITA	9	Bianchi, Bruno	168
ANNIE	33	Birch	103, 106, 122
Annisland	91	Birmabright	62, 73
Apache	143	Bishop, Stan	48, 50

Blundell, Jack	115, 121, 147, 164, 204	Capio, Mario	167
Blyton, Enid	12	Cargreen	29
BOADICEA	174	CARMELA	34
BOLERO	117, 119, 204, 206	Cassell, Andy	131
Bond, David	108, 161	Cat House	126, 129
BONNIE JEAN	126	Caulder, Johnny	21
Bosham	65, 95, 183	Cawsand Bay	27, 48
Boston Whaler	184	CAYENNE	75
BOUNDS	94	Cellon	122
Boxhall, Gerry	143	Central Council for Physical Recreation	126, 200
Boyd, David	137	CERIGO	54
Brabazon, Lord	121	Chamier, John	105
Bramford	8, 12	Chapman Sands Sailing Club	173
Brazilian mahogany	110	Chapman, Bill	55
Breon	150	Chapman, Colin	188
Brierly, Tony	132	Chatham Dockyard	194, 200
Brightlingsea	10, 16, 84, 94, 142, 146, 178, 197	Chichester Harbour	67, 78, 94, 102, 123, 163, 200
BRITANNIA	10, 15, 43, 51, 109	Chichester-Smith, Colin	76, 117
British Aerospace	144	Chichester-Smith, Nora	76
BRITISH AIRWAYS	133, 145	Chiggiatu, Artu	168
British Guiana	11, 15, 19	Chinese Rig	123
BRITISH OXYGEN	145, 182	Chippendale, Jack	194, 195
British Power Boat Company	23, 61	Churchill, Winston	41, 85
BRITOMART	16	Ciba	103
Brixham	34, 37, 42, 101, 157, 160	CLAMSHELL	125
Brixham Yacht Club	101	Clarence	18
Brown, F.B.R. (Buster)	72	Clark & Synnott	69
BRYNHILD	68	Clarke, Cyril	94
Build Your Own Dinghy Conference	126	Clark, Robert	35, 63, 70, 73, 78, 79, 83, 159, 212
Bumble	112, 122, 149, 157, 190, 196	Cliff Quay	14
Bunbery, Sir Charles	187, 188	Cluston, Harold	78
Burnham-on-Crouch	11, 74, 83, 127, 200, 214	Coe, Lawrence	187
Burns Ship Yard	65	Cold moulded	103, 107, 115, 117, 123, 171, 184, 187
Burton Cup	16, 128, 129	Coleman, Tim	182
Burton, Sir William	11, 15, 17, 41, 45, 52, 80	Commanche	143
Burton, Son and Sanders	16	CONQUEST	123
Bury St Edmunds Grammar School	8	CONSUTA	103
BUTTERCUP of Colchester	70	Cooper, Fred	59
Buttermans Bay	14	Coprolite	8
		Corke, C	10
C		CORONA	148
C Class Catamaran	121, 146, 171, 179, 180, 184	CORONET	163, 165
Cadet	167	Corry, John	76
CALETA	17, 43, 47, 53	Cowes	10, 42, 59, 63, 69, 73, 80, 121, 159
CAMBRIA	44, 51	Cowes Corinthian Yacht Club	148
CAMPEADOR	41, 45	Cracknell, Judy	100
Camper & Nicholson	10, 74, 80	Crane, Clinton	80
Canadian Canoe	105	Creagh-Osborne, Richard	148
CANDIDA	44, 51	Crews Union	119
CANETON	164	Crossbow	181, 182
CANTITOE	80	Crossly	17
Canvey Island	119	Crouch One Design	11

Cunningham 142, 174
CURACO 93
Currey, Captain C N E 85, 93, 103
Currey, Charles 60, 65, 76, 89, 94, 102, 106, 112
    115, 136, 147, 157, 162, 164, 170, 183
Curry, Manfred 209
Custom Boatbuilders 188

D
Daddyhole Plain 162
DARING 158
Dart One Design 31, 38, 45, 101, 207
Dartmouth 17, 25, 35, 42, 52, 61, 184, 193, 220
Davey & Co 87
David, Mr 129
Davis, T B 44
Dawes, Slotty 167
De Forest (Shorty) 112
De Quincy, Billy 121
De Quincy, Roger 120
Debbage, Mr 129
DEFIANT 121
Demant, Jimmy 63
Demon Yachts 185
Denmark 75, 162, 172, 176, 193
Department of Electrical Engineering 89
Dinghy Sailing Show, the 126
Ditton, George 84
Ditton, Lizzie 84
DOLLY VARDEN 63
Donkey 119, 120
Donkey Riding 120
Dorchester Hotel 149
Dragon 136, 159, 165, 168
Drake's Island 26, 49
Du Cane, Peter 61
Duke of Edinburgh 132
Dunlop, Scotty 29, 31
Dyke, Bob 189

E
EARLY BIRD 179
East Anglian Daily Times 12
East Anglian Offshore Racing Ass. 126
Eastern Multihull Sailing Ass. 172
Eastney Barracks 89
EASTWIND 121, 124
Edmunds, K (Corky) 94
Egyptian cotton 122, 139
ELAN 102
Ellis, Greer 176
Ellison, Mike 102, 205

Elvstrom 130, 162, 169, 170
EMMA HAMILTON 171, 174, 175
Emsworth 66, 93, 102
ENDEAVOUR 44, 47, 51, 80, 145
Engineering Council 191
ENIADÆ 27
Enterprise 131
ERIVALE 73, 75,
EVADNE 52
EVELYN 33, 34
Exchange & Mart 148
EXPDNC 55

F
Fairey Aviation Company 104
Fairey Marine 62, 102, 104, 106, 108, 117, 148, 164
Fairey, Richard 104
FAIRWIND 108
Falcus, Hugh 36, 37
Falmouth 30, 45, 76, 206
FARANDOLE 129
Farrant, Ralph 158
Farrar, Norman 12, 84, 188
Felixstowe 12, 55, 61, 94, 98, 117, 127, 128, 149, 156
Felixstowe Ferry Sailing Club 128
Fertilizer 7, 8, 9
FFV 148, 163
FIERY CROSS 65, 66, 97, 76
Fife, William 54
Finn 147, 162, 169, 183, 211
Firefly 62, 104, 109, 117, 148, 162, 170
FIRETAIL 117
Fisk, John 119, 136, 172, 174, 206
Fison 8
Flahraty, Jack 34
FLAMING ONION 65
FLEETWING 164
FLICA 48, 50, 51
FLICA II 80
Flying Dutchman 105, 125, 131, 135, 136, 140
    163, 165, 166, 170, 183
Flying Fifteen 164
FLYING FOX 114
Flying Junior 136
Flying Trapeze 76
Ford, Johnny 122
Foster, Glenn 120
Fowey 30
Fox, Henry 100
Fox, Uffa 35, 68, 74, 76, 81, 96, 102, 108, 110
    120, 121, 157, 163, 207
Frederiksen, Gert 176

Freston Hill	99	Hart, Richard	183
Frost, Honour	193, 194	Harwich	9, 14, 15, 26, 42, 51, 82, 156,
Fryer, Angus	167	Harwich & Dovercourt Sailing Club	128
		Harwich Town Sailing Club	148
G		HAWK	77
Gaastra	147	Hayling Island	95, 117, 120, 122, 188
Gabbiano	169	Haylock, Bernard	94
Gamblin, Bill	151, 153	Helensburgh	91, 92, 96
GAMECOCK	175	Helford River	30, 31
GARGANY	158	HELLCAT	142, 173, 174, 175, 177
Gartocharn	91, 92, 93	Helsinki	162, 183
George V	15, 44	Henslow, Professor	7
George, Keith	76	Herbulot, Jean Jacques	137
GHOST III	169	Herreshoff	44, 80
Gick, Phil	77, 157	Herve	148
Giles, Morgan	38, 40, 70, 72, 159	Hickman Sea Sled	184
Gironde	153, 154	Hills, Mabel	69
GLEAM	80	HMS Dolphin	90
Goffe, Michael	129	HMS Vernon	93
Gold medal	108, 162, 170, 171	Holloway, Bertie	173, 174
GOLDEN EYE	158	Holman, Kim	150
Goldsmith, Admiral	26, 31, 41	Holt, Jack	123, 129, 63
GOOD NEWS	117	Honduras mahogany	110, 118, 166
Goodson, Graham	124	Hood	137, 141
Goodson, Hugh	50, 80	Hooten, Bill	176
Goodson, Sir Alfred	43	HOPS	94
Gore-Lloyd, Ted	74, 75	Hornet	163
GOSSIP	136	Horsa Glider	104
Gourock	93	Hubbard Brothers	174
Greenbank Hotel	76	Hunloke, Sir Philip	44
Grey Marine Engine	55, 61	Hunstanton	112, 147, 206
Griffiths, Peter	124, 125	Hunt, Ray	184
Grove House	9	Hunts Yachting Magazine	9
Guinea Challenge Cup	10	Hurricane	182
Gulcher, Conrad	164	Hussy, Frank	127
GULVAIN	94	Hyde, Eddie	131, 135, 183
Gurley	133	Hythe	24, 60, 63
GYRINUS	157, 158, 160		
		I	
H		ICARUS	182, 198
H M S Beehive	61	Ijsselmeer	24, 63
H.D.M.L.	79	Illingworth, Captain	93
Hadleigh	129, 130, 132, 177	ILYS II	117, 203, 204
Hags Tooth	114	Imperial Service College, Windsor	13
HALCYON	84	International Canoe Trophy	96, 123
Hamble	104, 160	International Catamaran Challenge Trophy	
HAPPY RETURN	157		172, 173
HARPADO	40	International Fourteen	39, 76, 102, 108, 112
Harris, Bob	172, 173		121, 129, 164, 202, 203
Harrison-Butler, Dr	68, 69	International Sailing Federation	16
Harry King Boatbuilders	83	International Yacht Racing Union	16, 53
Hart, Norman	41	Ipswich 16, 100, 129, 133, 142, 147, 151, 166, 187	

Ipswich Boat Building Partnership	133
Iroquois	142, 143, 177
Island Sailing Club	60, 63, 66, 68
Isotta	61
Itchen Ferry	64
Itchenor Gallon	102
Itchenor Ship Yard	65, 94
IYRUNA	46, 53,

J

J Class	44, 49, 51, 80
James Piper	158
Jardine, Adrian	133, 167, 170
Jecketo	37
Judge	11
Jeltes, Cle	183
JENETTA	80
John Samuel White Ltd	59
John Wright Veneers	106, 110
Johnson, Max	148
Johnson, Peter	185
Jolly Boat	163
Jonas, Chris	151
Jonas, Harry	149, 150
JUMPS	94
JUNE	11, 14, 84

K

Kelvin	28, 100
Kendall, Martin	188
Khaya	118
KING DUCK	157, 160, 161, 162
King Harry Ferry	30
King, Colonel	70, 72
King's	75, 83, 98
Kings College London	7, 8
Kingston	171
Kingston Valve	20
Kingswear	17, 27
Knox-Johnston, Robin	133, 143
KURREWA	132, 137, 140, 141

L

La Baule	154, 163, 164, 165
Ladder Rack Seat	124
LADY BLANCHE	40
LADY DAPHNE	27
LADY HELMSMAN	171, 175, 176, 179, 180, 182
LADY MAY	43
Lamb, Bert	117
Lambert McCarthy, Lily	52
Lambert, Gerald	51, 80

Lancewood Splines	86
Langmaid, Alf	55
LAUGHTER	129
Lawes, Sir J B	8
LEAPS	94
Leather, John	186
Leckie, Peter	102
Ledwith, Jimmy	122
Lennox Garage, Southsea	85
Liberty Ships	93
Lidstone, Phil	55, 57, 66
LIGHTNING	76
Lipsett, Percy	129
Lipton, Sir Thomas	16
Little America's Cup	171, 172, 180
LITTLE ASTRA	80
Livingstone	137
Lloyds	10, 28, 53, 54
Loch Lomond	91
LOLLIPOP	16
Loosdrecht Lake	163
Lotus	188
Lowestoft	114, 115, 117, 149, 155
Lucas	94, 131
LUCILLA	136
Luders	104

M

Maas, Frans	150, 151
Macalpine-Downie, Rod	142, 144, 172
	173, 174, 177
MacAndrew, Vernon	39, 45, 71, 81
Mackenzie, Rear Admiral W B	95, 92
Mackinnon, P. V. (Bee)	121, 122, 123
MADALENA	28, 30, 31
MADGE	9
Maginnis, Joe	20, 55
Maharoo of Kutch	24, 220
Mainsty, Harry	30
MALAHNE	45
MANTA C	175
March, Rodney	171, 180
MARIANNE	163
Marsh, Mrs	132
Martin, Marco	31, 41
Martlesham	132, 150
MARTLET	40, 102, 108, 112
MARY ROSE	197, 198
MATILDA	174
MAY	11
McDonald, Sir Arthur	129
McGruer, James	28, 97, 168

Meakin, Jim	21, 22	Nunn, Ernie	165
Merlin Rocket	103, 122		
Metacentric Shelf Theory	68	**O**	
MIKADO	76	OCELOT	175, 176
Millers of St Monance	74, 212	OCTAVIA	16, 17
MIMULUS	129	Olympics	16, 104, 108, 118, 131, 135
MINDY	73		147, 159, 162, 168, 183, 200
MIRAGE	76, 206	OPUS	176
MIRANDA	83	Ordzonikidze	167
MIRROR CAT	143	Orford Sailing Club	128
MISS SENIOR SERVICE	175	ORTAC	70, 196
Mitchell	94	Orvis, W & Co	11
Mitchell, Tiny	148	Orwell Corinthian One Design	11, 14, 16, 82
MITENA	80	Orwell Corinthian Yacht Club	9
Monel	27, 31	Osborne, Bob	176
Monkey House, The	76, 77	Osborne, John	175
Moore, Beecher	77, 129	OSPREY	163
Morris, Stewart	77, 102, 108, 112, 116, 126	Ostara	16
	136, 161, 204, 206	Ouisetreham	148
MORWENNA	46, 47	Oulton Broad	114
Mosquito	103	Oxalic Acid	101
MOUETTE	80		
Mountcharles, Earl	10	**P**	
MOUSE OF MALHAM	93	Packard, A	84
MTB	60, 61	Packard, Celia	10, 11, 12, 69
Mudlark	37, 38	Packard, Edward	7, 8
Mulka, Rolf	167	Packard, Edward Jnr	8, 9, 10, 11
Murdoch, Frank	47	Packard, Henry	8, 9
Musto, Keith	131, 135	Packard, John	7
Mylar	146	Packard, Nina	11, 14
Mylne, Alfred	17, 42, 63	Packard, Thomas	7
MYNONIE R KIRBY	37	Packard, Walter	84, 98
MYSTERY	68, 73, 78	Parham, General	177
		Payne, Johnny	44, 80
N		Peep Holes	139
NAGMATI	24, 220	PENITENT	16
Naples Olympics	135, 168, 170, 200	Pepper, Dr	75
NATICA	40	Perry, Barry	136
National Physics Laboratory	85	Perry, Stug	137, 140
National Twelve Class	16, 65, 102	PHILANTE	45
Nautilus Rowing Club	9	Philip & Son	17, 25, 30, 41, 59, 184
Naval Construction Department	79	Philip, Alec	23
Navigators & General	117, 202	Philip, George	23
Nevern Square	69	Pier Hotel	98
Newport Maritime Museum	10	Pin Mill	14, 98
Nicholson	41, 45, 150	PINTAIL	158
Norris, Ian	173	Pitt-Pitts, Derek	148
NORSAGA	41	Planimeter	35
North Sea Flood	126	Plymouth	23, 46, 51, 100, 112, 144, 206
North Sea 24	150	Plywood	103, 122, 130, 163, 94
Noss Yard	17, 19, 31	Pollock, David	77
Nunn, Derek	189	Polyester	136, 205, 206

Pope, Nick	173	Roscoe, Richard	65
Port Edgar	93	ROSEBUD	9
Portsmouth	66, 85, 90, 190, 195, 197	Round Britain & Ireland Race	143
Potter, Gerald,	34	Rowhedge Ironworks	69
Powell, John	88, 90, 93, 95, 96	Royal Aeronautical Society	177, 178
Price, Arnold	22	Royal Canoe Club	90, 95, 105, 123
Priest, Frank	103, 126	Royal College of Agriculture	8
Primo Tacker	107	Royal Cornwall Yacht Club	76
Prince of Wales Cup	76, 101, 113, 129, 136 157, 162, 165, 206	Royal Dart Yacht Club	40
		Royal Harwich One Design	11, 16, 81, 127, 196
Prince of Wales Yacht Club	10	Royal Harwich Yacht Club	9, 16, 81, 84, 98 127, 129, 147, 162, 196, 198
Proctor, Ian	129, 163		
Proportional dividers	86	Royal Institute of Naval Architects	191
Prout, Roland	126, 145	Royal Mail Steam Packet Company	19
Pulpit	72, 75	Royal Naval College	38, 39, 41
Punic Ship	196	Royal Norfolk & Suffolk Yacht Club	114, 116
PURITAN	10	Royal Ocean Racing Club	64, 69
Pushpit	73	Royal Thames Yacht Club	16
Putney	67, 76	Royal Victoria Yacht Club	16
Pye's of Cambridge	127	Royal Yachting Association 16, 126, 172, 181, 185, 186	
Q			
Quantrill, Geoff	99, 11, 129	Rutherford, Tony	121, 147
Queen Anne's Mansions	87	**S**	
QUEEN BEE	84	S36 Lerwick	62
QUEEN MARY	93	Sailcraft	142, 174, 17, 184
QUEST	174, 175, 176	Sailspar	146
		Sainty, Peter	10
R		Saltash Bridge	29
RAF	23, 112, 122, 128, 152	Saltonstall, Bill	173
Rackham, Harry	13	Sanderson & Hickok	173
RAINBOW	51	Sanderson Paints	176
Ranelagh Sailing Club	65, 76	SANDHOPPER	125
RANGER	80	SANDPIPER	84
Ransome & Rapier	166	Sandquay Yard	17, 20, 24, 32
Ratsey & Lapthorn	63, 131, 138	Sandringham Yacht Club	174
Ratsey, Chris	63	SAPPHIRE	127
Ratsey, Colin	77	Saunders, Sam	103
Ratsey, Tom	63	Saunders-Roe	62
RAVEN	39	Sauter, Mr	20
Rawlings, Jack	73	Saxmundham	7, 9
Read, Bill	11, 14	SCARLET RUNNER	55, 56
REBEL	150	SCAUP	159
Red Crag	7	SCEPTRE	139, 140
Restronguet Creek	30, 77	Schenley, G A	10
Richardson, Mike	133	Scott, Peter	76, 101, 109, 157, 159, 163
Richardson, Phyllis	157	Scott-Paine, Hubert	60, 61
Rix, John	61	SEA PANTHER	147
RNVR	41, 78, 87, 189	Sea Cliff Yacht Club	172, 173
Robb, Arthur	93	Seahorse	195, 196
Robertson, E	10	Seahorse Offshore	132
Rogers, Jeremy	130	Seahorse Sails	129, 131, 133, 135, 138, 141, 177

SEA LION	174
Seaview Boarding House	92
Seel, Euan	35, 182, 185, 190
Seine Net Boats	56, 57
SEVEN SEAS	80
Seven Stones Lightship	25
Shackleton, Keith	113, 120
SHADOW	76, 77
SHAMROCK IV	16
SHAMROCK V	44, 46, 51, 52
Shark	142
Shaw, T E	24, 56
SHEARWATER	145, 171, 204
Shed 105	186, 190
Ship & Boatbuilders Federation	156
Shoreham	73, 78, 85, 95, 190
Shotley	15, 129, 188
Sierra Leone	12
Simpleton Pram	126
Simpson Strickland	17
Sir John Beale Trophy	114
Sittingbourne Ship Building Company	83
Skaneateles Boat Company	103, 104
Skene, Norman	35
Skipper Dinghies	107
Skips	94, 107
Slapton Sands	56, 57
Slaughden	124
Small Craft Committee	138, 191, 195
Smith, H C	11
Snape	8
Society of Nautical Research	193
Solent	60, 64, 69, 76, 81, 144, 213
Sopwith, Sir Thomas	44, 47, 80
Southampton	15, 60, 86, 138, 176, 179, 189, 198
Southampton Wind Tunnel	138, 176, 180
SOVEREIGN	41, 137, 141
Sparkman & Stephens	68, 104
Sparkman, Dave	68
Speed Sailing Organisation	181
Spurling, Rowe	116, 203, 204
St Catherine's Point	65
Standard Ten	188
Starbury	133
Stephens, Olin	68, 80
Stephens, Rod	81
Stevenson, Bill	44, 51
Stock Tug	19, l 20, 21, 22, 23
Stuart Turner	22, 47, 58, 100
Stutton	98, 101, 184, 189
Suffolk Canoe Company	186, 187
Sullivan, Captain	32
SUNBURN	115
SUNRISE	102, 109, 119
Supermarine	61
Sussex Yacht Works	73, 78, 85, 88
Swallow	36, 108, 159
SWIFT	161, 162, 170
Swordfish	104, 106, 127, 147, 162, 178
Symonds, W R	9
SYMPHONY	159
Synnott, Eric	63, 68, 78

T

Tamar	29
Teddington	85, 90, 85, 121
Teignmouth	38, 46, 70, 72, 160
Tempest, Frank	84
TERN IV	30
Terylene	130, 131, 132, 133
Tester, Rita	90, 97
THAI IV	142, 171
Thames A Rater, the	82
Thames Sailing Barge	27
Thames Sailing Club	118
THOR	102
Thornycroft, Tom	138, 142, 157
Thorpe Bay Yacht Club	173, 174
Thorpe Hall	7
THUNDER	76, 97, 101, 109, 136, 157
THUNDER & LIGHTNING	76, 101, 109, 157
Tigercat	172
TOMAHAWK	80
Torbay	39, 42, 45, 52, 63, 101, 104, 108, 157, 160, 164
Tormentor Yachts	105, 125
Tornado	146, 171, 179, 180, 182
Torpoint	18, 19
TOUCAN TOO	159
Trimingham	112, 164
Trinity House	24, 25
TRIVIA	41, 80, 81
Tufnol	111, 112
Turner, Admiral	68
Turner, Ellen	9
Tushingham	147
Tyler	150
Typhoon	146, 163

U

Una Class	10
Underwood, Wilfred	151
Usborne, Francis	68, 171

V

V I Flying Bombs	90
VALENTINE	10
VALIANT	90, 95, 120, 124
Van Allen Clark, Junior	173
Van de Stadt	150
Van Essen, U	164
Vanderbuilt	51
VANITY	44, 45
VANITY V	80
VELSHEDA	44
Vercoe, Stanley	41, 49, 51
VERONICA	42, 46, 53
Victory Medal, the	198
Victory, H.M.S.	25, 52, 194, 198
VIGIA	10
VIM	41, 80, 81
VISION	137
VITA	45, 47
Vosper's	61
Vosper-Thornycroft	61

W

Wadham, Ralph	148
Wagner Smitt, Leif	176
WAKE	95, 96, 123
Waldringfield	165
Waldringfield Sailing Club	128
WANTON	129
Warden-Owen, Eddie	131
WARRIGAL	115, 147, 162, 203, 204, 205
Warrington-Smythe	31
Warrior, H.M.S.	198
Warsash	105
Wash Bowl	144
Waters, Sam	114, 147, 162, 203
Watson G L	9, 10, 109
Watts, Captain O.M.	32
Way, Ken	147
Webb, Roy	151, 152
Welland, Jim	132
West Cromwell Road	69
West Mersea	78
West Solent Restricted Class	40
Westall, John	126, 148, 163, 165
WESTWARD	44, 55
Wey, Gordon	147
Weymouth Speed Week	181, 198
WHITE HEATHER	44, 51
White Steam Car	189
White, Dave	133
White, Pete	133
White, Reg	142, 145, 171, 174, 180, 182, 184
Whitlock, Peter	194
Whitman, Lou	123, 124, 125
Whitmore	133
Whitstable	83, 136, 166
Widdicombe, Leslie	130, 132, 133
WILDCAT	173
WILDFIRE	116
Williams, Ivor	111, 134
Willis, Eric	118, 151, 154, 205
Wills Venturer	175, 176
Wilson, Captain H P	88, 90, 91, 92
WINDSPRITE	109, 115, 118, 136, 203, 206, 233
WINDSTAR	108
WINGLIDER	147
Winter, John	76, 77, 101, 109, 157
Wishbone Rig	207, 209, 210
Wivenhoe	61
Wolfe, Bruce	120
Women's Institute	12
Woodbridge	7, 10
Wooden Boat	186
Woolston	61
Woolverstone Hall	12
Woolworth	44 51
World Youth Sailing Championships	185
Worth, Claude	30, 31
Wykeham Martin	146

Y

Yacht Racing Association	16, 53, 159
Yachting	172
Yachting Press	148, 207, 211
Yachting World	35, 38, 59, 65, 74, 82, 94, 109, 200, 205, 207, 209, 212, 216
Yachting World Cat	142
Yachts and Yachting	165
YANDY	148
YANKEE	51, 52, 80, 145
YANKEE FLYER	176
Young, John	133

Z

ZEELUST	151, 154, 155
Z-spar	133

www.ingramcontent.com/pod-product-compliance
Lightning Source LLC
Chambersburg PA
CBHW071232080526
44587CB00013BA/1584